Recording My Life

Printed in the United Kingdom by Biddles Ltd, Surrey

CD production and manufacture: Sound Performance, London

Published by Sanctuary Publishing Limited, Sanctuary House, 45-53 Sinclair Road, London W14 0NS, United Kingdom

www.sanctuarypublishing.com

ISBN: 1-86074-327-7

Recording My Life

*with Elgar, Chaliapin, Caballé,
von Karajan, Furtwängler,
Mountbatten and Menuhin*

Isabella Wallich

To my sons, Richard and Roger Corbett, and their sons, Eric, Daniel, Christopher and Philip, and to my daughter-in-law Jean, without whose skill and confident support I might never have had the courage to finish this story. I can only say thank you!

CD Track Listing

TRACK 1
John Williams Guitar Recital (Delysé, ECB 3149)
Étude No 1 in E minor by Heitor Villa-Lobos...1.55

TRACK 2
A Concert Of Welsh Songs (Delysé, ECB 3161)
Meredydd Evans (baritone), Maria Korchinska (harp) and The Tryfan Octet
(arrangements by Peter Donner)
'Y Ferch O Blwy Penderyn' 2.34

TRACK 3
Geraint Evans Sings In Landaff Cathedral (Delysé, DS 6063)
BBC Welsh Orchestra conducted by Mansel Thomas
'Lord God Of Abraham', from *Elijah* by Felix Mendelssohn 3.55

TRACK 4
Des Knaben Wunderhorn, Gustav Mahler (Symphonica, IMP CD PCD 2020)
Geraint Evans (baritone), Janet Baker (mezzo-soprano). London Philharmonic
Orchestra conducted by Wyn Morris
'Lob Des Hohen Verstands' 2.22
'Antonius Von Padua Fischpredigt' 4.05
'Verlorne Muh' 2.15

TRACK 5
Piano Concerto No 2 In B Flat, Opus 19, Ludwig van Beethoven (Symphonica,
IMP CD 30367 00162)
Charles Rosen (piano) and Symphonica of London, conducted by Wyn Morris
First movement: *Allegro Con Brio*..13.44

TRACK 6
Symphony No 5 In C Sharp Minor, Gustav Mahler (Symphonica, Collins Classic
CD 10372)
Symphonica of London conducted by Wyn Morris
Third movement: *Adagietto* 8.11

TRACK 7
Symphony No 9 In D, Gustav Mahler (Symphonica, IMP Classics CD DPCD 1025)
Symphonica of London conducted by Wyn Morris
Third movement: *Rondo Burleske*..14.43

Contents

Overture

From my earliest days, my life was filled with music. My mother, Louise, was the blessed possessor of a beautiful light soprano voice, as well as a talented and accomplished violinist. Our home was filled with the sound of the great Beethoven and César Franck sonatas for violin and piano, which she played with her partner, a gifted young *professore*, who was to be my first teacher when I reached the age of four.

I was born in Milan, oh so long ago, on 12 March 1916, two years after the outbreak of the First World War, and my brother, Mondy, followed me into the world 18 months later. My father was Camillo Constant Valli, and my mother an American girl, Louise Gaisberg, who came from Washington DC. Our flat was in a large apartment building in the Via Serbellone, in which my father had lived before his marriage. Her brother FW Gaisberg, Uncle Fred – who had already gained a considerable reputation in the early days of the Gramophone company – had deemed her voice to be sufficiently promising to encourage her to go to Milan in 1909 and develop her vocal talent there. It was whilst she was living in the famous Pensione Rieger, chaperoned by her elder sister, Belle, that she met my father, Camillo, a handsome and successful young Milanese businessman who had taken temporary residence there.

Her early story is unusual, for in 1903, on a short visit to his family in Washington, her brother Fred decided that his sister Louise was talented enough to pursue her musical studies in London and under his supervision. On thinking of this now, it's almost unbelievable that her mother, recently widowed, allowed this young girl, still under 15, not only to leave her home and country but also to live in the sole care of two young men, her brothers Will and Fred, who, however devoted they might have been, were deeply involved in pursuing their own adventurous careers. Indeed, at this time Fred was travelling constantly all over the world in search of artists to record and new markets to explore. Luckily for Louise, Will had a far more static position in the Gramophone company in London, and was therefore able to keep a careful eye on her welfare.

She was admitted to the Royal College of Music as a violin student and became one of its star pupils, working under the guidance of Professor Rivard, who was then the leading violin teacher in the college. Living up to his demands was in itself an arduous task, but in addition to practising for many hours a day she also did her best to look after her brothers' flat and provide meals, not only for the two young men but often for their friends as well, some of whom also hailed from America. Inevitably, disaster struck. Louise became very ill and had to return to Washington, where she underwent an operation on her neck, which shattered any hopes she had of taking up the violin as a professional career.

Once again, her brother Fred played an active part in influencing her life by bringing her back to London some years later, in 1909, this time to pursue her studies in vocal training. In his capacity as recording manager and chief talent scout for the young Gramophone company, he must have heard something in his sister's voice which caught his attention, for he arranged for her to go to Milan to continue her training. His brother Will demurred, for even though Fred was frequently in Milan, Will felt that Louise was unsuited to being alone in the hurly burly of life in that city full of ambitious young aspirants to the glorious stage of La Scala. It was finally settled that a member of the family should accompany her, and her older sister, Belle, was chosen to act as her *duenna*.

Louise must have worked very hard to develop her lovely voice, and Fred's instinct proved correct, for in 1912 she was offered the difficult role of the leading flower maiden in the first-ever performance at La Scala, indeed in Italy, of Wagner's *Parsifal*, with the great Tullio Serafin conducting. What a triumph, and how proud of her Fred must have been. As to the handsome young Camillo, family history relates that he had a seat in the stalls for every performance!

Louise remained in Milan during the run of *Parsifal*. The management at La Scala then offered to send her on a tour with the company to Johannesburg. However, Camillo and Louise sensed that war was very near. They became officially engaged, and departed from Milan for London in order to talk things over with the Gaisberg family, who were then living in a large house in Fitzjohns Avenue. The house now accommodated Grandmother Gaisberg, as well as my mother's eldest sister, Carrie, and her two brothers, Will and Fred. It was decided that she and Camillo should be married at Christ Church, their parish church in Hampstead, but first Louise insisted that her future husband – who was, of course, a Catholic – should be converted to the Protestant faith. He took instruction from the local parson and was confirmed by the Bishop of London just in time for them to marry before the actual declaration of war, on 14 July 1914. They left for Milan at once, as my father had already been called up in the Italian Army. The journey across panic-stricken Europe was horrible, but they finally reached the beautiful flat in the Via Serbellone where Mondy and I were later born. With his fluency in English and German, Camillo was immediately attached to act as interpreter to British Command in Milan.

Our young lives were blissfully happy. The flat was on the fifth floor of the building, and we had a spacious *terrazza* in which to play. Mondy had a little red pedal car that he drove at a fiendish speed (a forecast of the future, perhaps), and finally crashed it and broke his arm. I can remember the poor little boy sitting on a small stool while the kindly doctor strapped his arm to his body after the accident.

I, too, met with disaster when I forced my hand through the glass door to the *terrazza* in a temper, when I was denied my birthday right of dipping my finger into the dough of my cake. I had to have my wrist stitched. The Valli family, who had all been invited to the party that afternoon, smothered me in sympathetic kisses and gifts.

Our *baglia* (nurse) was a pretty, fair girl called Ida, from the Veneto district. She wore the colourful costume of an Italian children's nurse, and I remember that she was always smiling and spoiled us delightfully. Rina was our cook, who created the most delicious dishes in the large kitchen, with its doors leading onto the *terrazza*. It was furnished with a huge table, on which she kneaded the dough to make the pasta dishes, which were a weakness of mine then and have been ever since. There was also a laundry room in which all of the household washing and ironing took place, supervised by Madalena, Daddy's old housekeeper, who would come in especially to carry out this household task. I remember that she was a very disagreeable old lady indeed!

Every morning, weather permitting, our *baglia* would take Mondy and me to the Giardini Publici. When he was very small, Mondy would sit in the pram and I would trot along beside him. In the gardens, there was quiet and space in which we could safely play all sorts of games with the other children while our *baglias* sat and gossiped together, but our special delight was to be allowed to drive around the gardens in a little cart drawn by goats. Oh, that was bliss! There was a charming man with whom we have been photographed in the Giardini who was known as the "handsome photographer". I was a little chatterbox, and I can hear myself now, informing him that *"mio papa e Italiano e la mia mamma, Americana"*. I think that really he just wanted to flirt with our pretty *baglia*!

On our way home, we had to pass a building site. We would usually approach it at midday, just as the workmen stopped for lunch and sat on the pavement with their backs to the wall, eating the most enormous ham-and-cheese rolls. They would always hold them out and offer me a bite. Had I not been in the charge of Ida, I would certainly have succumbed to temptation, for their lunch looked delicious, and by that time I would be very hungry. On reaching home, as our old lift creaked slowly up to the fifth floor, I would hear the sound of music. As soon as we entered the hall I would dash into the drawing room, where my mother would be standing with her violin, throw my arms around her legs and implore her to stop. I remember these scenes so vividly, and I wonder why I behaved in this strange way. I suppose that I was jealous to think that she should be so absorbed in an interest not directly concerned with me. Or perhaps the music upset me emotionally. Who knows?

When I reached the advanced age of four, I was placed on a seat at the piano and told that I was now a big enough girl to begin to play. I remember no difficulties of any sort, and the young *professore*, my mother's partner, was engaged to give me lessons. It all came so naturally, just like learning to eat or walk. In a very short while, so I am told, I was playing an early Mozart sonata. I have no recollection of thinking this in any way unusual. I just took it for granted and enjoyed it.

Our home was often full of visitors. Uncle Fred, who throughout the war had spent many months travelling to Russia, and sometimes as far as China, was often in Milan, which was still the centre of musical activities at that time. In spite of the hardship of travelling during that period, Aunt Carrie often accompanied him. It is a constant source of amazement to me, considering the impossibility of private travel during World War II, how often she managed to travel with Fred to Milan at that time. In fact, Aunt Carrie and my mother proved to be too venturesome, and they became the victim of two very painful and unfortunate incidents whilst travelling to London from Milan with myself and Mondy, who was still a babe in arms. For what reason this journey was undertaken I cannot imagine; I only know that all of my mother's jewellery was stolen, and that it wasn't insured.

Far worse, however, was the accident which befell Aunt Carrie, who, while she was descending the stairs of the wagon-lit as it drew into the platform on reaching Paris, slipped and fell between the train and the tracks. She sustained a severe fracture of one of her legs, but was fortunate enough to be tended by a surgeon in the British Army, who set the break so successfully that she never had any further trouble from this accident for the rest of her long life. Why my father was in London to meet the two girls when they finally arrived history does not relate, but it is a well-known fact in family sagas that, on being told of these dramas by his tearful wife, his only comment was, "Bother the jewellery. Is Carrie all right, and are the babies safe?"

There is, however, one tragic event in the family for which Uncle Fred and Aunt Carrie never forgave themselves. Whilst they were staying with us in Milan in 1918, towards the end of the war, Uncle Will remained in London. He was instructed by the Gramophone company to go to the Western Front to supervise the recording of the sound of a German gas attack. He was not a strong man, and the conditions and dangers he faced were severe. On his return to London, he became a victim of the raging 'flu epidemic which was then decimating the civilian population, and died quite alone before Carrie and Fred could get back from Milan. Much to my regret, I never knew my Uncle Will, but he was greatly loved by the family, as well as by all of those who knew him and worked with him.

For Uncle Fred, it was a double tragedy, for not only had he lost his much-loved brother but he had also depended to a great extent on Will's calm good sense and his talents as a businessman. Will had assumed the responsibilities with which Fred did not wish to be burdened, leaving him the freedom to carry out his work as an impresario and the producer of recordings. I have been told in later years that Uncle Fred was so angry and bitter with those who had taken the decision to send Will – who was, after all, an American subject, well over military age and in delicate health – on this dangerous and extraordinary mission that he very nearly resigned from the company and returned to the USA. I knew nothing at the time of this awful family loss, and Mondy and I continued to live happily in our Milan home.

As soon as the war came to an end, there were many visitors from America, which delighted us, for we felt ourselves to be the centre of much family attention. To Mondy and me, the most important of these visitors was our cousin Warren Forster, the son of Mummy's elder sister, Emma, and Rudolf Forster. He was virtually of another generation, and to our delight was reputedly the twelfth strongest man in America. I don't know where this story came from, but we saw him lift both his mother and ours at the same time, each suspended from an outstretched arm. Our admiration knew no limits, and we implored him to repeat this *tour de force* over and over again. Warren won us over completely when, on returning to Milan from a quick visit to Switzerland, he arrived with two St Bernard puppies which he intended to take back with him to America. I remember well that the faces of the poor little things were black from coal dust, as the railway authorities had insisted that they were placed in a cage outside Warren's carriage. We heard that the male didn't survive his transfer to the hot climate of Washington, but the female puppy lived to reach a good age.

I haven't spoken yet of our grandmother Valli, Nonna, who was a Brugnatelli before her marriage, and the other members of the Italian side of the family. Nonna lived in a rather sombre apartment filled with heavy antique furniture, and all of the walls were lined with literally thousands of books. She shared her home with her eldest son, my dear Uncle Leo, after my grandfather had died many years ago. Zio Leo, who had graduated in Chemistry from one of the great universities, ran the family business with my father, which consisted of a factory on the outskirts of Milan – where pharmaceutical products were manufactured under Leo's direction – and a shop, which was in the centre of Milan, near the Galleria. It was a well-known landmark in the city, and in later years Daddy explained that it was a miniature and elegant version of the English chain Boots. He delighted in carrying expensive perfumes and toilet articles in his stock, which he purchased from abroad. It was through the contacts which he made at this stage in his career that he was headhunted, first by Sir Ernest Cooper, chairman of the Valet-Autostrop company, and later by François Coty, when they were seeking the help of a brilliant young businessman to launch their new companies in foreign countries.

Zio Leo was quite different in every way to my father. He had no ambition to make a successful career in business, and felt that he would rather spend his life in the study of philosophy. I was told that his experiences in the Italian Army during the war had been very painful, and probably had much to do with his desire to live his life as something of a recluse. I loved him dearly, and because I was the only girl in my generation of the family he spoiled me outrageously.

In recent years, thanks to the intellectual diligence and competence of my cousin Vermondo Brugnatelli, I have learned much of interest concerning the history of our Italian background. Of the Vallis, little seems to be known. Our grandfather, Vermondo Valli, was born in Pontida, a village not far from Bergamo. When still very young, he was sent by his father to London in order to acquire business training of some sort. How this was to be achieved is not explained, but we do know that he was employed in a cosmetics factory. He returned to Milan and eventually created his own company, Societa Anonima Valli, which grew into a well-known business. I can hardly remember Daddy speaking of his father, who died before I was born, and nor did Zio Leo ever mention his name to me, although Nonna would occasionally refer to him as *"il povero papa"*. It was thus that I have always thought of him.

Nonna's ancestry is quite different and very interesting. My information begins with Filippo Cartellieri, who was born in Milan in 1795 and who died in 1880. His long life encompassed the dreadful struggles against the Austrian occupation, but in spite of the fact that his son, Fernando, was a *Garibaldino*, he, as a *ragionare* (chartered accountant), managed to live life without experiencing excessive oppression from the Austrian enemy. His wife, Teresa Antongini, was the daughter of Tom Antongini, private secretary to the great d'Annunzio. It was their daughter, Marietta Cartellieri, who married a Brugnatelli, and their daughter, Enrichetta Brugnatelli, who married Vermondo Valli and thus became our grandmother. I don't know how they met, nor have I ever heard anything of the reaction in the Brugnatelli family to this marriage, which they may have considered to be a *mésalliance*. Nevertheless, the mysterious "Nonno" created and established a highly respected business, from which my father was able to launch a successful career in England.

Through my cousin's industrious investigations, I have also learned that a German colonel in command of troops stationed in Como during World

War II was also a Cartellieri. It appears that a branch of the family must have left Italy to settle in Germany, where they became distinguished members of the great universities there, as well as in Austria and Switzerland, with a considerable list of learned publications to their names.

Our happy life in Milan came to an abrupt end in 1921, when I was five years old and Mondy was three, for we were suddenly packed off to England to live in the charge of Uncle Fred. I can still vividly remember our departure from the Via Serbellone, waving a cheerful farewell to our weeping mother from the *carrozza*, in which Uncle Fred, Mondy and I were driven to the station. To us, it was another adventure. We loved Uncle Fred, and we were told that he was taking us to London in a big train to see Aunt Carrie, who was waiting for us there. In fact – heartless little beasts – we were quite thrilled!

It was only later that I learned the reason for this upheaval in our lives. My father had been feeling increasingly uncomfortable under the obvious growth of the Fascist Party. He could see no future in remaining in a country under the rule of a despot, and in any case he had never felt very comfortable in Italy. He had loved England ever since he had spent some years there as a student, and had made up his mind then that one day he would return there to live, and so he handed over his share of the Valli business to Nonna and Zio Leo and accepted a position that had been offered to him in Paris by Sir Ernest Cooper, who wanted him to form the new Valet-Autostrop company in France as the first step towards freedom from his native land. The fact that I was at the age at which my education should have begun must have also been a factor in their decision to leave Milan so that I could begin my schooling in England.

And so my poor mother was forced to part from her children, leave her beautiful home and place her furniture in storage until she knew where she would finally pitch her tent. She accompanied her husband to Paris to stay in a *pension* in the Avenue Victor Hugo until fate revealed where they were finally to settle.

1 *Early Days And Holidays*

My parents had been living in Paris since the break-up of our home in Milan in 1921, while Uncle Fred and Aunt Carrie looked after Mondy and me in London. As soon as they were settled, however, they came over to collect Mondy and take him with them to Paris, while I remained in London with Aunt Carrie and Uncle Fred. I only realised later what an act of devotion it was on Aunt Carrie's part to undertake the responsibility of caring for such a young child. It was a very happy and enjoyable time for me, and music played an important part in my life from a very early age. Uncle Fred not only supervised my piano practice but he also found me an excellent teacher in Mabel Rutland, with whom I studied for a number of years. Above all, he opened the magic doors of opportunity to hear great music interpreted by international artists – with many of whom he was on terms of intimate friendship – who flocked to London after the war.

Uncle Fred seemed to be constantly on call for visiting artists, who were forever asking for his help and advice. Very often he would take me with him when he called to see them. To this day, whenever I visit the Savoy Hotel, I recall the feel of my little feet sinking into the pile of the soft carpets in the seemingly endless corridors leading to the suite occupied by Louisa Tetrazzini, and hearing her infectious laughter and beautiful trills as she tried out her voice. She and my uncle were old friends from their days in Milan before the war, and she always gave him a loving embrace of welcome. I don't know how he had the patience to take me with him on these visits, but perhaps my childish presence sometimes eased difficult situations. On looking back, I think that the kindness lavished upon me by both my aunt and uncle was astonishing.

I remained in London so that I could begin my education in England. I had been put on the waiting list to attend Threave House, an excellent girls' school in Hampstead. However, as I had to learn to read and write in English before I could be accepted, in the meantime I attended a kindergarten run by Mary Vernor-Miles, which was both delightful and efficient, and I was very happy there.

In time, a totally unexpected event occurred which changed the course of our family life again. Uncle Fred received a telegram for my father in London, and immediately telephoned him in Paris to tell him that François Coty wished to contact him. As Coty was the founder and owner of what was then the most famous perfume house in the world, the excitement must have been intense. During the course of the meeting (which took place at once, as Daddy was already in Paris), Monsieur Coty offered my father the chance to create and direct the Coty company in England. This was not only a wonderful business offer but also the answer to a prayer, as we could then all be reunited as a family, and it must have been a moment of great relief to my mother, who could now have her two children living with her again and could look forward to having her own home. This wouldn't take place at once, however, for it was decided in the meantime that we should share the flat in Avenue Mansions with Aunt Carrie and Uncle Fred, presumably until my father was convinced of the permanency of his new position. Everything happened with such unexpected speed that both of my parents must have been rather bewildered. In the event, they moved to London very shortly, and Mondy – who was then five years old – went with me every day to Miss Miles's little school.

The school was in a very large house at the top of Heath Drive, and it was a long walk from where we lived. It was quite rural, being situated in Heysham Lane, which connected Heath Drive with the completely open area of nearby Hampstead Heath. There was a large garden, in which we were allowed to play during the summer term, and there were about 20 pupils there, who were supervised by a kindly and experienced staff whose charm I have not forgotten, even after all these years. It was very much a family affair, with the mother of the headmistress, Mrs Miles, playing a very active role. The second-in-command was Miss Lockhead, a typical Girl Guide leader, but very kind indeed. Most memorable and indeed influential in our future lives, though, was Mademoiselle, a French lady who taught us her language and became our governess when we had left Miss Miles's school a long way behind us.

Mummy, who had a passion for acquiring as much knowledge as possible, decided that Mademoiselle should come to us at home for two hours every day during the school holidays to teach us French, and as she was a brilliant teacher she succeeded. How we resented those lessons, and how grateful we have been in later life, both to her and to my mother's insistence that we endured them for quite a number of years! Mademoiselle sometimes took us for long walks, which nearly always included a visit to the local cemetery. This seemed to hold a great fascination for her, and filled Mondy and me with extreme boredom. (I wonder if Mummy knew of these gruesome visits?) Mademoiselle was incredibly plain, but very intelligent and a brilliant teacher. She must have held our interest, although I can remember her chasing Mondy around and around the dining-room table with a ruler in her hand! But she taught us the rules of the language, which we have never forgotten and which we have had occasion to use many times in our lives.

I entered Threave House School when I was eight years old, and I was happy there from the very first day. Mondy must have remained with Miss Miles for nearly another two years, until he was old enough to enter his prep school, the Hall, at Swiss Cottage.

Threave House School was built on a steep slope, so we seemed to be forever climbing stairs to the various classrooms. At first I was in the junior school, in the basement, which was a bit gloomy but near the kitchens, which pleased me, as I was always hungry and I found the delicious aromas coming from them very comforting. When I moved to the upper school, we would have to line up along the banisters of the beautiful staircase from the entrance hall to the first floor until we were called in to prayers, which were held in the largest classroom. This must have been the drawing room of the beautiful house before it became a school, and I would try to imagine what it had been like when a family had lived there.

The headmistress was Miss Jean Macmillan, and the second-in-command was Miss Nina. These two elderly Scottish ladies lived in two bedrooms at the top of the house and in a large and elegant drawing room on the entrance floor, where parents and dignitaries were received and where I was occasionally sent in disgrace to be reprimanded by Miss Macmillan. Miss Macmillan was gentle and kind, but if it was our fate to fall into the hands of Miss Nina it was a different story altogether, for she was both severe and unyielding in her punishments.

The teaching staff was of an exceptionally high order, and as I progressed in the school I realised how fortunate I was to be taught by intelligent and dedicated women. They must have been understanding, too, for they allowed me frequent leave to play in piano competitions and small concerts and to go home and practise whenever I had free periods. Besides granting these concessions, they also accepted the interruptions to my studies that occurred when Uncle Fred invited me to the studios in Abbey Road if a great pianist was being recorded. Apparently, they were also reconciled to the fact that I was occasionally allowed to stay up late so that I could attend concerts in the Queen's Hall, and even on occasion to go to the opera during the season. It must have been difficult for the staff to cope with this unusual situation, but I don't remember having to deal with any problems. In fact, I enjoyed my lessons enormously, and in spite of the liberties I was allowed I somehow managed to obtain all of the necessary scholastic certificates.

I am reminded here of an incident which occurred when I was about twelve years old. Uncle Fred, no doubt inspired by a desire to please me as well as to keep one of his favourite artists happy, took me with him behind the scenes at Covent Garden after the first act of Wagner's *Die Walküre*. He guided me to Lauritz Melchior's dressing room, where Kleinchen, Melchior's pretty little wife, was trying to keep him amused so that he wouldn't think too much about how hungry he was during the long dinner interval between the first and second acts. He couldn't eat anything, of course, and so in order to distract him Uncle Fred had conceived the idea of bringing me with him to make a fourth hand at bridge, as he knew that Kleinchen always carried a pack of cards with her on their travels. So there we were, the huge singer dressed only in his bearskin, little Kleinchen, my uncle (who was a small man) and me (the smallest of all), solemnly sitting down to a game of bridge. If the standard of play were to be judged by my game, it must have been very poor indeed, but we did succeed in keeping the great singer amused and his mind off the delicious Danish sandwiches that Kleinchen provided. Poor man! I can't imagine what they thought of all these events at school. Perhaps they never knew.

It was at school that I met three of my lifelong friends. The Margetson sisters, Stella and Colleen (always known as Coggie), were nearing the end of their school days when I was just beginning mine. I think that I was noticed by them as their father – a most charming man, whom I remember well – walked down Heath Drive with his two daughters on the way to his office every morning, and he made friends with me in the first instance by greeting me as his "little Italian girl". The Margetsons were interested in the arts and were very talented. Coggie became a distinguished painter and caricaturist, and Stella published many historical articles and books about London, as well as two novels. My third friend was Gildie Crawford, who was my age and with me in all of my classes, and it was through her that I later met my husband.

These friendships endured after we had left school, and I met Coggie frequently at the opera and concerts. She was a born hero-worshipper, and with her passion for music and singers she became quite an authority on the voice and the intimate friend of many of the great international artists whom she met during their seasons in London. Gildie Crawford, on the other hand, wasn't at all musical, but we shared a love of games, especially tennis, and we played together as first couple, representing Threave House in matches against other schools. We also had rather similar fathers, both of whom were successful businessmen.

Unbeknownst to us, Gildie's father, Sir William Crawford, and mine had been briefly associated in business. Sir William, who was one of the top advertising men in the country, had undertaken certain projects for Coty of which my father apparently did not approve. The first time I met Sir William was at a tennis party at Heath House, the Crawford home, when he sat at the head of the immense table around which we had all gathered for tea while I was at the opposite end, small and rather nervous of this formidable man. My name suddenly seemed to mean something to him, for he called out, "Valli. Valli. Not any relation to Camillo Valli?"

"Yes. I am his daughter," I answered.

"Well, that's a fine thing. We've just had a terrific row, and we've broken off our business association," he thundered.

This was my rather unfortunate introduction to Gildie's father, which caused some slight embarrassment for a short while, but he soon laughed and was kind to me, and the incident was tactfully forgotten.

There were frequent tennis parties at the Crawford house on Saturday afternoons, and good tennis it was, too, especially when Gildie's elder brother, Stewart, was down from Oxford. He was a fine player, as indeed was Gildie, and we enjoyed some wonderful hours of play. Lady Crawford was a most generous hostess, and in the winter she gave many dances and cocktail parties for her children's friends, and it was at one of these that I met my future husband, Dick Corbett, for Stewart had married Mary

Corbett, who was a fellow undergraduate at Oxford. All of this was in the future, however, for Dick and I met many times when I was a schoolgirl, and we weren't even remotely interested in one another. At this time, he was already a member of a major East India company, and was spending many months – years, even – in Ceylon and Malaya. I was still at school, and engrossed in my musical activities, which were so demanding that I had no time to think of marriage.

Because of the increasing importance of Uncle Fred's position both in the Gramophone company and throughout the musical world in general, he was constantly in demand by artists when they visited London for concerts or for the opera season at Covent Garden. He was particularly busy at these times, taking advantage of their presence in London to complete recording programmes. They would tell him about their troubles and the intrigues that they often imagined were taking place, and we looked forward to hearing about the latest scandals when he came home.

My greatest joy was to be invited to the studios, when Uncle Fred would allow me into the engineer's room to watch the delicate operation of cutting the grooves into the recording wax. Even after the advent of electrical recording in 1925, artists still had to endure the agony and nervous strain of making as near a perfect take as possible, as there was no editing in existence. Often, when recording particularly difficult material, the music had to be recorded many times, making the operation exhausting and nerve-wracking for all concerned. This is where my uncle was so brilliant, for he handled the artists with sensitive skill and good humour. Even at a very young age, I was absolutely fascinated by the process of recording, and was proud to be allowed to attend sessions. I realise now that I was taking everything in, storing knowledge that would be very valuable to me in the future.

There were many concerts to attend, and great soloists flocked to London. Among these were my two idols, Artur Schnabel and Edwin Fischer, both of whom gave recitals at the Wigmore Hall and performed with the orchestra at the Queen's Hall. Not only was I lucky enough to be allowed to attend these concerts but, most wonderful of all, Uncle Fred also invited me to the studios to be present at Schnabel's marathon recording of all of the Beethoven piano sonatas, and not just to listen but also to sit beside him and turn the pages of his music. It was an unheard-of privilege, as well as a great responsibility, but apparently I rose to the occasion successfully, for I was present at nearly every session and Schnabel gave me a signed photograph to thank me for my help, of which I am proud to this day.

My other hero, dear Edwin Fischer, a gentle, genial man who was such an inspired musician, shortly followed Schnabel into the studios. Once again, I had the privilege of turning the pages during his recording sessions of the Schubert impromptus, opus 90. He also undertook the task of recording all of JS Bach's preludes and fugues, and I took my place beside him at the piano as often as I was able to escape from school. What a feast of wonderful music-making, and how fortunate I was to have been present! He also gave me a signed photograph, which I keep among my treasures. His kindly modesty was quite astonishing, and when I turned the pages for him during his recording of the Mozart piano concerto in G, K453, with John Barbirolli conducting the London Symphony Orchestra, he said, "The next time, you will play and I shall turn the pages." Imagine my confusion, then a mere 15-year-old student, when this great and kindly master made this wonderful remark to me.

Until Mondy and I reached the ages of about 13 and 14, we had spent every summer holiday at the Hotel Victoria in Menaggio, on Lake Como. We went there year after year from our early childhood, and met the same families whenever we returned to this paradise. From England came the Glikstens, three maiden ladies who were delightful company, and with them was their niece, Joan, whom I had met when we had both attended Miss Miles's little school in Hampstead. They travelled to Menaggio in a superb maroon Rolls Royce, driven by their faithful chauffeur, Davie, who was very popular with us children. I remember that, when Mondy was still a little fellow, Davie would allow him to sit on his lap and steer the beautiful car when no one was around.

From Paris came the Gimpels, a family of art dealers who also visited Menaggio every summer. There was Monsieur and Madame Gimpel and their three sons, Erneste, Pierre and Jean, as well as the dog, Saida, and I can hear Mme Gimpel even now calling after Saida in her high-pitched voice when he ran away, which was very frequently.

Faithful visitors, too, were the Dutch baroness and her sister, who were very kind to me when I was recovering from the typhoid fever that I had contracted after buying lemon ices in the village, which were delicious but, alas, not clean. After my illness, they showed sympathy by giving me a beautiful little silver box set with an amber stone in the lid, which sits on my dressing table to this day.

The hotel owned a good tennis court beside the Protestant chapel, which was also part of the hotel. A service was held there every Sunday during the holiday season, at which an English padre officiated, who was also staying in the hotel. When Uncle Fred was with us, he would play the organ for the Sunday morning service.

High up in the mountains was the famous Menaggio/Cadennabia golf club. Its 18 holes were hewn out of its steep slopes, and it was unbelievably beautiful. We would drive up there in a coach, and the hotel would provide each of us with a delicious cold lunch. I never attempted to play, but Mondy was a natural sportsman and was very good indeed, even when he was quite young, much to the disgust of the grown-up golfers who failed to match the shots that he played with utmost ease.

As we went to the Hotel Victoria every year, we grew to know the staff very well. The most important and dignified employee was Guiseppe, a handsome blond Swiss who was the head porter. He was a charming, capable man who could arrange anything and everything. He was known as "Signor Dunque" because, before answering any question put to him, he would shake his head and say, "*Dunque*," which roughly means, "Let's see." He was quite severe with us children, but we were very fond of him, in spite of his vigilant eye. The head waiter was called Frederico, a large and kindly man with a black beard who was known as "Spinach". There was also a dear little flat-footed waiter whom we called "Charlie", who was kind to us and endlessly patient. All of these men were our dear friends, and they would welcome us warmly on our arrival every summer.

Gennaro the boatman, who looked after the beautiful rowing boats that belonged to the hotel and supervised the bathing activities, managed the outside staff. He was led a terrible dance by Mondy, who swam like a fish and was utterly fearless in the water. Mondy's speciality was diving from the raft and coming up under the fat stomach of some elderly guest, who certainly didn't appreciate this aquatic behaviour!

Dear, beautiful Menaggio. What a happy place! And how we loved our wonderful holidays there, year after year. I can remember weeping when it was time to return to London and school. Many years later, just after my marriage and shortly before the outbreak of World War II, I returned there with Dick, and much later we visited the Hotel Victoria with our two boys for a brief holiday just after the war.

Towards the end of 1931, when I was 15 years old, we were all shocked by the news that Threave House School was to close. Miss Nina had died, and Miss Macmillan didn't wish to carry on alone. We were all very sad, for the school was much loved, but it was particularly hard on the girls of my age, who were studying to pass their final school-leaving certificates (later known as A-levels). It was a severe blow to both pupils and staff, and I can remember deciding that, as I now no longer needed to behave as a prefect – a status which, despite everyone's amazement, I had nevertheless attained – I could now do something really naughty. I decided to paint all of the flowers on the dingy wallpaper in the prefects' study in vivid colours, for their gloominess had long offended me. My crime was never discovered.

Discussions took place to determine my future. My parents felt that I should sit for the final exams, and sent me to Queen's College in Harley Street, which was a famous finishing school. I agreed to go there, if only to sit for the school certificate. To my surprise, I enjoyed my term there, as it was the summer and my tennis was good enough to represent the school with Betty Bond as first couple. At the end of the term, though, I held my parents to their promise to allow me to concentrate entirely on my music studies. I had been with Mabel Rutland for many years, and she was a fine teacher, but the time had come for a change. I had passed all of the Royal College exams year by year, and had entered nearly every available piano competition. It was now time to move on.

Paris was the obvious choice, since one of the finest teachers in Europe was the head of the piano school at the conservatoire, and thanks to my mother's determination and Mademoiselle's skill I was fluent in French. It was therefore decided that I should go to Paris, and early in 1932 Mummy and Aunt Carrie accompanied me there, leaving me at 14 Avenue Wagram in the care the Picards.

2 Elgar And Menuhin In Paris

I was 16 years old when I went to Paris to study with Isidor Philipp, who was then the foremost professor of piano at the conservatoire. I lived in the home of two delightful ladies: Mme Picard, the widow of Colonel Picard, who was formerly the official historian of the French Army; and Madeleine, their daughter, who was to be my *répétitrice* and would prepare me for my lessons with "*le grand maître* Philipp". She was a fine musician and an intellectual woman who spoke fluent Russian, and as a relief from her musical work she translated Tolstoy's novels into French.

There was an upright Erard piano in my bedroom, and I practised on this for nearly eight hours a day. On the opposite side of the corridor was Madeleine's room, which contained her piano and in which she gave lessons to the children of the *petites classes* of the conservatoire. The apartment at 14 Avenue Wagram was on the fifth floor, and there was no lift, so I would tear madly up the stairs, until one day the doctor who lived on the *rez de chaussée* stopped me and told me that I would die young if I continued in that way. I replied that Mme Picard – "Maman Poule", as she was affectionately known – had been doing this for 50 years with no ill effects, but presumably not at the same speed! I remember that I was later less hasty on my way to the fifth floor so that I didn't offend him.

The third member of the household was Eliane, their pretty maid, who came from the Normandy countryside and who slept in the attic rooms of the building along with the other servants. On summer evenings, I would watch her walking up and down the Avenue Wagram from my little balcony, and I'm afraid that she was up to no good. Of course, I never mentioned her nocturnal wandering to the Picards, and she continued to enjoy the freedom of life in the attics. In this, she was better off than I, for I was nearly always strictly chaperoned when I went out.

I sometimes managed to escape on my own, however. I remember that, on one occasion, when I had succeeded in getting out for a little walk, I met a girlfriend from school in London, and we decided to sit on a *café terrace* to enjoy a cup of coffee. As luck would have it, Mme Picard spotted us on her way home from a shopping expedition, and I was severely reprimanded. (What would she have said if I'd been with a young man? How times have changed.)

Life wasn't all hard work, however, and the food – supervised by Mme Picard and cooked by Eliane – was delicious. Alas, there was never enough of it to satisfy my young appetite, and I became quite run down, for my hours of work at the piano needed a lot of food to sustain the effort, and what I was given never seemed enough to satisfy me.

The two years that I spent in Paris were both valuable and delightful. I grew very fond of the Picards, who were consistently good to me. Not only was Madeleine an excellent teacher but she was also kind enough to introduce me to a group of her friends, the Weill-Reynal family, who were most congenial. The father was a professor at the Sorbonne and, I believe, a communist deputé, while Mme Weill-Reynal was a doctor. They had six children, the eldest of whom was François, an officer in one of the grand French regiments. He was exceedingly handsome, and was, needless to say, my favourite of all the family. Poor Mme Weill-Reynal was permanently exhausted, and she would retire early at the end of her long day. (I can still remember her sitting in bed with a typewriter, surrounded by papers.) Yet she always seemed to find the energy to give me a warm smile of welcome when I visited the family. During the war, many years later, I would often think of these kind friends and wonder what became of them, as they were Jewish and intellectuals, and the professor's political affiliations were in direct opposition to those of the Nazis.

I was taking two or three lessons a week with Madeleine, and these were a great help, but she was very strict and unyielding in her adherence to the Philipp method, which at times made me feel rather uneasy. It was as though she were more concerned with instilling technique than in engendering an understanding of the music that we were studying. Maître Philipp himself had published a vast quantity of technical studies, which he insisted that she should follow, as his *répétitrice*. Some of these exercises, which I had to practise for considerable periods of time every day, involved using contorted fingering, called *doigtés*, to play scales and arpeggios, as well as endless rounds of playing them in different rhythms. These were physically dangerous to the hands, and unless extreme care was taken they could create tension in the arms, which could cause endless trouble in the future. There is no doubt, however, that the technical potential that these exercises developed was extraordinary, because, if the student could acquire facility using these *doigtés* in practice, there was nothing to fear in tackling music such as Liszt, Chopin or Schumann when using conventional fingering. I was amazed by the improvement in my technical abilities and the confidence that this ability fostered.

There were also private lessons with le Maître, which I attended with much awe, as well as those held in public classes at the conservatoire, at which all of his pupils were present. In the beginning, these were a dreadful ordeal, but I got used to them and really began to enjoy the experience of listening and comparing my work with that of my fellow students. It seemed to me that there was a set pattern in le Maître's teaching: he spoke softly, rarely showing any emotion, as though he was leading us through a sophisticated performance pattern, and he also took it for granted (and rightly so) that we were capable of meeting all of his demands. To me, however, the sheer excitement of making music was absent. Something very important seemed to be missing.

At the end of May, I received a very exciting letter from Uncle Fred in which he told me that he was bringing Sir Edward Elgar to Paris to conduct his violin concerto at the Salle Pleyel, with Yehudi Menuhin as the soloist. I knew that Uncle Fred had just recorded this wonderful piece, and that its success meant more to him than anything he had previously attempted in his whole career, for he worshipped Elgar as a composer and loved him as a man. This would be the first performance of the work in France, and I realised that Uncle was embarking on a great undertaking and that its success meant much to all concerned. I was touched and proud that Uncle Fred had asked for my help with Sir Edward during the visit. The protagonists in this great adventure – Sir Edward, Yehudi and Uncle – were in fine heart, for immediately after the recording of this great work there had followed a concert at the Royal Albert Hall in London, which had been a triumphant success.

Uncle Fred, Sir Edward and Richard, his valet, travelled to Paris by air, and as this was Sir Edward's first flight their excitement was intense. Just before their departure, Uncle phoned to ask me to make myself available during the visit, as my knowledge of French would be very useful. When they arrived, after a successful and uneventful flight, they drove straight to the Royal Monceau in the Avenue Hoche, one of the most beautiful of the old Parisian hotels, which had been recommended by my father, who always stayed there on his business visits to Paris.

I was intensely excited when Uncle phoned and told me of their safe arrival and invited me to join them for dinner that evening. A car was sent for me, and when I walked into the hotel foyer my uncle and Sir Edward were there waiting to greet me! The memory of that moment, and of the warm welcome that I received from them both, is one that I will treasure for as long as I live.

We went into the restaurant, and I can remember the table at which we sat, which was to the right and near a window. The dinner was delicious, although I was almost too excited to eat. Sir Edward, I remember, thoroughly enjoyed it. He was in splendid form, and told many humorous stories, not only to do with his musical experiences but also concerned with incidents involving his dogs and his enjoyment of country life. This didn't surprise me much, as he appeared to be a typical English country gentleman whose interests lay with his garden and his animals. It was when he teased my uncle, whom he called "Frederic Barbarossa", that one saw the humour and wit shine in his eyes and glimpsed the shrewd analytical brain of the creator of the *Enigma Variations*, which so brilliantly reveal his profound understanding of human beings.

After dinner, Uncle Fred told me how I could help him the next day. He explained that George Enesco had already undertaken the main work of rehearsing the orchestra, but that he would take Sir Edward to the Salle Pleyel the next morning, where the Menuhins would be waiting for him and Yehudi to rehearse the concerto with the orchestra at 10am. Then, for reasons which to this day I still find amazing, he placed upon my young shoulders the responsibility of looking after Sir Edward, of collecting him from the hotel and accompanying him to the Salle Pleyel in time for the performance in the evening. Imagine my intense excitement and nervousness on the next night, when the car arrived at the Avenue Wagram to take me to the Royal Monceau, where I found Sir Edward with Richard waiting for me. I still remember vividly how elegant and distinguished he looked in his tails.

To say that I was overawed by the extraordinary trust that had been placed in me would be an understatement. I knew that I had to justify this trust by ensuring that Sir Edward arrived at the concert hall quietly and safely. We sat side by side in the car, holding hands as we made our way through the heavy evening traffic of Paris. I understood very well how nervous and preoccupied he had to have been about the ordeal before him, and so I hardly uttered a word, as I didn't want to disturb his concentration.

When we arrived, there were vast crowds besieging the Salle Pleyel and an enormous number of policemen blowing whistles. This was a great cultural and social event, and as members of the government and the diplomatic corps were present it was necessary that the police were there in force. We pulled up at the main entrance, and with Richard's help we forced our way through the crowds into the main foyer, through which we had to pass in order to reach the artists' room. Imagine my horror when the ushers didn't recognise Sir Edward and refused to let us through. Uncle had omitted to provide us with tickets! Luckily I spoke fluent French, and made such a scene that the box-office manager was called, who of course let us through at once. I was very upset and embarrassed by this incident, but luckily Sir Edward was so preoccupied that he hardly noticed the little drama. We were rather overdue when we finally reached the artists' room, and we found the Menuhin family and Uncle Fred anxiously awaiting our arrival. Thankful that my mission was successfully accomplished, I joined Madeleine Picard, who was waiting for me with her mother in the foyer, and we took our places in the hall for the concert.

This was undoubtedly an event of great historic interest in the world of music, and the hall was packed with a deeply attentive audience awaiting the first hearing of this work, about which so much had been written by the critics in Britain, the United States and Germany. I, who knew how different the French were in their musical taste, anxiously awaited the arrival on the platform of our two artists. In the event, I needn't have feared, for Elgar conducted his great concerto superbly and with complete confidence, and Yehudi played as one inspired. It would have been hard indeed not to have been moved by the sight of these two hugely gifted human beings, the distinguished elderly gentleman and the handsome youth, giving themselves completely to the performance of this great work. Even the blasé Parisian audience responded with enthusiasm, although I feared that Sir Edward and Yehudi might have felt that the applause lacked the warmth to which they were both accustomed. I needn't have worried, however, for the reception and the brilliance of the occasion delighted them, and Uncle Fred was vastly relieved that everything turned out so successfully.

There is no doubt that this historic visit to Paris was inspired by my uncle, and was therefore his responsibility. Its success caused much gratification and pride for all concerned. In essence, it was a highly sophisticated promotion of the recording made by the Gramophone company, but Uncle Fred's warm geniality transformed the whole undertaking into an occasion of great satisfaction and pleasure for Sir Edward and the Menuhins. As soon as they returned to London, Uncle phoned to tell me that Sir Edward had been awarded the GCVO by the King. What a triumph, and what a wonderful homecoming!

After this exciting time, I had to settle down once again to hard work, but Uncle Fred's great kindness didn't end with the Elgar visit. Perhaps he feared that I might have been feeling lonely, away from the family for the first time. He took advantage of his close friendship with the Chaliapins to ask them to include me occasionally in their family life.

The family lived in an enormous apartment in the Avenue d'Eylau, and theirs was nearly always an open house. As Uncle Fred's niece, I always seemed to be welcome, and when I became too homesick I would ask Madame Chaliapin if I could visit them. It was a joy to receive their warm welcome and to sit at their huge table, where lunch and dinner was served, with Feodor Chaliapin at the head, either involved in a loud and boisterous conversation in Russian with his guests or quietly pondering some problem. At the same time the young ones in the family carried on conversations and laughed with friends or amongst themselves. The huge table presented a vivid picture, with Mme Chaliapin, the daughters Marina and Dacia, and the beautiful Stella, Madame's daughter from a previous marriage, seated around it. (Marfa, the eldest of the Chaliapin girls, was already married and living in England.)

Also seated at the table were the resident governesses and tutors and, very often, Sergei Rachmaninov with his wife and two daughters. The two Russians talked endlessly together, perhaps reminiscing about their lives before the revolution, and frequently there were bursts of laughter. Rachmaninov appeared very austere, and of course I was in great awe of his presence, but he was kind and friendly, as were his wife and daughters. They would always greet me warmly and ask after Uncle Fred's health.

What an extraordinary experience it was for a young girl to share even briefly in the lives of these wonderful people! I owed all of this to Uncle Fred, of course, for whom these great artists felt so much affection and respect. Now that I am at an advanced age in my life and living in Paris once again, I feel that I really must find the apartment in the Avenue d'Eylau and enquire if any of the Chaliapin family are still living there. I know that, after his death in 1938, Maria, his wife, and Dacia, the youngest daughter, went to live in New York, while Stella married a Frenchman, the Comte de Limur. Marina, the second daughter, was living in Rome, and Marfa – married to an Englishman – was in England during the war.

The only member of the family with whom I have had contact in recent years is Marfa, who wrote to me after hearing one of my series of broadcasts for the BBC about Uncle Fred's life and career. By that time, she had married again, and had become Lady Hudson-Davis. I also heard from her at a later date, after her return from Russia during the '80s, where she and Chaliapin's descendants had been invited by the Russian government to transfer their father's remains to St Petersburg for reburial. During the great ceremony there, when many of her father's recordings were played, she couldn't help but think how much their family and the world owed to "Uncle Fred", as the Chaliapin children always thought of him. I needn't say more of how deeply touched I was by her affectionate tribute.

As kind as the Picards and their friends were, there were still times when I missed my family and longed for home, and so, when my father came to Paris on business, I would greet him with great enthusiasm and delight. (I suppose that it must have been hard for them at home, too, to be without me.) When he came to Paris, he would spoil me by taking me to the most delightful restaurants, my favourite being La Perigourdine, across the river from Notre Dame, where he would indulge me in my love of artichokes, which were always prepared in the most delicious cheese sauce. These were a *spécialité* of the restaurant, and I loved them. Daddy would say, "How can you eat so much? How is it possible that you're not fat?" I would explain that, if I had eaten frequently at La Perigourdine, I surely would have become fat, but that, although Madame Picard's fare was excellent, there wasn't enough of it. At times, we were joined for dinner by Raymond Greilshamer, the French director of Coty, and often – joy of joys – would visit the theatre. It's little wonder that I anticipated my father's visits with enthusiasm.

The mention of M Greilshamer's name brings to mind another incident that occurred during my student years in Paris. On one evening during the summer he very kindly asked me out. He sent his car to collect me from the Avenue Wagram, and the chauffeur had been instructed to drive me to his flat in the Avenue Raphaël to collect him in time to reach the theatre. As we were somewhat late, the chauffeur had been told to leave me in the car while he went to tell the concièrge to phone M Greilshamer and ask him to come downstairs. While the chauffeur was out of sight, the door of the car was violently wrenched open and a man brandishing a knife jumped in. I screamed in terror, and luckily the chauffeur – who was on his way back – heard me and rushed to the car. The man saw him coming and ran. I don't remember what happened after this, but although I was certainly very shaken I insisted on being taken to the show. After this, I was convinced that Paris was a sinister city, and for a while I was very nervous. Of course, M Greilshamer was more upset than I was, but I made him promise not to tell my father because I knew that he would insist that I should return to London immediately. M Greilshamer kept his word, and I stayed on for many more happy months.

Sometimes, when I stopped practising in the late afternoon, Mme Picard would take me across the Seine to the Rue du Bac and the Rue des Saints Pères to search for *antiquités*. She was a great one for picking up *objéts d'art* which were of little financial value but nevertheless of great prettiness. I enjoyed these expeditions immensely. After spending a couple of hours visiting the shops, we would end these trips with what she called a *goûter* in a patisserie. We also bought the most delicious cakes, wrapped in pink paper on little trays, bound with gold cord, which I took home to share with Madeleine after dinner.

Sometimes we visited her old schoolfriend Mme la Général Dubail, the wife of Général Dubail, who was then head of the Legion d'Honneur. They lived in the Legion's official residence, a beautiful old house on the Quai d'Orsay, which had an enormous number of reception rooms, all of which were filled with beautiful furniture covered in dust-sheets. After passing through these rooms, one would reach a little parlour where Mme Dubail would be sitting, with her parrot on a perch. She was always very charming and welcoming, and would offer us a *goûter* of tea and little cakes.

3 Music Versus Drama

The family seemed to be missing me, and felt that I had been away from home for long enough, and so my return to London was arranged. Also, Uncle Fred may have wanted to keep an eye on my musical training. My health had been affected during the previous few months, probably due to the long hours of practising and the rather light (yet delicious) diet provided by Madame Picard. Indeed, I had been suffering from a series of boils which developed in my armpits and were so painful that I sought help from Sally, the wife of Fred Tyler, one of Uncle's friends and a long-standing colleague in the Gramophone company, who was then resident in Paris, and I dare say that Mrs Tyler had probably reported my plight to the family. In any case, I decided that it was time to go home.

When I returned to London from Paris in the spring of 1934, I immediately arranged lessons with Grace McKnight-Kauffer, who had been highly recommended to me by Philipp. She had been a pupil of his and also of Paderewski's, and began her musical life as a child prodigy. She was a fine musician and a brilliant teacher, and I soon realised that the tuition that I would receive from her would be quite different to that which I had experienced in Paris. Philipp told me that she had been married to the eminent American artist E McKnight-Kauffer, although she was now divorced, and he warned me that she was very bitter about men and not an easy character to deal with. I soon discovered this to be true. However, she was such a fine musician and teacher that I decided to endure any difficulties that might occasionally arise in order to profit from her great musical talents.

Mrs McKnight taught me to speak in music, and that nothing was too difficult if one knew what one wanted to say and, more importantly, if one studied what the composer wished to convey. I stopped playing the gruelling technical exercises from my Paris days, and instead I practised very relaxed scales and other technical exercises every morning before I began the serious study of repertoire. I soon lost the pains in my arms that had worried me greatly by the end of my time in Paris. Mrs McKnight persuaded me that, as soon as I was convinced of the true meaning of the music, nothing would be technically too difficult or impossible. When I had grasped this, the difficulties seemed to fade away. To this day, I have never forgotten what she taught me, and when I'm working in music I think of her advice, and it helps me to overcome the many musical problems which arise.

In 1935, when I was preparing and studying for my first recital in London, I was taking two or sometimes three lessons a week with Mrs McKnight. These were invaluable but exhausting, as she would often get carried away in her enthusiasm, and could be very demanding. My family was grateful for what she was doing for me, although I knew that my mother in particular feared that I had to struggle too hard against her dominating personality. It was perhaps because of this that, on my return from Paris, she reminded me that, when I was twelve years old, Elsie Fogerty, the principal of the Central School of Dramatic Art, had said that there would be a place there for me when I reached a suitable age. Mummy asked me whether I would like to take her up on this. A number of years previously, I had won the coveted annual verse-speaking contest in London, at which the adjudicators were John Masefield, John Drinkwater and John Gielgud, as well as Elsie Fogerty herself. My mother now worked hard to persuade me to add at least a year at the Central School to my musical training programme.

I also thought that maybe it would be a good idea to bring some other interests into my life, and so I agreed to give it a try, but I never stopped the many hours of practising and continued to attend major musical events. I just added my time at the Albert Hall (where the Central School was situated, at the very top of the building) to the hours that I spent at my piano. It was quite spooky up at the school. I was amazed to find that, between the gallery and the outer walls, there was room enough for a small theatre, dressing rooms, classrooms and fencing and dancing rooms – a little world of theatre, in fact!

It was an amusing and happy period, and came as a refreshing break from the rigorous concentration that I devoted to my musical studies. It was also good for me to be with young people of my own age. However, I found that I didn't really like acting, and I never took very much to actors. What actually happened was obvious: I became deeply immersed in the "sound" of poetry. Elsie Fogerty showed interest in me, and became excited at the idea of speaking verse to music. She went on to work with me, and entered me for a number of performances, at which I spoke verse to a musical accompaniment. I quite enjoyed these events, and I remember one in particular that took place at Oxford, with John Drinkwater presiding. I admired his poetry, and so this occasion remains vivid in my memory. I knew that I wasn't going to continue studying at the Central School, but I nevertheless enjoyed it and found myself gravitating toward arranging music for plays and acting less and less. I did play one or two Shakespearean roles, which was very exciting, and both Elsie Fogerty and my mother were disappointed when I decided to return to working exclusively in music.

I was at the Central School for nearly all of 1934. After leaving, I had occasional meetings with two of the girls with whom I had been friends. They were very different in type: Jennifer Skinner was plump and blonde, while Rosemarie Wilder was slim and dark – "Miss Wilder, Wilder and Wilder", as our speech coach, Clifford Turner, said when she was called upon to perform. Jennifer was talented and ambitious, and at that time was beginning to get quite a few jobs on the professional stage. Rosemarie, meanwhile, wasn't pretty, but she was elegant and dressed very well in a rather exotic fashion. I understood that her parents had separated when she was very young, and that she had been brought up by her grandmother. She was a delightful human being, and showed considerable common sense. Curiously enough, she didn't continue with her acting, and I heard that she married a cousin who was an Australian airline pilot, and gave birth to a number of sons. Perhaps this compensated for her own lonely childhood.

Another of my friends at the Central School was Jill Furze. She was an exquisite creature, very small, slight and delicate, and was born to play Juliet. She was a highly gifted actress, certainly the star of the students of that year. I lost touch with her during the war, but some years later I heard that she had married Laurence Whistler, the glass engraver and brother of Rex Whistler, the famous artist. Alas, Jill died in childbirth during the war, and Rex, her brother-in-law, was killed on active service. Many years later, I read in *The Daily Telegraph* that Laurence Whistler had designed and created some beautiful engravings on glass windows for an ancient church in Morton, in Dorset, in memory of Jill, and I resolved to find this little church. I'm so thankful that I did, for the engravings were exquisite and a perfect tribute to her. What a sad fate for this highly gifted family! I'm afraid that the war intervened in all of our lives, and many were doomed to tragedy.

Another friend was Tony Bazelle, who seemed to enjoy a much happier fate. After the war, I read that he was working pretty regularly on the stage, and doing well. I remember him as a most amusing fellow. He and I shared a dreadful weakness: during our days at the Central School, we couldn't appear on the same stage without collapsing into the most idiotic giggles. It was very painful, and we were severely reprimanded by the producers for our corpsing, which I believe is a form of hysteria. In the end, we were forbidden to act in the same plays.

I was nearly 19 years old when I decided that I'd had enough frivolity at the Central School, and I knew that the time had come to resume my concentration exclusively on the piano. My mother was very upset at my decision, for she wanted me to continue acting, and I think that she must have had quite a battle with Mrs McKnight. It wasn't a question of who won; I had always been involved in music, and my year at the drama school was just a sort of relief interlude, which I'm sure did me good. In any case, most of the time I had been practising and arranging music for plays. It certainly wasn't time wasted, as I enjoyed the company of young people, and learned that there were ways of living other than being entirely absorbed in music.

4 *Music At Home And Abroad*

When the musical seasons of 1934-6 were in full swing, I took advantage of the feast of great concerts and operas that were offered to the public. The Berlin Philharmonic, conducted by Furtwängler, gave wonderful concerts at the Queen's Hall, which were enthusiastically supported by the public in spite of the growing anti-German feeling, and the opening of the Glyndebourne Opera Festival at Major Christie's beautiful home in Sussex was perhaps even more exciting. When Uncle Fred heard of this astonishing project, he entered immediately into an exclusive agreement for the recording rights, and *Così Fan Tutte* was recorded on location. I was very much involved, and was wild with excitement at the prospect of attending a number of performances in the charming theatre, as well as one or two of the sessions. It was wonderful to hear the great musician Fritz Busch working with the cast of fine young singers, and I took full advantage of the opportunity. I remember that I was struck by his manner of musical thinking and his method of conveying this to the cast in a manner which closely resembled the musical thoughts expressed by both Edwin Fischer and Mrs McKnight.

I must have thrown myself into the autumn season in London with great enthusiasm. My diary shows that not only was I working with Mrs McKnight but that I was also rehearsing with Olga Hegedus in preparation for her recital at the London Cello School, where I was to play the Grieg sonata with her. I was also practising two-piano works with the French actress Yvonne Arnaud, who had been a pupil of Philipp's at the conservatoire and who had embarked on a career as a pianist until she decided to go onto the stage, where she enjoyed great success as a *comédienne*. She had married an Englishman, and she and I met in Boulogne, curiously enough, while we were awaiting the ferry to take us across the Channel.

I was very relaxed and happy at this time, as I was beginning to give recitals around the country at various schools, which I found to be highly enjoyable. My first performance with Olga Hegedus had been a success, and further concerts together were planned for the following year. I was thus gaining confidence all the time, and was beginning to enjoy playing in public.

As a result of this euphoric state, I decided to persuade my parents to throw a New Year's Eve party at Wayside. To my great pleasure, they agreed. They pretended to be long-suffering when the idea was first suggested, but I knew that they were really looking forward to it, and certainly they enjoyed the event when it took place. All of the family were there, including Aunt Carrie and Uncle Fred, as well as Mondy, who was down from Oxford for the Christmas vacation. A number of his friends were also invited, including Bill Younger, Ralph Instone and John Sherriff. My friends who attended included Mrs Margetson, Coggie and Stella, as well as some of the girls who had been with me at drama school. Many of our guests were musicians from the symphony orchestras, including Laurie Kennedy, the principal cellist of the BBC, and Tony Pini, who led the cellos in the London Philharmonic. (I seem to have had a passion for cellists in those days!)

There were also old friends amongst the singers: the formidable Maggie Teyte, the only artist known to have been feared by Uncle Fred; Peggy Sheridan, who had known my family in Milan long before I was born; Eva Turner; and many others. It was a very happy evening, which drew to a climax when Big Ben struck midnight, when a small fountain which I had insisted on installing in the middle of the drawing room sprayed not water but champagne. It was certainly a huge success, and after this the fun grew fast and furious.

Laurie Kennedy and Tony Pini were sufficiently inspired by the champagne to display their orchestral rivalry by fighting a duel with Frankfurter sausages. We had engaged a little Zigeuner band to play Viennese waltzes throughout the evening, but things really went with a swing when Uncle Fred sent the band home, sat down at the piano and got everyone singing old favourites. There was no doubt that the party was great fun, and was remembered with nostalgia by my friends when I met them in later years.

I enjoyed my family life, which was full of vitality and interest, and I can't remember feeling restricted in any way, probably because I shared many interests with my parents. My enthusiasm must have been boundless, for I was practising for many hours a day and going to hear as much music as I could. I was in training for my concert on 5 December 1936, which was drawing near, and I was concentrating on preparing myself for this trial. I was also playing sonatas with Eleanor Warren, as well as with Olga Hegedus, and I shared their recitals at the cello school and at the Wigmore Hall.

I remember a bizarre incident that occurred when I was practising with Eleanor. We were working in her home in Kensington when Eleanor's father, Colonel Warren, knocked on the door. He told us that we had to stop playing for a few minutes as Emperor Haile Selassie had just arrived to view the house, which was up for sale, and he wanted to inspect the drawing room. My consternation was considerable. This was in 1936, at the height of the war in Abyssinia, which Italy had just invaded. With my Italian name, I wasn't at all happy to meet the Emperor at this time. However, when Colonel Warren introduced us and we made our curtseys, the Emperor never even blinked when he heard my name, and the incident passed off peacefully.

From my very young days, Walter Legge and I had always shared a close friendship. In fact, the story goes that Uncle Fred introduced me to him when I was about six years old, shortly after my arrival in England from Italy. He was then a youth of 16 or so, just joining the staff of the Gramophone company's in-house magazine, *The Voice*. It seems that I remarked to my uncle that he was "a funny boy", so obviously I had taken notice of him from a very young age. He showed early ability, both as a knowledgeable musician and as a talented writer, and as he gained experience in the world of music, by coming into contact with the great artists, his potential as a powerful personality also grew. Walter and David Bicknell acted as Uncle Fred's assistants for a while, and David remained a faithful supporter over the years. Indeed, he was one of the last people to visit him before his death, in 1951.

Walter, however, was another character altogether. He could be difficult to deal with, because his ambition and undoubted brilliance certainly caused trouble at times. He quarrelled frequently with Rex Palmer, who had joined the artists' department at a later date, and often these young men nearly came to blows. It was always left to Uncle to deal with these tiresome situations, which were somewhat exhausting and exasperating.

I had always found Walter very attractive. He began to develop as an impresario almost as soon as he joined the company, and he was also the possessor of a delightful sense of humour, which made him an amusing companion. Many people disliked him, but most of them had to admit that they enjoyed his company. I can remember my mother saying that she didn't really want to invite Walter to our Sunday evening *soirées*, but if he wasn't there she was disappointed. My parents, Uncle Fred and Aunt Carrie really feared that a serious attachment might develop between Walter and myself. However, common sense prevailed.

In the meantime, I was working hard in preparing for my concert, and was also attending magnificent performances at Covent Garden. I was fortunate to hear both cycles of Wagner's *Ring* when Melchior, Lehmann, Frida Leider, Olczewska and Friedrich Schorr and artists of a similar calibre were singing. In addition to these musical feasts, I was also lucky enough to hear Toscanini perform three times at the Queen's Hall, as well as at the Vienna Philharmonic. (How I miss that wonderful hall, with its superb acoustics! What a tragic loss it was to London's musical life when it was later completely destroyed by a German bomb.) There was also an unforgettable performance of Strauss's *Der Rosenkavalier* at Covent Garden, performed with Lotte Lehmann, Elizabeth Schumann and Olczewska.

During the international season, our house would be quite a mecca for artists. They loved coming to visit us on Sunday evenings to escape from hotel life and to enjoy a warm welcome and good food in our family atmosphere. From 1935 until the outbreak of the war, Villa Valli lived up to its reputation as being a home from home for many artists, including some of those escaping from Nazi Germany.

In that summer, we spent our first holiday in Austria, at St Gilgen, on the Wolfgangsee, which was a truly beautiful place. It was perfect – there was something there for everyone. Mondy and I enjoyed the companionship of the other young people – plenty of pretty girls for Mondy, and handsome young Austrians for me. One of these was Bucca Furstenberg, whose family had a summer place on the lake, and another was Rudolph Adamcyk von Baranssky, a goalkeeper for the Austrian ice-hockey team, who seemed particularly glamorous, possibly because of his long name! It was delightful fun to go swimming and boating with them, and in my memory the weather remained fine, which is admittedly unusual in the Tyrol.

Most wonderful of all was the Salzburg Festival. In the late afternoon, we would don our evening clothes and set off on the perilous mountain drive to attend the opera. First of all, on our arrival in Salzburg, we would usually go for a drink at the Café Bazaar, where the famous gathered, and would then move on to the *Festspielhaus* in time to enjoy a delicious "snack". This usually consisted of *Wienerwürstel* in a crusty roll, which was washed down with either beer or champagne depending on our financial position at the time. Then came the great and glorious performances, which were the purpose of our being there. As I write, I can see a programme on my desk, yellow and rather tattered, advertising a performance of Beethoven's *Fidelio*, conducted by Arturo Toscanini. Looking back, I can hardly believe that I was present at such a magical musical event, and when I open the old programme – a very modest leaflet – I read that Lotte Lehmann was Leonora. It just seems too wonderful to be true!

I remember that Feodor and Maria Chaliapin and Stella Petzol, Maria's daughter, motored from Salzburg to have lunch with us at our hotel at St Gilgen, which caused great excitement amongst the other guests. After a very happy day spent enjoying an excellent but simple lunch (for Chaliapin was diabetic), we took a short stroll to the lake. Then, after sitting in an admiring circle, listening to the great man telling us stories of his fabulous career, it was time to change and get ready for the drive to Salzburg for the performance of *Don Giovanni*, with Pinza in the lead role.

After this, the Chaliapins invited me to ride in their car to Salzburg. My parents weren't very happy, for they feared the wild driving of Vincenzo, the Chaliapins' Italian chauffeur. However, they couldn't stand against my delight at the invitation, nor the Chaliapins' insistent promises that they would look after me with the greatest care, and so off we went on this dangerous mountain road, hurtling around bends, with Feodor sitting by Vincenzo and me in the back with Madame Chaliapin and Stella. It was wild indeed, and Vincenzo drove as though we were competing in a grand prix, whilst Chaliapin sang all the way, gesticulating and acting out some great role. I was a bit frightened to start with, but as Madame Chaliapin took it all in her stride I decided that there was only one thing I could do, and that was to enjoy the experience to the full.

When we arrived, the Chaliapins must have gone to their hotel to change, but not before M Chaliapin had insisted that I should accompany him to the performance and sit with him. Imagine my reaction to this invitation, for I knew that the great artist would be the focus of everyone's attention. I must say that I was filled with some trepidation. I certainly had reason for my fears, for from the moment we entered the auditorium the whisper went around, "Chaliapin, Chaliapin," like a strong gust of wind, and all eyes were on us. I sat between him and his wife, for which I was grateful, for Madame Chaliapin's calm acceptance of the commotion caused by our entrance gave me courage.

I needed reassurance, for my fears were amply justified. At every entry of Pinza, the great bass who was singing the role of the Don, Chaliapin made comments in a loud whisper. His opening gambit was nearly always, "Non, non, non cosi," and then a *sotto voce* demonstration of how *he* would sing it! To my amazement, Pinza took it in good heart, as indeed did the audience. In fact, I think that it added to the thrill of the performance. I can't remember which of the distinguished conductors was in command, but he must have been very patient, for no violence occurred. I remember excusing myself in the interval so that I could sit with the family, and I think that Uncle took my place. Chaliapin was probably showing off, like the great child that he could be, and because he was so adored nobody seemed to mind, not even Pinza!

After a wonderful *Falstaff*, with Stabile and Toscanini conducting, and a performance of *Così Fan Tutte* that I don't remember very clearly, we spent a further week enjoying ourselves at St Gilgen. After that it was back to London, passing through Vienna, Budapest, Innsbruck and Zurich on the way, reaching home on 30 August.

There were now only four months to go before my first recital at the American Women's Club. I can't help but think that it would have been wiser, in view of Uncle Fred's position in the world of music, if I had first given concerts at many more of the big schools around the country and recitals in the provinces before tackling a London audience. Admittedly, the recital wasn't going to be a professional affair, as it would have been if held in the Wigmore Hall, and no critics were invited in their professional capacity, but nevertheless it was a tremendous ordeal that lay before me, and I must admit that I was very frightened.

The actual event had a dream-like quality about it, and yet it was very vivid. I remember driving to Grosvenor Square with my mother and father, dressed in my first concert gown, which had been made for me by our French dressmaker, Mme Fernande. I was wrapped in a fur coat, and my hands were clad in woollen gloves because it was very cold, and in any case I was frozen within from fear. The hall was packed, for everyone present wanted to hear what Fred Gaisberg's niece could do. To this day, I can remember walking onto the stage in my beautiful white gown and sitting before this great friendly instrument and beginning to play. I opened with a Bach prelude and fugue in B minor, followed by Beethoven's sonata in E major opus 31, number three, and then the very difficult group of Brahms waltzes, opus 39, followed by Rachmaninov's prelude in G minor, opus 23, before ending with a group of pieces by Scriabin, opus eleven. As I played, I began to settle down, and I don't think that I did too badly. The audience – many of whom were my friends and had known me since childhood – was warm and kind. They wished me well, and their warmth gave me courage.

In the years before the war, I played in many concerts in England and Scotland, in large and famous schools. Every concert increased my experience, and I grew more and more confident. After my recitals abroad in 1938, I found that I actually enjoyed playing in public. These were three years of endeavour, happiness and great interest, as the shadow of war that loomed over us was still too unbelievably awful to even consider seriously.

The first of these concerts took place at Westminster School in the beautiful ancient "Up-school". Mondy was in his last year there, and so of course he was present. He must have been very concerned that I should do well, and indeed my playing there was quite a responsibility for both of us. As far as I can remember, all went well. This was my first concert of a tour, and a few days later, on 6 March, I left Euston Station early in the morning to travel to Chester, where I was due to give a recital that afternoon. I can't remember whether I went alone or whether my mother was with me, but I do remember a beautiful old hall, playing well, and leaving by train immediately after the concert, arriving in London late at night. These two recitals were very important, as they served to bolster my confidence. Only by frequently performing in public could I achieve this.

The next concerts on my schedule were far more crucial, for I was due to perform in two very well-known musical centres. My programme was heavy, beginning with the Bach *Italian Concerto* and an early Beethoven sonata, possibly opus 31 number three again, followed by the entire Brahms opus 76, which demands both mental and physical endurance. Not content with this hefty undertaking, I completed my programme with three Chopin nocturnes and the great ballade in G minor. It was fortunate indeed that the Chester concert had gone so well, and that it had built up my confidence, for two days later, on 8 March, my mother and I left by train for Manchester, where I was to give my first truly public recital, in the Houldsworth Hall. This was a big undertaking, as Manchester was the home of the fine Hallé Orchestra and the centre of a sophisticated and knowledgeable public. John Barbirolli had asked a number of friends to come and hear me, and so this was a considerable trial to overcome. In the event, it went well, and my mother and I left for Glasgow by train the next day feeling pretty confident. The journey was very pleasant, and I remember that we both fell in love with the beautiful scenery of the north of England.

My next recital was in Glasgow, at the Stevenson Hall on 12 March, my 20th birthday. This concert was also important, as John Barbirolli – who had just left Glasgow to take over from Toscanini in New York – had arranged for friends to be there to help us. Imagine how relieved I was to know that John himself wouldn't be there, which he would have been if he'd been in the country. That would have been too much for my nerves! On the morning of my ordeal, I went alone to the Stevenson Hall to try out the piano and to listen to the acoustics. The hall was quite large, and I can remember feeling quietly comfortable on the tram coming back to our hotel, thinking that the constant public appearances were doing their work and that I was actually beginning to enjoy myself. I played well that night, and received good reviews from the critics in both Manchester and Glasgow. We returned to London feeling relieved and happy.

It was wonderful to have my mother with me. As an artist herself, she was both critical and helpful. It must have been strange for her to see her daughter embarking on a musical career, and at times quite a nervous strain, but she was a great help and comfort to me.

As usual, London was the centre of the most exciting musical season. We took the train back from Glasgow after the concert, and on the very next night I attended a Horowitz concert at the Queen's Hall. I was very tired after so much travelling, but I remember how excited and thrilled I was by his wonderful playing. The feast of music seemed endless, for on 30 April I was once again in the Queen's Hall for a concert by Rachmaninov. How incredible it is to remember that I was actually present to hear these masters, world renowned and remembered forever. It seems like a dream, and it makes me wonder whether it was my youth and enthusiasm which made them appear to be of a quite superb calibre or whether – as it seems to me now – I have never heard performances of such greatness since.

Life wasn't all hard work and going to the opera and concerts. I had many friends, such as the Crawfords, to whose home I was often invited to enjoy cocktail parties and dances. There was also the Robertson family, who entertained most generously in their large house in Hampstead, and whose daughter Margaret, known as Woppets, was a particular friend of mine. Billy Robertson, her brother, was at Oxford with Stewart Crawford, and so we were a happy little band.

There were other friends, too, who were immensely kind and supportive to me as a young artist. Most memorable, because of her outstanding character and intellect, was Miriam Sacher, of the Marks & Spencer family (I don't remember which), whom I had met at Hendaye whilst on holiday, and who remained a staunch supporter of mine until my marriage. I remember that she and her husband, Harry Sacher, both came to my wedding.

Other friends were Aksarova, the Russian singer, and dear Eva Turner, the great British soprano, who was a friend of the family from our Milan days. She was warm, generous and wonderfully encouraging and supportive to me as a young artist. She gave me much advice on how to overcome the dreaded nerves which struck during performances, but agreed that experience was the only real cure.

1937 was a very full and fruitful year for me. The music world was particularly brilliant, as everything possible had been arranged to make the coronation year as glamorous as possible. Many great artists and orchestras visited London, including the Berlin Philharmonic, under Furtwängler, and there were wonderful performances of the *Ring* cycles at Covent Garden, again with Furtwängler in command of the greatest Wagnerian singers in the world. The first cycle starred Völker as Siegmund, Frida Leider as Brünhilde, Maria Müller as Sieglinde, Max Lorenz as Siegfried, Bockelmann as Wotan and Weber as Hunding, and in the second cycle, the beloved Melchior played Siegfried, and Kirsten Flagstad, on her first appearance in London, was Brünhilde. These were heady days indeed, and even then the cup was not yet full, for Toscanini also arrived in London to conduct a series of concerts with the BBC Symphony Orchestra, and many international instrumentalists were also present to make their contribution to the coronation festivities.

It seemed to be an endless feast, and one simply didn't know where to draw the line. In fact, one didn't, for fear of missing some unforgettable musical event. Indeed, we were right to feel this way, since this year was to prove the end of an era. Those of us who had contacts in Europe – particularly in Germany and Austria – were only too conscious of the perilous situation. There were endless stories of artists being thrown out of musical institutions in Germany because they were Jewish, leaving everything behind them except – thank God! – their great talent, from which we benefited. It was hard to believe that Germany, the home of such great music-making, could behave in such a way.

From my diary, I see that on 6 May I tore myself away from London to go to Vienna with Uncle Fred for six days or so, where I believe that he had arranged to help one of the Gramophone company's Jewish artists. It must have been very important, in any case, to have forced him away from the coronation season, in which he was very much involved. I remember that visit to Vienna very well, for a beautiful ring that was given to me as a 21st birthday gift by my godmother, Drusilla Bossi, was stolen. (I have other bad memories of losing things in Vienna, including a Stradivarius violin, a story I shall recount later.) As I remember, it was a sinister visit, and I was happy and relieved to get back to dear old London.

When Toscanini was conducting his series of concerts with the BBC Symphony Orchestra at the Queen's Hall, obtaining tickets for these events was almost impossible. However, because Uncle Fred had played an important part in helping the BBC to arrange them, our family was fortunate to attend at least some of these superb performances.

During his visit, Toscanini generously offered to conduct a concert in Oxford as a tribute to the great university and as a gracious gesture of thanks for the wonderful reception that he was receiving in England. When he heard of this, Mondy was determined to obtain tickets, which were like nuggets of gold. He succeeded and invited me to come to the concert, which was to take place at the Playhouse Theatre, the only sizeable hall in Oxford. I was thrilled at the thought, and on the appointed day, on instructions from Mondy, I was at Paddington Station in plenty of time for the train, which left at 11am. I remember that I was dressed in a pretty new spring coat and feeling rather pleased with myself. However, when I arrived at Oxford, expecting to find Mondy waiting for me, I saw no sign of him. I thought that there must have been some misunderstanding, and so I decided to take a taxi to Christ Church, thinking that he would be there. He wasn't, though, and Bill Younger, who happened to be in Mondy's rooms, told me that he had gone to the station as arranged to meet me.

In a state of panic I took another taxi back to the station, where I found Mondy looking grey with anxiety. Apparently he had met the special train, which had been laid on for the occasion and about which I hadn't been told, and so of course I wasn't on it. Poor boy. He told me that he had rushed around, opening carriage doors in his search for his missing sister. Finally, he had said to a porter, "Have you seen my sister? She's not on the train. Have you looked under the seats?" Luckily, I appeared at this moment, and all ended well.

On the way back to Mondy's rooms, which overlooked Meadows and where lunch was waiting, we saw a large black limousine with Toscanini sitting in it. He was on his way to the theatre, I supposed, to see the hall before the concert, which was due to begin at three o'clock. It was a remarkable gesture on Toscanini's part to take the time to leave London in the midst of his heavy schedule at the Queen's Hall and to give this unique performance. It was unforgettable, and I'm grateful to Mondy for having made it possible, in spite of the drama of fearing that he would find his sister's body under a seat on the Paddington train!

5 *Mausi Wagner, Menuhins And Motors*

"What on Earth are you doing here? Nobody is allowed to be at the Toscanini rehearsals."

These were the first words I ever heard spoken by Friedelind "Mausi" Wagner, and they heralded a friendship that began on 2 June 1937 and lasted until she died on 8 May 1991. Mausi was incurably generous, and I received many gifts from her over the years, but the one that I value the most is a handsome volume entitled *The Life Of Franz Liszt In Pictures And Documents* by Ernst Burger. The inscription that she wrote inside the cover touched me deeply: "For a very happy birthday, dearest Isabella, as well as in celebration and appreciation of 50 years of friendship. With loving wishes, Mausi. Lucerne, 12 March 1987 – Toscanini rehearsal, June 1937."

The rehearsal to which she refers was the one at the Queen's Hall. She was present at Toscanini's invitation, and I had been smuggled in by Uncle Fred, who was determined that I should hear as much of Toscanini as possible, with strict instructions for me to stay hidden at the back of the stalls, under the balcony. It was when I emerged during the break in the rehearsal that I heard Mausi's clear, light soprano voice challenging my right to be there. She had brought Coggie Margetson with her, and of course in a few moments Coggie introduced us. Although I pretended to be rather affronted by Mausi's teasing, we decided to shake hands and go to Yarners, the famous coffee shop next door to the hall, to celebrate our meeting.

I was interested in meeting Mausi, for Coggie had told me so much about Richard Wagner's granddaughter. It was fascinating to see her resemblance to the great composer, and although she was a handsome girl she had nevertheless inherited the Wagner nose. This was a feature shared by most of the Wagner descendants of her generation, except for the youngest, Verena, who resembled her great-grandfather, Franz Liszt, and who was certainly prettier than Mausi, although she appeared to lack her forceful personality.

I had heard much from Coggie about her friendship with Friedelind, but although we both attended many performances at Covent Garden and the Queen's Hall, somehow I had just missed being there at the same time. As I said, Coggie was a hero-worshipper, and her life centred on the adoration of famous artists, with some of whom she became close friends. The most important of these was Frida Leider, the great portrayer of Brünhilde, and it was through her that Coggie met Mausi. At the time of their meeting, Mausi had still been a schoolgirl, sent to England by her mother, Winifred, really to get rid of her, as Mausi's indiscreetly-proclaimed anti-Nazi feelings were an embarrassment to the pro-Nazi entourage in Bayreuth, headed by her mother. Leaders of the Nazi party, including Adolf Hitler himself, filled their house, Wahnfried, during the festivals, and Mausi had grown to hate and fear them.

She was living in London on the modest allowance that her mother sent her, on Hitler's own permission, but mostly she was supported by her many generous friends. I well remember poor Mausi's nervousness growing as the day for the monthly arrival of the cheque from Germany drew near, and how she would wonder whether or not it would actually turn up. As she explained, she didn't know what she would do if it didn't, for she feared to return to her home in Bayreuth. She was a frequent guest at Wayside, and became very much part of the family, calling those close to her Uncle Fred, Aunt Carrie, Mummy, etc, just as I did. She was at that time rather a lost soul. It's neither easy nor safe to openly declare against one's country's politics, especially those preached by Nazi fanatics. We spent hours listening to her stories about the Nazi leaders, and it was fascinating to be on the inside at such a critical time in history.

At the end of July 1937, my parents, Mondy and I went to America to visit my mother's family, as by now we all felt in our hearts that war with Germany was inevitable, and it seemed right to see the American relations again. We had a delightful ten days on the Atlantic, crossing the ocean in Cunard's great liner the *Adriatic*. We enjoyed this immensely, but when we arrived in New York the incredible heat knocked us out, particularly Daddy and Mondy, who simply couldn't bear it. We were met by Mr Brookes, the chief executive of Coty in America, and taken on board his yacht, on which we sailed for a week on Long Island Sound. In prospect this seemed a marvellous idea, but in fact the heat on board the small vessel was unbearable. Our menfolk in particular didn't enjoy themselves. It was rather embarrassing; poor Mr Brookes was so kind and hospitable, but he couldn't reduce the temperature. We were thankful when the cruise ended and we were free to escape to Massachusetts to join our cousins, "the twins", in Attleboro, a pleasant small New England town, where it was cooler, thank goodness.

It was a delightful and happy visit, and we all enjoyed it. Mummy was especially happy to see her sister, Belle, for we feared that it would prove to be the last time for many years.

We saw much of Mausi during the autumn of that year, and on reading the letters which she later wrote she reminded me of some of the events that we had enjoyed during the late summer of 1937. One in particular stands out in my memory. The Menuhin family was in London, staying as usual at the Grosvenor House, where I would visit them with Uncle Fred. I felt sorry for Yaltah, the youngest, who seemed to be leading a rather dismal life, being dragged about in their strange nomadic existence. I thought that she would enjoy some happy hours with young people, and so I decided to organise a visit to see Mondy at Oxford, with Yaltah and Mausi as our guests. When I broke the news to my uncle, he was horrified at first at the thought of taking such a risk with one of the precious Menuhin children, but he said that he would put the idea to Papa and Mama Menuhin. Much to everyone's amazement, they agreed to the trip. Mondy was delighted with the prospect of hosting such a prestigious luncheon party, and set about organising the meal, which would be sent up to his rooms from the famous Christ Church kitchens, and choosing the other guests whom they were to meet.

I could only observe, however. I wasn't allowed to drive them to Oxford in my old Ford, Sieglinde. Daddy kindly allowed Waylett to drive us in the family car, and off we went on 3 June 1937, on a beautiful summer's day, Mausi, Yaltah and me sitting sedately on the back seat of the family's Armstrong Siddeley. Yaltah, who was very pretty, wore a pale blue cap with a long feather, and to the best of my remembrance she didn't take it off for the whole day! We were greeted on our arrival by Mondy, his great friend Bill Younger, Ralph Instone and a young German, Jobst von der Gröben, who on hearing that Mondy was to be host to Yaltah Menuhin had practically thrown himself at his feet, begging to be invited to meet her. He was a fine musician himself, and a passionate admirer of Yehudi. So there we were, gathered together in Mondy's rooms overlooking Meadows and sitting down to a delicious lunch, which I'm sure ended with the famous Christ Church meringues.

It was a happy and rather dream-like day, and it had a very unexpected outcome, for Yaltah and Jobst fell deeply in love with one other, in a manner reminiscent of Romeo and Juliet. The lunch was very jolly and amusing, even though Jobst and Yaltah were strangely silent. After lunch, Jobst said to me, "Do you think Yaltah and Miss Wagner would like to come to my rooms in New College? I think that they would enjoy their beauty, and they could also see my piano, which has just been sent over from Germany." We agreed, of course, and so Mausi, Yaltah and I walked with him through the beautiful gardens to his rooms in New College, where he proudly showed us his fine grand piano and asked Yaltah if she would like to play.

Without another word she sat down and began with the orchestral opening of Beethoven's *Emperor* concerto, and proceeded to play through the whole work, both the orchestral and the solo parts. It was a magnificent and inspired performance, and one which I have never forgotten. Afterwards, I said to Mausi, "I think that she's the most talented of all the Menuhins." Yaltah and Jobst were in such a euphoric state that I could hardly separate them. Finally, after she had begged Jobst to come to London to visit her at the Grosvenor House (she felt that her parents would be happy to welcome him), we persuaded her to start back on the journey to London.

We three girls sat on the back seat once again, with Yaltah in the middle, still in her little blue cap with the feather, which was rather drooping by this time. Suddenly, quite out of the blue, she pulled from around her neck a gold chain with a small ring attached, and told us that it was her engagement ring. Imagine how astonished Mausi and I felt on receiving this totally unexpected news. Her behaviour with Jobst certainly hadn't indicated that she was involved with anyone else, and as she was only 16 years old I wondered what I'd started, and what Uncle would say to me now. Mausi and I said, "Explain, please."

Yaltah was only too happy to tell us then that she was engaged to a young man in New York – a scientist, I believe – and that he was an Australian, related to the "Aspro" family, whose son and daughter were engaged to Yehudi and Hepzibah! This fact in itself caused much comment, as nobody could understand why on Earth such apparently unsuitable marriages had been arranged. Perhaps Papa and Mama Menuhin thought that it was time for Yehudi to marry, and the "Aspro" family (whose name I cannot remember) was highly respected. Meanwhile, Mausi and I gathered from Yaltah that Yehudi and Hepzibah thought that it would be rather amusing if Yaltah married the young New York relative. Yaltah, however, didn't want this. She knew nothing about marriage at that stage in her life, and she told Mausi and me that she had no intention of going through with the wedding. The Menuhins had lived in such an extraordinary way, utterly removed from normal life, and I was sure that such marriages would prove to be disastrous, as indeed they were. Goodness, I thought. This is a situation. How am I going to cope when we return her to her parents?

On the way home, Yaltah begged me not to say anything about Jobst, and so, when we reached the Grosvenor House, Mausi and I went up to the suite and handed her over to the family. We stayed for only a few minutes, during which time Yaltah thanked me prettily for the happy day, and Mausi and I soon took our departure. I heard from Uncle Fred a few days later, after he had visited the Menuhins, that Jobst had been to see Yaltah – not once, in fact, but on a number of occasions, before the Menuhins left to go back to America – and that he was very much liked by them. As things turned out, nothing came of their meeting, for war broke out and Jobst vanished back to Germany. Yaltah ended up marrying the young scientist, and their marriage indeed turned out to be unsuccessful.

After our return from the holiday in America, we found that the excitement of the coronation was calming down and that the awful worrying about the gathering clouds of war was becoming more and more evident. London was still enjoying a brilliant season of concerts and theatrical activities, and I had to settle down to hours of hard work at the piano to prepare my programme of concert repertoire. Toscanini came back to London to conduct a series of concerts, and Mausi immediately appeared from who knows where to be with her beloved maestro, whom she adored both as a conductor and a friend. He had known her from her very early years in Bayreuth, and she had always had a special place in his affections. She also attended performances at Covent Garden, where so many of her friends amongst the German singers were performing. From them she heard of the terrible way that artists were being treated in Germany, and she was filled with horror. I know that she didn't go back to Bayreuth, as I have an entry in my diary, dated 20 July, in which I note that

I had arranged to meet her for lunch in London. After that, I went away and didn't hear from her until I received a letter from Paris, dated 10 October, in which she wrote that she had gone with Toscanini and his family to Lucerne for the festival and then with them to his home in Milan, where he remained. She then went on with friends to Venice, which she absolutely adored. She told me that she had never known anything more wonderful than riding in a gondola. "It was the perfection of locomotion."

When in London, Mausi spent much time in our home, and she seemed to feel that she had a place there where she felt completely safe. Many were the hours that we spent discussing the terrible situation, which was growing more threatening by the day. She described vividly the fanatical zeal of the Nazis, so we were perhaps more *au fait* about the situation than most people.

In the meantime, Mondy was back at Christ Church for the autumn term, trying (and probably succeeding) to put all thoughts of war behind him. In this, I suppose that he was like all of the young men that were there during that time. Our home was always full of friends, and we were determined to enjoy life as much as possible in spite of the gathering clouds. Our Sunday-evening suppers when visiting artists were in London were as popular as ever, and I spent many happy hours in the studios when great pianists were recording.

There was one ordeal to which Uncle Fred subjected me, however, which I have never forgotten. He asked Wilhelm Backhaus – for whom I had the deepest respect – to listen to my piano playing. He and my uncle were good friends, and Backhaus was one of the kindest people in the world of music. Nevertheless, I was filled with dread at the prospect. As it turned out, though, the occasion went very well. He came to our house, and I'm sure that he was as nervous as I was, for he wouldn't wish to hurt my feelings if it were necessary to give an adverse opinion. I remember that I practised up until the moment of his arrival, and that I was actually playing one of the Brahms Rhapsodies opus 79 when he rang the front doorbell. I needn't have been worried, however, for he was so kind and encouraging that I almost enjoyed myself. He too was relieved to be able to praise my work, and so we were both happy, as indeed was Uncle Fred, who had taken a considerable risk in asking this favour of the great pianist. He would never have done so had they not been friends for many years.

On looking through my diary of 1938, I realise now – perhaps more than I did then – that our lives were dominated by the approaching menace of war. I can remember sitting on the stairs at Wayside with Mondy, Ralph Instone and Walter Legge, looking at one another in despair and saying over and over, "Surely it isn't possible. It can't happen again." Those involved in the international music world were perhaps more conscious than others of what was really going on; more and more artists were leaving Germany and Austria and quietly slipping away to England and America.

That year, Uncle Fred went to Vienna to record a concert on 19 January in the beautiful old Musikverein Hall, in which Bruno Walter conducted Mahler's ninth symphony. He had persuaded his company that this was a golden opportunity, as it could be the last chance of recording this great conductor with his own orchestra. Indeed, this proved to be the case, as two months later the Germans marched into Austria. By this time, Bruno Walter had left, and he listened to the masters of the recording in Paris when Uncle took them over from London for his approval.

There seemed to be a great concert every night in London. Furtwängler arrived in January with the Berlin Philharmonic, Mengelberg came to conduct the LPO, and this is to say nothing of Toscanini, who arrived to conduct concerts with the BBC Symphony Orchestra in May and June. Covent Garden also welcomed many of the great stars who were leaving Germany for political reasons, including Frida Leider, whose husband was Jewish; Elizabeth Schumann, who came to London with her family; and Lotte Lehmann, who collapsed on stage during a performance of Richard Strauss's *Der Rosenkavalier* because of the agony of worry that she was enduring at the thought of her husband's fate in Germany. One performance I can never forget was of Mozart's *Die Zauberflöte*, in which Richard Tauber sang Tamino and the incomparable Tiana Lemnitz was Tamina. Never have I heard such perfection before or since. Sir Thomas Beecham conducted this sublime performance, and he was on magnificent form. He also triumphed in his production of Strauss's *Elektra*.

In spite of the stress under which we were living, our lives consisted of the usual routine of work and pleasure. I was preparing programmes for my European tour, which was scheduled to begin in Holland in February of the following year, while Mondy returned to Oxford after Christmas for the spring term. He seemed to be in good form, and enjoyed his time spent in the beautiful ageless surroundings of Christ Church. Meanwhile, I was also busy with rehearsals and performances with my cellist friends, and taking and giving lessons. I enjoyed these very much, especially those with Coggie Margetson, whose enthusiasm made up for her lack of technical ability. I had kept to my routine of four hours practising in the morning and again in the afternoon, interrupted by a walk over Hampstead Heath, very often in Coggie's company, during which we would gossip about the musical scandals and events of the moment. I also went over to Paris once or twice to study a particular work with Philipp.

At the end of July, Mondy borrowed my old Ford, Sieglinde, and went off with Ralph Instone to drive to Rome, spending time wandering through France on the way. Although Sieglinde was a gallant steed, she was by now pretty ancient, and so it was something of an adventure. It was planned that my parents and I would meet Mondy in Rome, and that I would drive back to England with him in Sieglinde, as Ralph had made other arrangements. All went well, and we spent some delightful days sightseeing in that fabulous city.

One incident remains vividly in my memory. We decided to visit the Vatican, and drove there in the old car. As we had already spent some days inside the Vatican Museum, we decided that this time we would devote ourselves to the gardens. When we arrived – my parents, Mondy and me, all packed into the old Ford V8 – we were greeted by a handsome and magnificently uniformed Swiss papal guard. When we explained to him that we wished to visit the Pope's private gardens, he volunteered at once to go with us and give us a conducted tour. What a funny sight we must have been, five adults, including our handsome escort, all squeezed into the old jalopy and driving through the Pope's own gardens. It was hilarious, and we all laughed and enjoyed ourselves immensely, including the guard! This was the last holiday that I would ever spend with my family. We didn't realise this, of course, but I'm sure that the hidden anxiety of our fate loomed behind our happy laughter.

After the Vatican expedition, Mondy and I left Rome on 15 August to begin the return journey to England in Sieglinde. We started off in great spirits. The car carried us gallantly during the first days, and we stopped first of all at Rimini and then at Venice, that beautiful and fantastic city. It was after this that Sieglinde began to rebel, and the old engine started making strange noises. Mondy began to look more and more harassed. I wasn't worrying too much at this stage because I was enjoying myself so much that I didn't care where we broke down.

Then, not very far from Milan, disaster struck. Luckily, we were able to telephone our grandmother's home, and when we got there we found Uncle Vermondo there alone, as the other members of the family were away in the mountains. He came to our rescue, organising a tow to his garage and inviting us to stay until the car was repaired. We were lucky, and enjoyed our visit very much. Uncle Vermondo suggested that, while the car was in the garage, we should go up to San Vito di Cadore, where our grandmother and the rest of the family were staying. He must have driven us there and then arranged for the mechanic to drive Sieglinde to meet us at San Vito as soon as she was ready. I thoroughly enjoyed our extra and unexpected time with our family in the beautiful Trentino Mountains, but Mondy remained concerned, doubtful that Sieglinde would recover sufficiently to get us back to England.

He was right to be concerned, for we had no sooner set off when once again the old car packed up, and we were stuck again. This time we were rescued by my godmother, Drusilla Bossi, and her husband, Achille, who arranged for a mechanic to try and fix Sieglinde while Mondy and I spent the night in their beautiful villa on Lake Maggiore. I shall never forget the sight of the full moon shining on the waters of the lake when I came out onto the balcony from my bedroom. It was quite magical. The beauty was further enhanced when an incredibly handsome young lawyer – one of Uncle Achille's assistants – walked out onto his balcony at the same time. I couldn't help wishing that Sieglinde would still be unable to proceed the next morning!

The car was fine, however, and off we went again, this time to cross the Simplon Pass into Switzerland. We hoped and prayed that the old car would survive this ordeal and get us safely over the mighty mountains. In fact, not only did she do this but we actually reached the outskirts of Paris before she collapsed again, near Fontainebleau. This time there was no one to telephone for help, but fortunately we were rescued by a little Algerian man who was a genius mechanic. He put Sieglinde right and we never had any trouble with her again.

Meanwhile, we telephoned the family in London. They had been hearing of our misadventures all over Europe, and so we told them that we were very comfortable, spending a day or two in one of the most beautiful hotels near Paris while waiting for Sieglinde to recover before we attempted the last leg of our journey to the Channel and back to London. My father's only comment was, "Well, you are a cheeky pair, I must say."

6 A New Family And Marriage

1938 was a year that those of us who lived through it can never forget. It was as though a great black cloud was hanging over us, which we tried to dispel so that we could get on with our normal lives. It's hard to believe, on looking through my diaries, that we continued to enjoy our social lives, going to concerts and the opera and even taking holidays in Europe, in spite of Hitler's sabre-rattling, his terrible threats against the Czechs and the frequent broadcasts of his sinister rallies, during which he whipped his audience to a frenzy. How did I ever imagine that I would be able to go on my European tour at the beginning of 1939? The panic caused by the Munich crisis put an end to any hopes I might have had of giving a recital in Prague, even though Chamberlain came back waving a piece of paper and announcing that there would be "peace in our time".

It was in the autumn of that fateful year that Dick Corbett and I began to see something of one another. It was at a cocktail party given by Lady Crawford at Heath House that we really spoke for the first time, and although we had previously met on a number of social occasions, we'd never felt any particular interest in one another. Perhaps it was because of the heady times in which we were living, or perhaps because I'd just returned from a few days in Paris, where I had gone to take lessons from "*le maître* Philipp", and I was feeling rather exhilarated. Whatever the reason, something happened between us, and Dick invited me to dine with him at the Ecu de France the next evening. I can't say that it was love at first sight, for we argued quite heatedly throughout the evening about many things, including music and the political situation. The only subject upon which we agreed was our love of France, for Dick's mother had been born in Antibes, which he visited every year and enjoyed immensely. It wasn't a particularly peaceful meeting, and I remember that we weren't very happy with each other when it ended. It was strange, almost as though we were afraid that our relationship might become serious and neither of us was ready for this to happen.

My thoughts at that time were much involved with the preparations for my imminent concert tour, scheduled in Holland, and I was worried that the situation in Europe would prevent me from proceeding, and so there was no mention in my diaries of a further meeting with Dick until after my return from Holland. In the meantime, as the date of my departure approached, I was working for hours on my programmes and taking lessons nearly every day.

My programme was a heavy one. I would open with Bach's *Italian Concerto*, and then follow this with the great Mozart fantasie and sonata in C minor, K 457, which lasts for nearly 45 minutes and is very arduous in every way. After the interval, I would play all of Brahms's opus 76 capriccios and intermezzi, another mammoth undertaking, so I obviously wasn't afraid of over-taxing my strength, and I dearly loved playing these dramatic pieces. I would finish the programme with the *Suite Bergamasque*, which wasn't my choice, but Mrs McKnight thought that it made a light musical contrast to the rest of the programme. She was probably right, but I didn't feel very happy playing Debussy at that period in my life.

I rehearsed the programme a number of times by playing it to friends and finally my mother, and I set off on our great adventure on 8 February 1938, crossing the North Sea via Harwich to the Hook of Holland. I well remember arriving early in the morning at Den Haag, feeling rather low and seeing my photograph on large placards that were announcing the concert plastered all over the city. It was terrifying to come face to face with this sort of thing for the first time, and I remember Mummy and I looking at each other and wondering if we should turn around and go back on the next boat to England! However, after a large Dutch breakfast consisting of excellent bread and delicious cheeses we felt much better, and set about the business of meeting my agent and visiting the concert hall to try the piano. In spite of our fears, we managed to enjoy ourselves. I think that my mother was pleased to get away from the domestic routine, and perhaps it brought back memories of her own career as a concert artist. It was always fun to be together, and in spite of the ordeals ahead we managed to tuck away quite a few delicious Javanese meals, although I took great care not to over-indulge.

My first concert was in Den Haag on 10 February. On the previous day, I had practised my programme on the piano that I was to use, and on the morning of the concert I played in the hall itself so that I could get used to the acoustics. I must confess to being very nervous indeed, and to not being able to decide whether to spend the afternoon resting in my hotel room or to go out into the town. In the end, I chose to rest. This is a common problem; one has to get into a routine of behaviour on the day of a concert. As this was my first recital abroad it was something of an ordeal, but on the whole I think that it went pretty well – at least, my mother seemed to be satisfied.

Knowing that I had the experience of playing on a broadcast at Hilversum the next day, I went to bed immediately after the concert to try and rest as much as possible. Needless to say, I hardly slept at all, going over every single note of the programme. This is always so, I am afraid, as one is strung to such a pitch that it takes hours to wind down after a performance. Although very demanding, I loved the Mozart fantasie and sonata and the group of Brahms pieces. They suited me well.

For my broadcast at Hilversum, I played another programme, lasting for exactly one hour, which consisted of the Beethoven sonata opus 31, number three, and the Schubert impromptus opus 90. This was broadcast to England and other European countries, and I must say that I thoroughly enjoyed it, as I played very well and I loved the programme. I received many telegrams and phone calls and congratulations from home, which cheered me enormously and put Mummy and me in great spirits, ready to face the important concert in Amsterdam.

We went on to Amsterdam the following morning, and once again I went through the routine of trying out the piano in the large hall on the morning of the concert. I remember going there alone and returning to the hotel on a tram, thinking how pleased I was to be actually getting into a routine. The experience of my first concert at Den Haag and my following success at Hilversum made me feel so much more confident and much more able to face the performance that evening, although I reminded myself that I had to keep at concert pitch and not relax at all. Things went well at this last concert, and I played my programme with so much more confidence and even pleasure. A number of our Dutch friends came to hear me, and one family took us all to supper at the famous Kempinsky restaurant – with disastrous results. There were great bowls of oysters on the table, and I decided to try some. This turned out to be a grave mistake, for I became very ill and really thought that I was going to die! I've never eaten an oyster since that night. It may have been because I was so excited after the ordeal of the concert, but I never gave oysters another try. Apart from this contretemps, I was very pleased with the way in which the first part of my tour had gone, and so was my mother. We returned to London feeling pretty pleased, ready to prepare for the next adventure, which was to take place in Milan, after which we were scheduled to travel to Prague.

On my return, my first duty was to visit Mrs McKnight and tell her everything in detail about my playing. This was not easy, and I was glad when it was over. I could then talk to my friends and family, who had heard my broadcast, and bask a little in the pleasure of my success. I received a lovely letter from Mondy, who had listened to the broadcast in Oxford and said that I had played so well that he had forgotten to be nervous and enjoyed the programme. Uncle Fred was pleased, too, as were all of the family, and this gave me great encouragement for the concerts to come in about a month's time.

On the first Friday after my return from Holland, Lady Crawford gave another party, and once again Dick was there. I hadn't seen him since our rather unsatisfactory meeting at the end of the previous year. This time things went much more smoothly, probably because I was more relaxed after my success in Holland, and Dick gave the impression that seeing me again meant a great deal to him. On the first Sunday after our return, Mummy, Daddy and I went up to Oxford to see Mondy, and I was given a triumphal welcome by him and his friends, which gave me immense satisfaction and pleasure. It was at this time that I came to realise that the whole course of my life was about to change. As well as the certainty of having to face up to war, my feelings for Dick were growing and, although our meetings had been relatively few, it was becoming clear that we loved one another, and that we should probably marry. At every meeting we felt more secure, and although nothing was said we knew that our decision had been taken. Dick now came frequently to Wayside, and was beginning to feel very much at home with the family.

When Dick escorted me to the wonderful dinner at the Savoy Hotel on 21 April in honour of Uncle Fred, this served as being almost a formal declaration to our friends. That evening was a tribute by the world of music to the man who had virtually created His Master's Voice's great red label catalogue, and by his talent, courage and faith had pioneered the greatest record company in the world. Everyone who meant anything in the international world of music was at the Savoy on that night. World-famous musicians came to London for the event to pay tribute to my dear uncle. Modest as ever, we had a dreadful time getting him there to make a speech and face this extraordinarily emotional crowd, but he did it beautifully and we were all deeply proud. His sister Carrie – who had devoted her life to making his achievements possible – was there, of course, looking very pretty with a pink feather boa draped over her evening gown. Also present were his youngest sister, my mother, Louise; my father; Mondy; Lady Crawford and Gildie; and Mausi, who had come over from Paris to pay her tribute to "dear Uncle Fred". There was such an extraordinary atmosphere of affection and respect, including messages from artists who had worked with my uncle but who could not be present. The event signalled the end of an era, the end of my uncle's career and the end of peace. As I write these words, I remember clearly the emotions I felt: pride in his achievements and sadness that it now had to come to an end. However, he left behind him the records of his wonderful work, and the gratitude of so many artists, who, by his faith in them, he had launched on their careers.

Shortly after the dinner, Uncle Fred and Aunt Carrie left to take a holiday in America, but he had no intention of retiring there. He was planning to continue to work for the company as a consultant, and also to write his memoirs. I don't think that he could face leaving his wonderful life and his family completely, for we in England were his family.

Despite my decision not to go to Prague because of the imminence of war, I was still working very hard and practising many hours each day. Although I continued my lessons with Mrs McKnight, she knew nothing of the arrival of Dick in my life, but I'm sure that she suspected something, for she warned me frequently about the stupidity of getting married, and I had to endure many lectures on the subject. This wasn't surprising, as the poor woman's own experiences with love had been disastrous.

In the meantime, Hitler slammed the door on all hopes of peace when, on 15 March, his armies marched into Prague. This was the end. Now it could only be a matter of time – days, perhaps – before we would have to fight Germany. I had been preparing to leave for my concert in Milan on 31 March. Life was very hectic indeed, as I was working hard and seeing Dick more and more frequently. Mondy had now come down from Oxford for the spring vacation, and we were all deeply preoccupied with the thought of what lay before us. My brother was now in his last year at Christ Church, and he and his friends were already planning what they would do when hostilities began. The atmosphere was fraught with tension. I often saw Dick, who was becoming increasingly important in my life, but there were also many occasions when I met with other friends, who seemed to be asking for comfort and reassurance by talking about the awful situation in which we found ourselves. It was becoming increasingly obvious that I would be unable to leave at the end of March, as planned, and all thought of giving my concerts in Milan was now quite out of the question.

Even so, I must have clung to some hope of being able to carry out my plans, but much to everyone's relief at this stage I was taken ill with a severe attack of influenza and was forced to retire to my bed. Dick had been imploring me to give up my tour, and was overjoyed when I telephoned him to tell him that I was ill and that all hope of going to Milan was gone. Indeed, with Italy on the brink of joining the war on Germany's side, it would have been madness to think of going there for my concert, particularly as I had been born in the country.

There were times when discussions became very heated, particularly when young people came to the house. The older folk couldn't believe that they were facing war once again, and the young were angry because they felt that we had let down the Czechs during the Munich crisis. Many had joined a voluntary force at the time, including Dick, who was totally opposed to appeasement with the Germans. Much to my dismay, he and my father became very angry indeed with one another, and my mother told me that she had remonstrated with Father when he had once said, in the height of temper, "I never want to see that young man in our house again!"

"I think that you'd better change your tune," Mother had replied, "since I'm sure that Isabella is going to marry him."

In spite of our disbelief that it could really happen, trenches were being dug in parks and balloons called Colonel Blimps were going up to protect us from low-flying dive-bombers. It really came home to me one day when I drove through Regent's Park and saw hundreds of troops and volunteers digging up the carefully-tended lawns ready for the planting of vegetables. I realised then that all hope was gone.

Meanwhile, the international opera season opened at Covent Garden on 2 May with *Die Verkaufte Braut*, followed by *Parsifal*. Beecham and Furtwängler conducted the *Ring* cycles, while Weingartner covered other

German operas. It was an act of faith on Beecham's part to go ahead and stage the season, but luckily his gamble paid off. Dick accompanied me to hear *Tosca* and *Die Verkaufte Braut* but absolutely refused to sit through a Wagner opera. In June, Toscanini arrived for his concerts at the Queen's Hall, and needless to say Mausi appeared at the same time, coming over from Paris, where she had been living.

Mausi told me later that she'd heard no whisper of Dick's arrival in my life, and she was amazed on coming into my room one day to see a photograph of a very handsome young man on the table by my bed. My romantic activities had been the subject of some gossip in the music world during the past year, and so I decided to keep Dick's name a very close secret, even from my most intimate friends.

In the beginning of May, Dick's mother invited me over to Gorse Hill for the weekend. The Corbett home stood high on the Surrey/Sussex hills, and overlooked the South Downs for many miles. It was a beautiful place, and Dick adored it. As I was packing to leave for the visit, I remember my mother saying to me, "You know, Isabella, you're going to have to make a very important decision this weekend." This was indeed a serious thought, but my feelings for Dick were such that I had little doubt of the outcome.

Meeting one's future mother-in-law is a rather awe-inspiring occasion, and Katie was a formidable personality. There were also three French cousins staying there at the same time, which didn't help matters as all three girls eyed me with interest and some suspicion. Everyone was immensely kind to me, but on the Saturday, after realising that meeting so many of his female relatives all at once had to be something of an ordeal, Dick drove me to Corfe Castle in Dorset for a picnic. During the heavenly hours we spent there, we decided, without any definite declaration, that we would marry, and in view of the imminence of war the sooner the better. Nothing was said of our decision when we returned, and I spent the rest of my time at Gorse Hill getting to know Katie, for whom I was already beginning to feel a warm interest, and Old Lizzie, the sister of Katie's nanny and a Leicestershire farmer's widow, who looked after the domestic side of things for the family. I felt that I had passed a test when she told Dick that she liked me very much and that she hoped that we were going to marry!

The two months before our marriage were blissfully happy. I seemed to be floating on air, loved and appreciated by all. Even Daddy had given up his political tussles with Dick, and they all felt that it was a marriage that would bring happiness not only for Dick and me but also for the whole family. This came about after my parents visited Katie, driving to Gorse Hill very formally with Waylett at the wheel, when it was decided that the families approved highly of each other. The young Corbetts – including Dick's younger brother, Patrick; Susan; and her husband, Henry Walcot, who was normally pretty wild – behaved in an exemplary fashion, no doubt having been threatened by Dick before our arrival. Katie and my parents found that they had much in common, for her family – the Dracopolis, who lived at Antibes – came from Italian stock, and her relatives were as cosmopolitan as we were. However, it was a bit of a shock to both sides when we told them that we intended to get married sooner than we had originally planned because we felt that war was very near and we longed to have a holiday in Europe before it was too late. So our marriage took place on 8 July 1939 at Christ Church, in Hampstead, where my mother and father had married at the outbreak of the First World War in 1914.

7 War And Children

We went off on a marvellous two-week holiday in Dick's 2.5 litre MG, which was his pride and joy. We drove through France to Milan, where we stayed for three days so that Dick could meet my family, and then went on for a blissful rest at the Hotel Victoria, in beloved Menaggio, the scene of so many happy childhood holidays. Dick's pilgrimage came next, when we crossed the great mountains into France, arriving at the beautiful Villa Dracopoli at Cap d'Antibes, which was Katie's childhood home and where her sister, Marie, now lived with her husband, Raoul d'Aubas de Gratiollet, and their daughters, Antoinette, Annette, Nicole and Violette. They gave us a wonderful welcome.

Uncle Raoul was delighted to see Dick again, of whom, I gathered, he was very fond. He had been an officer in the French Army, and as a gascon he was typical of the very masculine men of his region. So, surrounded as he was by a very feminine wife ("Aunt Birdie" to the Corbett household) and four daughters, he was delighted to welcome a male member to his home.

Dick and his brother and sisters had spent many happy holidays in the company of his four cousins, and he was determined that I should catch even a brief glimpse of his childhood paradise. He had never known his grandfather, the artist Francesco Dracopoli, but he was very fond of his grandmother, who had spent much of her time in the villa, built by her husband, although she died in England.

Our visit gave me an enchanting glimpse of a beautiful place and delightful people, who welcomed me warmly as Dick's wife. It was fortunate indeed that we were able to spend a few happy hours with them, for alas war intervened, and everything changed. We were never to see the Villa Dracopoli again.

On our return to London, we moved into a charming little house that we rented in New End Square, high up in old Hampstead and very near the Heath. It was a delightful part of London in which to live, and convenient for Dick, as we were only a few minutes' walk from the tube station and on the direct line to the City and his office. Dick's father, Eric Corbett, who had died at the early age of 42, had founded the company Thompson Alston with Sir Clifford Figg, who was now the chairman, and Dick had been persuaded to join immediately after his father's tragic death from cancer. It was a terrible thing to lose his father, whom he had loved dearly, and it did nothing to lessen his grief when, under the influence of Sir Clifford Figg, his mother persuaded him to leave Oxford at the end of his second year to begin work as an office boy, ostensibly to learn the business, mainly concerned with the Far East. He never got over this dreadful episode, and he certainly had little affection for the company. It also meant that, once he had become a director, he had to go to Malaya and Ceylon on frequent and protracted visits. Of course, the war put an end to these activities for a while, and in a way Dick was delighted to escape from the routine of work. Had we known what the Far East was going to do to us after the war, his dislike of his City job would have been even stronger!

We were very happy when we moved into our little house, buying furniture and finding the right place for our wedding presents. I struggled with the housekeeping, about which I knew nothing, and I remember that Mummy sent our faithful helper, Mrs Millwood, who had helped in Wayside for years, to come to my assistance. I was very fond of her, and she trained me well. Knowing that war was inevitable unless a miracle occurred to save us, Dick volunteered to join the air force. He wasn't young enough to train as a pilot, nor did his sight pass the tests, and for this I was utterly thankful. Mondy, too, had signed up to join the army, as a gunner.

We tried to lead normal lives, attending concerts and visiting the theatre occasionally, inviting friends to visit us and spending weekends at Gorse Hill. I continued to take lessons from Mrs McKnight and to practise with Eleanor Warren, but with the ever-darkening shadow of war hanging over us it was very difficult to think about anything else. Uncle Fred had sent Aunt Carrie back to America, and he was living alone in his home in Crediton Hill. I saw as much of him as I could, for he must have been lonely, and it was a joy for us to talk about the musical life in which we had both been so involved.

It seemed as if we had hardly settled into our new home when we walked over the heath to Wayside on that fateful Sunday morning of 3

September to hear Prime Minister Neville Chamberlain announce that, as Germany had not accepted our ultimatum to withdraw its troops from Poland by 11am, Great Britain had declared war. It was a terrible thing to happen, and it seemed unbelievable, in spite of the fact that we had been anticipating it for a long time. We were soon obliged to believe it, though, as very shortly after the declaration the air-raid sirens began to wail. We looked at each other in utter consternation, unable for some seconds to think of what to do next. Was it possible that the Germans were going to attack us immediately? It was a false alarm, of course, but it was a bitter warning of what was to come.

Nobody knew what to do next. There was the blackout, of course. Most people had prepared horrible curtains in advance for this, but no one actually wanted to hang them. It seemed such a terrible acceptance of the fact that we were at war. Daddy wanted to begin painting the windows with some dreadful dark blue substance, which he had heard stopped glass from splintering, and I remember my mother weeping and asking what would happen to her beautiful home. I, too, was deeply concerned about my dear little house, and I knew also that Dick would soon be called up to join his command, and that Mondy would have to begin his training as a gunner. In the meantime, we carried on trying to live reasonably normal lives for as long as possible. We entered into the "phoney war" period, in which nothing seemed to be happening at all as we did voluntary work, took lessons in first aid and watched the blimps sailing over our heads. By the end of February, I was making plans for the birth of our baby. In spite of the awful uncertainty of our lives, we were overjoyed to welcome our child, as though by his coming we were asserting our faith in a future which at that time appeared to be uncertain.

On one Saturday, at the beginning of March, we had just finished our lunch, and we gazed idly from the window which faced New End Square. There, approaching us, we saw a rather large figure, dressed in a black cloak, walking slowly towards our door – "like a ship in full sail", as Dick said. To our amazement it turned out to be Mausi Wagner, of whom I had heard practically nothing since the outbreak of war. I had assumed that she hadn't gone back to Germany, but had received no news, and indeed I was very concerned about her. We were delighted to see her, for she was such a great friend, but I can't say that we welcomed her presence without some anxiety, for we could foresee many complications. After all, she was a

German, and well known to the general public for her intimate association with Hitler and the other Nazi leaders. We knew, as her friends did (of which she had many in very high places), that she was violently anti-Nazi, and indeed had suffered banishment from her home as a result. However, it was a dangerous time to have anyone around who, as far as the public knew, had been closely involved with the Nazis. Her arrival made our position particularly difficult, as my family was of Italian origin, and by then we were at war with Italy as well as Germany. It was also awkward for Dick and for Mondy, who were awaiting their call-up. (It says a lot for the loyalty of our friends and for the common sense of the government office that made these decisions that we never had any problems concerning our foreign birth, although it's true that Mondy had to wait rather a long time before he was accepted for officer training at Catterick. While he was waiting, he worked in a branch of the services in which his knowledge of languages was of great value.)

We could do nothing but give Mausi a warm welcome, for we were so fond of her. She told us that she had been to Switzerland, where she had been living in the Wagner house in Lucerne, and that her mother had warned her never to attempt to return to Germany, as she could not protect her daughter. She also told Mausi that she should remove herself as far as possible from the German frontier, as she was no longer safe, not even in Switzerland. I can't imagine what Mausi did for money during that period.

The story of how she managed to get into England is rather interesting. It was now the beginning of March 1940, and nothing was happening on the war front. The MP Beverly Baxter, who was well known in the world of music and apparently a friend of Mausi's, persuaded the authorities to grant her a visa. This occasioned a considerable outcry and much commotion, and questions were asked in the House of Commons about why this woman had been allowed to enter the country. It was awful for her and for her friends.

The phoney war was now over, and events were taking a very ugly turn. On 9 April, we heard that the Germans had invaded Denmark and Norway. This was indeed an unexpected move, and it changed the whole tempo of events. It was now all a matter of time. How much time had we gained in not declaring war on Germany when the Munich crisis occurred, and instead using the time to re-arm? Holland and Luxembourg were invaded on 10 May, and on 11 May Chamberlain resigned and Winston Churchill became prime minister and took over the leadership of the country. It's impossible to describe the relief we felt to know that he was at the helm at last.

On 17 May, Belgium capitulated and the Germans broke through at Sedan and entered France. I will never forget this, as Dick was just about to leave us to join his officer training squadron at RAF Burford, and Mausi was with us. We were looking at a large map of France, and when we heard of the breakthrough at Sedan she said, "This is it. We're finished." She was quite white, and added, "They'll have to intern me now." This indeed happened, and we heard nothing more about her until after the war, when she told me that she'd been taken to Holloway Prison, and afterwards to the Isle of Man. It was from there that Toscanini obtained permission for her to be released and sent to South America, under his guardianship.

After this, it was pandemonium. Dick had left to train with his squadron, and on 29 May the siege of Dunkirk began. Because I was pregnant, and the bombing of London was now growing serious, it was decided that I should move to Wayside to be with my family. Mondy was also there, awaiting his call-up, and the whole situation seemed unbelievably mad. They put a camp bed for me under the staircase at night, as it was thought to be the safest place if a bomb fell near the house. Mondy would lie on a blanket on the floor to be near me, and I can clearly remember saying to him, "Is it possible, or are we in some awful dream, lying here, listening to bombs whistling down?" While he was waiting for his call-up to Catterick, he was doing some sort of voluntary work. I would hear him coming in at all hours with other people, and there were strange whisperings, but I never asked what was going on.

It was at this time that the memorable battle was fought at Dunkirk, when we succeeded in transforming a terrible defeat into victory by withdrawing a huge number of our troops from the beaches in an armada of ships of all types, sizes and descriptions and bringing them back to England. Germany was thwarted from an attempted invasion of our shores, and never succeeded in this, thank God, although we feared on a number of occasions that Hitler was about to try again. We might have felt that things couldn't get worse, but on 10 June Italy declared war against Britain and on 14 June Paris fell. On 22 June, Pétain signed an armistice with Germany.

It was a beautiful summer's evening when we heard this news. I remember walking out of my parent's house with my little pekingese, Shi, and thinking in a calm and detached sort of way that now we stood alone, and that it was better that way. There were no more so-called Allies to let us down, and we had a large percentage of our men back at home with us. Now we had to use the time to prepare ourselves for the defence of our country. Strangely enough, I never doubted for one moment that we would win in the end, in spite of the terrible state of things at this time. We had complete faith in Churchill. His presence and his wonderful speeches gave us such courage, and I know that nearly everyone felt the same certainty and confidence as I did in our ultimate victory.

It was at this point that I announced that I was going to join Dick near Oxford, where he was in training. We were so happy to be together again. The decision to be near him whenever I could was absolutely the right one, and one to which I adhered throughout the war. At this stage in my pregnancy, however, I had to be near my surgeon, Mr Palmer, so my stay at Burford didn't last for very long. As Dick was posted to his first RAF station at Gosport, between Portsmouth and Southampton, I returned to London to await the birth of our child, who was due towards the end of August. We never doubted for one moment that it would be a son, and we were proved right.

As well as our preoccupation with our own concerns, we were desperately worried about Susan, Dick's youngest sister, whose husband, Henry Walcot, had been missing since Dunkirk. He was one of the brilliant young officers on the staff of General Gort. The last we heard of Henry was that he had been on board with the general staff on their naval vessel, and about to sail for England, when he was told that his own regiment, the King's Shropshire Light Infantry, was involved in fierce combat in a desperate attempt to hold off the Germans while our troops fought their way onto the ships waiting to pick them up from the beaches. Apparently, he went back to assist his regiment in a counter-attack and no further word was heard of him.

Susan behaved with the utmost courage, believing that he would have fought his way out of the battle and was in hiding somewhere in France. As he was a career intelligence officer and spoke perfect German, any of the strange stories that we heard of him being sighted could have been true, and Susan – who was also expecting a child – refused to give up hope of his return. Meanwhile, although she was not officially classed as a widow, the War Office paid her a pension. It was all most mysterious, but only one of the many extraordinary happenings which occurred in those mad days.

My poor mother-in-law, Madrina ("Katie"), must have endured the most awful anxieties, for not only was Dick in the air force (although not, admittedly, in combat service at the time) but also Patrick had joined the 31st Highland Division, and was shortly to be taken prisoner. Her beloved son-in-law, Henry, whom she had known since childhood, was also missing, and no one knew anything of him. Katie had immense courage, however, and never showed her anxiety.

Gorse Hill was commandeered as a training base – for undercover agents, we surmised, who were being prepared to parachute into enemy country. Curiously enough, Katie was allowed to remain there and live in the little flat over the garage, perhaps as a blind. She told me that she never saw the men who trained there, but she would hear soft voices speaking in many languages at night, when they were allowed to take exercise. I often thought of this when Dick and I lived at Gorse Hill for a short period after the war. I wondered if the strange discomfort that we felt while we were there was due to the atmosphere created by those poor souls who were being prepared for God knew what horrors after being plunged into some occupied territory in Europe.

Shortly after Susan gave birth to Elizabeth, on 13 August 1940, there was a most strange occurrence: Henry Walcot suddenly appeared some days later, without warning, and was able to spend a few hours with his little daughter. Then he disappeared again, as mysteriously as he had appeared. She never saw him again

Katie then decided that Gorse Hill wasn't a suitable place for Susan and her baby, and so she took a charming little old cottage in a nearby village called Brooke, which proved to be a haven of rest to many members of the family and friends in the months to come. However, after a short while Susan decided to move to Shropshire, to live with the Walcots, feeling that the distance from London made things safer for her little daughter.

Our son, Richard Sebastian, was born just before midnight on 7 September at 27 Welbeck Street, in the West End of London. I had planned to have the baby in my parents' home, and my labour began there on the morning of 6 September. It couldn't have begun at a more inopportune moment, however, as it coincided with the great air attack against London on 6 and 7 September, which the Germans launched as the prelude to invasion. The bombing of London went on day and night, without ceasing, and I was unable to make any progress in the business of giving birth. I was in too bad a state to know what was happening, but I hate to think what my poor family and Dick must have endured.

After 24 hours of struggling, I was still making no progress, and so Mr Palmer ordered that I should be rushed to a nursing home in the late afternoon of 7 September to have a Caesarean section. Mr Palmer went ahead to prepare the operating theatre, which was a nerve-wracking thing in itself for him, as the bombs were falling thick and fast and London was ablaze. The nursing home was empty, as all of the mothers and babies had been evacuated, but a skeleton staff was standing by and they opened the operating theatre. I was driven in my father's car by Mondy, who had been standing by in case he was needed, with Sister Mac, my nurse, holding the bottle of anaesthetic above my head and my mother sitting beside me. Dick must have been in the car, too, as his CO had been wonderfully kind in granting him compassionate leave. He had far exceeded his allotted time, but I don't think that anything would have forced Dick to leave before he knew that the baby was safely born.

It was a hair-raising drive. I can remember vague glimpses of familiar London streets alight with fires and explosions all around us, and being carried through the door of the nursing home. After that, I remember nothing until seeing my beautiful, huge son, Richard Sebastian, perfect in every way, in spite of the ordeal. I was told afterwards that, as soon as Dick had seen the baby and that all was well, he had driven back to RAF Gosport through that terrible night. What a time, and how bravely everyone had behaved, and how grateful I was to everyone who had looked after me. My family were heroes, as were the surgeon and my nurse, Sister McKenzie, a tall, strapping Scot. It must have been a dreadful experience for Mr Palmer, both as a man and a surgeon, and Dick and I could never thank him enough. In the years to come, I had cause to call on his help again, and he proved himself to be a faithful and highly skilled friend.

I and our son, who came always to be known as Pompy, were the only patients in the nursing home. I stayed there for a few days until I was strong enough to be moved. My mother and Sister Mac were with me all the time, with Pompy in a basket at my side, and every time they heard a bomb falling nearby they threw a blanket over us to protect us from flying glass. I remember Uncle Fred coming to visit us, and his horror at the danger from the huge unprotected window in my room. He tried to move a large wardrobe in front of it, all by himself, to make an impromptu shield.

After a few days, it was thought that this was ridiculously dangerous, and it was decided that I should be moved to Wayside, in Hampstead, away from the centre of London and therefore slightly safer. A sort of air-raid shelter had been constructed in the dining room, with four stout wooden pillars placed at the corners of a bed and sandbags piled up to the ceiling all around me. (To this day, since that time I've never seen or smelled a sandbag without shuddering.) A shelter had been built in the garden, and everyone – including our two maids, Annie and Jennie – slept there, except for my mother and my faithful Sister Mac, who stayed with Pompy and me.

As soon as I was strong enough, my mother, Sister Mac, Pompy and I travelled down to Brooke in an ambulance. There was really no alternative, as my father – who had moved his business to Leighton Buzzard – had to be there, and my mother wanted to be with me until I was able to join Dick. Annie and Jennie were sent to their homes to await their call-up. It was a hard decision for my mother to leave her home, and I knew nothing of what had happened to our little house and our possessions. There was no alternative, however, as I couldn't stay alone in London with the baby.

Dick was very thankful when he knew that we had reached the cottage at Brooke and that we were safe. He told me some time later that, when he had heard the German bombers flying over the coast on their way to drop bombs on London, he had spent almost the entire night on his knees, praying for our safety.

The cottage was a blessed haven, and Katie couldn't do enough to make us comfortable. It wasn't quiet, though, for it was bursting at the seams with all of those who had come to find some rest. To start with, there was me, still in bed and recovering from the operation; Pompy; Mummy; Sister Mac, who took up a lot of room; and Daddy, who would also come down from Leighton Buzzard as often as he could. To add to the numbers, there were some French officers who were on General de Gaulle's staff, friends of Katie from their childhood days at Antibes, who begged to be allowed a few hours of rest and relaxation away from London. Katie told me in later years that she couldn't understand how I could rest so quietly surrounded by so many people. I explained that I was so thankful to be there in the first place, and safe, that nothing in the way of human noise had worried me at all. Dick's HQ wasn't too far away, and his fellow officers generously contributed some of their petrol allowances so that he could visit me occasionally.

Two of the French officers were Richard Mallet and his son. The Mallets and Katie's family had lived next door to each other in Antibes, and much of their childhood had been shared with the Dracopoli children. Richard and his son had decided to leave France to continue the fight with de Gaulle, and their joy at finding Katie must have been great, as they had been very lonely. I remember that Richard slept under the dining room table, with his son in a sleeping bag next to him. My mother had a bed, I think, but Sister Mac was in a sleeping bag close to my bed. Pompy, meanwhile, was comfortable in his basket and doing well.

By this time, Mondy – now Gunner VF Valli 93136 – had been called up and was training at Catterick, and so the family was scattered all over England. As soon as I was sufficiently recovered, I announced that I was going to join Dick near his RAF station at Gosport, where he had found and rented a house at Lee-On-Solent, a typical south coast resort – or at least it had been before the war! Plans were made for me to move there. It wasn't a popular idea, but Dick and I were determined to be together for as long as possible.

My mother now had to join my father at Leighton Buzzard to set up home in a delightful house called Oak Bank, which had been bought by his company as a reasonably safe second base from which to operate, although she decided that she would first come with us to Lee-On-Solent to help me get settled into our new home. Her courage and cheerfulness were wonderful, and she was a tower of strength. I believe that, in spite of the danger and discomfort, she was enjoying being with us. She loved Dick, and doted on Pompy. When Daddy finally came to fetch her, I hated to see her go, for she had helped us through many bad moments, including shivering from lack of fuel, cooking our supper of tiny fish in a frying pan over the sitting-room fire, and laughing hysterically when we persuaded Dick to dance for us in order to keep warm.

When Daddy saw that the house in which we were living was only a few minutes' walk from the beach, that our garden was bounded by a wall surrounding the great naval base, and that on top of the wall were young naval ratings manning tom toms, his horror knew no bounds. "You can't stay here. It's ridiculous!" he shouted. When we explained that the German bombers crossed the coastline before dropping their loads, and that we were therefore reasonably safe, he nevertheless remained unconvinced.

Life at Lee-On-Solent was far from restful. One never knew when a stray Dornier would pop out of a low cloud and drop a few bombs on *HMS Daedalus*, our neighbourly naval base, and soon the attacks on the ports intensified as the Germans attempted to force through the blockade of our shipping.

I remember one occasion when Katie had come to stay, and she offered to take Pompy for a little walk in his pram in order to allow me to rest for a short time. I wasn't very happy about this idea, but I agreed, on the condition that she just walked once around the block and returned the moment she heard a warning. Shortly after their departure, I heard a low-flying aircraft making sinister noises. I rushed out of the house, looking wildly one way and then the other. By now the air-raid sirens were wailing, and I was panic-stricken. Suddenly, to my utter relief, I saw Katie running towards me with the pram. She had also heard the strange noises made by the raider, and had anxiously gone up to a gentleman walking in the street and said, "Excuse me, sir, do you think that these noises are due to enemy action?" He had answered, "Yes. Run for it!", and then of course the sirens had sounded. Knowing Katie, this made us laugh when we recounted the story to Dick, but it wasn't funny at the time.

The danger was now very acute, and when the great raid on Southampton took place in the early part of 1941 I really feared that our last hour had come, as we had no air-raid shelter, and in any case it would have been of little use. The noise was terrible, and the flames and flares made the town look like a scene from hell. To add to the eeriness, in the middle of the raid everything went suddenly quiet. I asked Dick what was happening. "Is it all over?"

"No," he replied. "Our radar probes are being used for the first time to seek out the enemy planes."

On the morning after the raid, we looked out on a scene of desolation. Dick had to return immediately to RAF Gosport, and I was left with no electricity and no milk for Pompy, which he needed for his feed. To my joy and intense relief, I saw our intrepid milkman picking his way through the rubble and calling, "Milko! Here I come!" I threw my arms around the dear man. I shall never forget his cheery greeting.

After another big raid, Katie, who was desperately anxious about our safety, managed to force her way through the army defences that had closed off the area by insisting that she had to find out if her family was still alive. They allowed her to pass, and she arrived laden with goodies, including candles, which were most important, for we had no electricity. How delighted I was to see her!

It must have been early in May 1941 that Dick was posted to RAF Uxbridge at West Drayton, and he found a little house in a suburb of London. Between moves, we always returned to Oak Bank, where we were given a wonderful welcome and the chance to rest and recuperate before we took up residence in one of the rather awful little rented houses into which we moved so frequently throughout the war. Dick, of course, went off immediately to his posting and lived in camp until I was able to join him. I was delighted to get away from the bombs on the coast, and our time at Ruislip was reasonably peaceful. By this time, Dick was a squadron leader, and he was working very intensively.

At around this time, the pattern of the war changed. The Germans gave up trying to bomb us into submission, and as a result the plan to invade us had been abandoned. The war at sea continued in all its ferocity, however, as they tried – often successfully – to sink our convoys and attacked our navy vessels. We were tremendously heartened, however, when the great German battleship *Bismarck* was sunk off the coast of Brest by *HMS George V* and *HMS Hood*. We were jubilant about this, as this great ship had been wreaking havoc on our shipping, as had the *Scharnhorst*.

On one summer's evening – 22 June, to be exact – I heard Dick's little old motorcycle pop-popping towards our house on his return from RAF Uxbridge. He was shouting with excitement, and I rushed out to meet him. His news was indeed electrifying: "The Germans have invaded Russia!" He kept saying, "We've won the war. Even if we have to keep fighting for years they can never win now!" Our relief was indescribable, for it meant that the Germans would have to shelve their plans to invade Britain. Indeed, the enemy had amassed 120 divisions on the Russian borders, and had a huge complement of air power supporting them. Now we understood the extraordinary event which had mystified us when we learnt that Rudolf Hess, Hitler's most favoured and intimate associate, had flown a single fighter plane to Scotland to the home of the Duke of Hamilton. Nobody could understand the reason for this extraordinary performance, least of all Hitler, I'm sure, but now we realised that, after being made party to Hitler's plan and unable to shake the Führer's determination to carry out the attack on Russia, Hess had decided in a mad moment to fly to Britain and attempt to negotiate a separate peace with Britain. Why he went to the

Duke of Hamilton, however, was a mystery. He never met Churchill, of course, and was shut up in the Tower until after the war.

The German invasion of Russia changed the whole course of the war. No one had believed that it could happen. In spite of our warnings to Stalin he refused to listen to Churchill and continued to conspire with Hitler against us up until the last moment of Nemesis. Stalin didn't prove to be a comfortable bedfellow throughout the war, but at least he took the heat off. It wasn't a free ride, though, as we had to use our hard-pressed Merchant Navy ships to supply Russia with much-needed raw materials. This was no joke, and we received precious little thanks for it from Stalin.

Our resources were stretched far and wide. We were fighting great battles in the desert, in Greece and in the Balkans, and very soon another shock awaited us when, on 7 December 1941, Japan attacked Pearl Harbor. The United States was taken completely by surprise, and immediately declared war on Japan. We did the same. Another theatre of war had opened, and we found ourselves with two great allies. Now we no longer stood alone. There was no doubt that we would ultimately triumph, but we couldn't imagine the horrors that lay before us in the war against Japan. The first shock came with the immediate loss of our two great battleships *HMS The Prince Of Wales* and *HMS Rodney* just off the coast of Singapore on 10 December 1942.

In January 1942, Dick was posted to RAF Glasgow, and after spending Christmas at Oak Bank Pompy and I moved there to join him. Dick had found a typical Scottish suburban house built of grey stone, the best thing about which was the view that it commanded of the mountains in the distance. From my point of view, it was a restful and healthy posting, but it was strange to be so far away from the war. My father had recently bought a delightful Adam house in St Vincent Street so that his company could have a second office in case the buildings in London and Leighton Buzzard were damaged by bombs, and so we often had the pleasure of him visiting us. It was a rather vague period for me, in spite of the terrible fighting and disasters that our troops were suffering in the Far East, and it's difficult to remember much about it. Pompy throve on the peaceful atmosphere that I suppose was reflected in us, and I was truly grateful for the rest. I remember that there was a Glaswegian lady who came in to help me with the housework, and who made us laugh when she called to us for a cup of tea by saying, "The tay is infusin'."

The most dramatic incident was caused by a rather evil cat we had mysteriously acquired. He somehow got into our next door neighbour's kitchen and stole their meat ration, which they had left on the table for a few moments. We heard the commotion, and soon afterwards the cat came into our kitchen with the meat in his mouth. I'm ashamed to say that we never owned up to this awful theft, as indeed it was, in those days, since we were rationed to only two ounces of meat per person per week!

In April 1943, Dick was posted to HQ Group at West Waltham, and once again we packed our bags and descended on Oak Bank while Dick found us somewhere to live. He eventually chose Holly Cottage, a small house in Farnham Common, once a rather smart suburb of London in the Thames Valley but now deserted, except for service families like ours. This was another quiet posting, as the war was currently being fought in North Africa and the Far East. It was a pleasant location, but somehow neither Dick nor I felt very well while we were there, maybe because the lack of sufficient food was affecting us, and the strain of Dick's job was probably telling on him. Had it not been for the wonderful parcels sent to us from Washington every few months by Aunt Carrie, I think that we would have fared badly, for not only did these parcels contain food but also often delightful items of clothing for each of us. It was like Christmas every time one of these packages arrived, and they did more good for our morale than one can imagine.

We had many friends at Farnham Common, some of whom moved on with us to our next posting. There was Tanbi Messenger, the CO of RAF West Waltham, who had a delightful wife and a little daughter; Squadron Leader Guiseppe, who was an eminent barrister in civilian life; and Teddy Cusdin and his wife. Teddy became one of England's most famous hospital architects after the war. John and Nucci Scott-Ellis were also living in the area, on serving duty like ourselves. She was German, and that was bad enough. I felt very sorry for her, especially as before the war I had known her mother-in-law, Lady Howard de Walden, a great patron of music but also a pretty formidable character. I believe that the Howard de Waldens were of Welsh origin, and probably staunch Protestants, which didn't help poor Nucci, who was a Roman Catholic from Southern Germany. I heard from her after the war, but I don't know what happened to the marriage.

Our time in Farnham Common ended in January 1944, when Dick was posted to RAF Chigwell, to the east of London on the Thames Estuary, and as things turned out this proved to be an important strategic base. He was also mentioned in dispatches on this appointment, which pleased us all very much indeed. Again, I stayed with Pompy at Oak Bank for a few weeks after this posting until Dick was able to find suitable accommodation. On 6 March, we moved into Rose Cottage on York Hill, Loughton, on the border of Essex and East London. It was a charming little old house with a beautiful, large garden, which was a delight for Pompy. However, the house was in the most filthy state. The walls were covered with spiders' webs, and the floors were caked with mice droppings. I needed help to cope with this, and found it by acquiring the services of Daisy, a tough Cockney woman who proved to be a tower of strength and good humour. She was very amusing, but she suffered from the rather powerful superstitions demonstrated by many Cockneys and couldn't bear it when I sighed, which she said I did far too frequently for her liking. I explained that this was probably due to the dust that we disturbed as we cleaned, and that my heart needed more air. I don't think that she was convinced, though, for she disappeared mysteriously one day. In her place I found a charming little schoolgirl, who kept an eye on Pompy as well as helping me, and this worked very well.

The furnishings in the house were very strange. Everything seemed to be dark red, including the curtains and carpets. In the dining room, there was a large mock-Tudor table and about twelve chairs, also covered in red leather. Pompy, who was going through a phase of playing steam engines, adored this room, and we would have to place the chairs in a line, representing the carriages of a train, with the front chair for the engine driver. His love of "choo-choos" was richly rewarded when we discovered that the father of our little schoolgirl helper was actually an engine-driver, and was in charge of the local railway. Imagine Pompy's delight when one day he was lifted into the cab of the engine and held in the arms of the kindly driver as the train shunted back and forth! He was also presented with a doll dressed as an engine-driver, which remained a treasured possession for many years.

This period of the war in England might be described as the lull before the storm. Everything was geared towards the invasion of Europe, wherever and whenever that might take place. Since we had moved to Loughton in March, we had been free from air raids and life seemed to be almost as though we were at peace. There were constant visits from our families, however, including Katie, who was now living again in the little flat at Gorse Hill; Susan and Elizabeth; and Mary Crawford, Dick's eldest sister, along with her son Mark, who had been born a few months before Pompy. Gildie Crawford was also a frequent visitor, when she was on leave from the WAAF, and of course my mother couldn't keep away from Pompy for long, and contrived to visit us pretty frequently. In fact, it was on her arrival on 13 June, when she announced with great excitement that she had seen the wreck of an extraordinary-looking plane lying beside the railway line, that we first learned of Hitler's secret weapon, with which he hoped to prevent our invasion of Europe. This was the hated V1, or "pilotless plane", which caused us dreadful suffering.

Dick had been working on the radar defence system that was being developed to intercept and destroy these monstrous machines. On his return from camp that evening, he confirmed that it was indeed the long-dreaded secret weapon, the production of which we had been launching enormous air attacks on factories in northern France and at Peenemunde, in Holland, to prevent. What we didn't know then was that an even more terrible weapon, the V2 rocket, would shortly be let loose on us, although the magnificently brave attacks of the RAF during the previous months had delayed the launch of these monsters until after D-Day. In fact, their launch would be postponed until September, thus thwarting the German attempt to prevent us from opening the Second Front on 6 June.

Until the start of the V1 and V2 attacks, Dick's posting to RAF Chigwell had been a happy one, for Loughton was a short distance by train from the centre of London, and this allowed me to live an almost normal life. When my mother was with us, I was able to go into town to have the occasional lesson with Mrs McKnight (I had my piano with me at Rose Cottage), and even to enjoy a concert and to meet my friends again. It was also very convenient because, as I was now expecting my second child, I had to pay monthly visits to my surgeon. After the awful experience he had endured at Pompy's birth, Mr Palmer was taking no risks, and I was scheduled to undergo a Caesarean operation in February.

The Allied invasion of Europe began on 6 June, and much to everyone's amazement, including that of the Germans, it was launched from the Isle of Wight and its neighbouring harbours, and the landings were on the shores of Normandy. How this secret was kept is one of the miracles of history, for it was generally expected that the attack on Europe would start from the eastern ports of England, and that the crossing would be at the narrowest part of the Channel. Apparently we perpetrated a huge hoax on the Germans by building mock aerodromes and camps and other war-like buildings in the eastern counties, and the secret was never revealed.

Loughton was not a safe place to be, for most of the V1s and, later, the V2s were targeted on the Thames Estuary because of the enormous concentration of shipping and troops. Life became terrifying and exceedingly dangerous, as these raids caused great damage and loss of life. They were also a shock to a nation that had already endured so many years of war. In September, we decided that Pompy – who was now showing signs of fear and nervous strain, as indeed were we all, by diving under the piano every time he heard the approach of a V1 – should go to Oak Bank while I should remain in Loughton to close down Rose Cottage, which proved to be the last house that we rented during the war.

During the short time that I spent alone in cleaning Rose Cottage, I was very lonely and often frightened. To get away from the silent house, I would sometimes wander down to Loughton village. It was on one such walk that I experienced the moving sight of a great procession of military vehicles, including huge tanks and field guns. When I realised that this seemingly endless stream was the First Polish Armoured Division, I was intensely excited, for Mondy was attached to this division as liaison officer, and they were obviously moving to the port from which they would depart to join our invading forces in northern France. Many years later, Mondy told me that they had sailed from a port near Dagenham shortly after D-Day, in an American vessel. By that time, he told me, the terrible weather of the initial landings had cleared, and the sun had been shining brightly. Because he had been the senior British officer on board, a nice young American officer allowed Mondy the use of his cabin, for which my brother had been grateful. They had landed in Normandy in the great Mulberry Harbour, and had then marched inland to Caen to join the battle of the Falaise Gap.

Mondy also told me how the Polish Armoured Division was ordered to capture Wilhemshaven, one of the last points of German resistance, just before the war ended. The Polish commander had decided to make one last offer to the Germans, who had been forced up the peninsular to the port. He decided that a British officer should be sent to negotiate with the general commanding that last remnant of the German Army. He ordered

Mondy to go off at four o'clock the next morning in his scout car with white handkerchiefs tied to his wireless aerial! Mondy motored along slowly until at last he sighted a German captain crouching by the side of the road. Mondy told him that he wanted to see the commanding German officer, and after some talk the German went off, presumably to a field telephone point. Mondy waited for what seemed a very long time. Eventually, the officer returned and told him that the general refused to surrender. As he had been instructed, Mondy then told the officer that, at eight o'clock the following morning, they would launch a full-scale attack against the German forces. Should the German general himself arrive at the rendezvous point before the designated time and offer surrender, there would be no further action; if not, a full attack, complete with air support, would commence at once. Mondy then returned to his Polish HQ, having seen no other Germans. "God knows where they all were," he said.

During the last months of 1944, Dick would come to Oak Bank whenever he could, and I see from my diary that we managed to spend a weekend at Gorse Hill in November. Katie was still living above the garage amidst her mysterious "lodgers", whose voices she heard in the night but whose faces she never saw. I think that it was a great tribute to her discretion and loyalty that the army allowed her to remain there.

During this period, I had an experience which is amusing to look back on but which wasn't that funny at the time. On a visit to London to see my surgeon, probably at the beginning of December, I went to Euston Station to catch the train for Leighton Buzzard. Travelling by train was very difficult, as the stations were blacked out and it was almost impossible to see the departure information. I went to the usual platform and entered a first-class carriage, which was full. The train pulled out almost immediately, which I thought rather strange, as I had given myself plenty of time. I assumed, however, that the train was leaving earlier than normal, and so thought nothing of it until I suddenly became aware that we should have stopped at one or two stations and hadn't. In the blackout, of course, there were no names on the platforms, and so one never knew where one was. I realised that something was amiss, and I asked if I was on the train that stopped at Leighton Buzzard. Everyone looked askance, for by this time I was obviously very pregnant. For a few seconds there was dead silence, and then one man – a very delightful one, at that – said, "No, this train doesn't stop until we reach Crewe."

I was very upset, as I knew that my mother must have come to Leighton Buzzard to meet the train on which I should have been travelling, and that she must have been frantic with worry when I failed to appear. The only person who offered to help me was the charming man who had spoken earlier, who turned out to be an eminent MP. He went to find the train guard and asked him if they would stop the train at Rugby, from which point I could get a local train to take me back to Leighton Buzzard. To add to my embarrassment, I suddenly remembered that I'd spent all of my money in London, and that I didn't have enough left to pay for my ticket from Rugby to Leighton Buzzard. This dear man also lent me enough money to pay for my ticket. I took down his address, and of course returned the loan with a warm letter of thanks the moment I reached home. During the wait for the local train at Rugby, I had the strange experience of seeing a group of Italian prisoners of war being marched through the station on their way to board a train to take them to their POW camp. In the blacked-out station, it was a very eerie sight, and I didn't like it at all.

From the beginning of September 1944, I was settled at Oak Bank, and Pompy's fourth birthday was celebrated there on the 7th. It was almost unbelievable that we had spent five years of our lives at war. Dick, now a wing commander, was living in the mess and getting back to Oak Bank as often as he could, while I braved the V2 attacks which rained down ceaselessly on London, as Hitler still hoped to cause so much destruction that we would be forced to stop our own bombing attacks and sue for a separate peace. London was a very dangerous place, but I was obliged to go for medical checks regularly, as the time of Roguey's birth was drawing rapidly nearer. One became philosophical about the danger from the V2 rockets, because when they struck there was no warning, and so one had no time to feel fear. The V1s, however, were far more terrifying, because their approach sounded so sinister. Even so, London was carrying on pretty normally, and from my diary I see that I took the risk of meeting friends and even hearing some music. I was always relieved, though, to return safely to the country.

Dick managed to get Christmas leave, and although we were very worried about Mondy, who was now with the Polish Armoured Division somewhere in northern France, we managed to forget about the war and shared Pompy's joy in the magical tree and the ritual family celebration. In our hearts we felt that this had to be the last Christmas of the war – at least, we prayed that it might be so. During these months, I spent many hours playing violin sonatas with my mother, and we were often joined by the very gifted young cellist Eileen Croxford to play trios whenever she managed to spend time with her family, who lived near us in Leighton Buzzard.

Our second son was born during the final stages of the war, on 8 February 1945. As he was to be born by Caesarean section, I knew pretty well in advance on which date he would enter this world. Mr Palmer, had arranged for the operation to take place at 27 Welbeck Street, and ordered me to be in London a good week before the agreed date in case of emergency. After the drama of Pompy's birth, he didn't have much faith in a smooth passage as far as I was concerned! I would be alone in London, as of course Dick couldn't get extended leave, and my mother would have to stay at Oak Bank with Pompy. I had no intimate friends that were still living nearby, and so arrangements had to be made for me to stay in a hotel while I awaited the operation. The difficulty was that every hotel within reasonable distance of the nursing home was fully booked. London was packed with foreign servicemen, and it was only after my father exerted some influence that I managed to get a room at the Savoy. So there I arrived, all alone, in a taxi from Euston Station, to be greeted by one of the tall, top-hatted commissionaires, who solemnly helped me into the foyer with my basket of baby clothes. Whenever I visited the Savoy in later days, I always remembered this extraordinary event with both amusement and amazement.

It wasn't pleasant to be alone at a time like this, in a huge hotel filled with foreigners. I was afraid to go too far afield in case I suddenly had to contact my surgeon, so I would stay in my room reading *Pride And Prejudice* or wander downstairs in the afternoons to watch the young officers dancing with their girlfriends in the restaurant overlooking the Thames. Katie came to have lunch with me in the grill room once, which we both enjoyed, in spite of every once in a while hearing the sound of exploding V2s, which the Germans were still sending over in large numbers. However, fate rescued me from this rather uncomfortable situation when, quite suddenly, I developed a severe cold on the evening of 7 February, and when I telephoned Mr Palmer he instantly booked me into the Samaritan Hospital as an emergency case. As dear Sister Mac wasn't free until 15 February, another nurse was assigned to me, a most amusing Irishwoman called, of all things, Sister Flood.

To my great relief, Mr Palmer ordered the operation for the next morning, and Roguey was safely delivered into the world on 8 February, a week earlier than planned. Oh, how thankful I was when it was all over! Now all I had to do was recover sufficiently to be able to return to Oak Bank and welcome Dick triumphantly home on his flying visit to meet his new son. I lay in my bed in the Samaritan Hospital, blissfully at peace, knowing that Roguey was safely and healthily in the world. My wild Irish nurse kept the baby in a small room of her own, from which rather suspicious odours of tobacco wafted on the air, and brought him to me only when he had to be fed. He thrived, nevertheless, and indeed gave lusty tongue to his demands. As he was the only baby in the hospital, the other patients weren't very pleased, and I received many notes suggesting that he should be given boiled water containing some sugar to calm him. Sister Flood thanked the lady patients for their advice but took little notice.

I can never forget the date of Mondy's and Catherine's wedding, for it was on 7 February, the day before Roguey was born. Only Daddy and Uncle Fred were able to go to Exeter for the ceremony in the beautiful cathedral, as my mother was looking after Pompy and I was certainly otherwise engaged in London! Mondy and Catherine had been fellow students at Oxford, but the war had separated them, as Catherine joined the navy as a Wren officer and Mondy became a gunner. It was only when he was posted to Topsham Barracks, near Exeter, that he remembered that Catherine's father was a canon at nearby Exeter Cathedral. When he went to visit her family, they gave him Catherine's address. She was stationed at Greenock, and Mondy and Catherine met again when the First Polish Armoured Division was posted to Scotland in 1943. Catherine had experienced an exciting war, ferrying American soldiers across the Atlantic to join the Allies in the invasion of Europe. Between them, they must have had many stories to recount since the carefree days that they had spent in Oxford as students.

On 15 February, as planned, Sister Mac arrived from her military nursing job to go with me to Oak Bank. I could hardly wait to see Pompy again and to introduce him to his little brother. I can well remember lying on a stretcher on the floor in the entrance hall of the Samaritan Hospital, waiting for the ambulance to arrive and praying that no V2 would come our way at the last moment. Roguey, Sister Mac and I drove in blissful happiness to Leighton Buzzard. Sister Mac was thankful to get away from nursing wounded serviceman for the time being, and she loved babies. There was also a strong bond of affection linking us from the dramatic time through which we had both passed during Pompy's birth. I was so thankful that the lonely ordeal was over successfully, and when we drove through the gates of Oak Bank and saw Pompy's face peering from the dining room window, where my mother, "Bam-Bam", was standing with him, I felt that there could be no greater happiness in life.

Dick wasn't very far away, and he would come over to Oak Bank as often as possible. It was a wonderful time, as we knew that the war had to be coming to an end soon, and the dear old house positively radiated happiness. Roguey seemed to find his place in the family from the very beginning. Pompy showed no jealousy of his little brother; in fact, he seemed to think that Roguey had been especially created for his own benefit. He even took his powerful yelling for his feeds with good humour, and did everything he could think of to amuse and comfort him. My mother and father and Uncle Fred absolutely adored the babies, and never seemed to mind the noise, commotion and extra work that their presence entailed. Indeed, I know that they dreaded the day when we had to go back to our own home, after the war was over.

The end of the war came with amazing rapidity and unbelievable drama. We used to run from the house to watch the seemingly endless procession of American bombers filled with troops trailing gliders behind them as they thundered over us on their terrible missions. At night, the whole procession would begin again, with our bombers setting off for raids on enemy cities to support our armies in Europe. It was an awesome and unforgettable spectacle, and I will never forget it. On 25 April, we learned that Mussolini had been captured and killed at Lake Como while attempting to escape to Switzerland, and on 29 April Hitler shot himself in his bunker HQ in Berlin. On 5 May, General Montgomery took the surrender of the German armies in north-west Europe.

We were all punch drunk with excitement, as one colossal event after another occurred, and on 8 May the end of the war with Germany was declared. This truly seemed to be the *Götterdämmerung* that Wagner had foreseen in his great operatic *Ring* cycle. We were still at war with Japan, though, and this didn't end until atomic bombs were dropped on Hiroshima and Nagasaki on 6 and 7 August – a terrible end to a terrible war.

In the meantime, we, the British people, perpetrated a fearful act of ingratitude towards our great war-time leader, Winston Churchill, to whom we largely owed our victory and our very existence as a nation, by throwing him out of office even before the cessation of hostilities against Japan. I was utterly shattered by this act of treachery and feared that the British people would never be forgiven for it. I made a solemn vow there and then that I would do everything in my small power to bring Winston Churchill back again to the head of a government.

8 Peace In The Country

Dick's demobilisation came through very soon after the defeat of Japan. I was amazed by the speed of this event, since I had understood that it could be months or even years before many were released. The reason for this became clear when, very soon after our return to Gorse Hill, Dick told me that he was being sent out to Malaya, ostensibly to investigate the condition of his rubber estates and the state of his company. My heart sank as I realised that I would have to endure further separation. Because the situation in Malaya was serious, due to the activities of the Chinese communist guerrillas fighting throughout the peninsula, I knew that once again I was facing a time of acute anxiety. Dick was a prominent man in the rubber industry, and as chairman of the Rubber Growers' Association in London he would be a sought-after target for the communist fighters.

I realised why he had been released so early, but I tried to ignore these presentiments and enjoy the end of the war and the move to Dick's beautiful family home, to which we had been looking forward, and which seemed almost to be an unattainable dream. The move took place in October, and although it was sad to say goodbye to Oak Bank, where we had been so wonderfully welcomed and cherished by my parents, we were wild with excitement at the prospect of returning to Gorse Hill and of being able to call it our home at last.

Gorse Hill was a very large house that my father-in-law had designed and built some 20 years before the war. There was a terrace with a pond and a fountain in front of the doors to the drawing room, and at one end of the terrace there was an artists' studio, which was built for Katie and which, I understand, she rarely used. At the other end were the servants' quarters and kitchens and the garage with the flat above it, where Katie had lived at times during the war.

We had little furniture with us, as our first home after our marriage at the beginning of the war had been a small cottage. We greeted the sight of each piece with enormous enthusiasm, and we placed nearly everything we possessed in the drawing room, including our numerous books, which we stacked on shelves lining the walls, and my concert grand piano in front of one of the windows. We decided that the large room was very beautiful, with its double doors and many windows overlooking the terrace. Unfortunately, we had few curtains, and there seemed to be hundreds of windows! There were two more reception rooms on the ground floor, the large dining room and a study, all of which had windows facing the south. There were also long, north-facing corridors on the ground floor and first floor. Each corridor had about ten windows, which had to be curtained to keep out the cold.

There was no possibility of buying furnishing material, for at this stage, and for many years afterwards, one needed ration coupons to purchase clothes, and so we resorted to buying thousands of yards of unrationed hessian to make the curtains and lining them with blackout stuff. We dyed the hessian a sort of orange colour, I'm not sure why, and it looked dreadful, but at least it kept out the howling gales that blew around the top of the hill. Our bedroom was delightful, however, as we had adorned it with our furniture and curtains that we had acquired on our marriage. This room was my consolation.

The boys' room was charming, too, as everyone contributed some of their clothing coupons towards the purchase of suitable material. Coggie Margetson painted all sorts of fascinating animals on whiteboard, a practice to which she had devoted a lot of time during her visits to Oak Bank during the war. These decorated the walls of the room, and the boys were delighted with them. The dining room was large and contained a beautiful Tudor oak table and Katie's ladder-back chairs, which she generously allowed us to use. Next to this room was the servants' hall, bedroom and kitchen, which containing a huge Aga cooker, which I loved, for it continually radiated a gentle heat. I can't remember how we fuelled it, unless our entire coal ration went to feed this hungry monster!

The main problem we encountered on our arrival at Gorse Hill in October was how to heat the house and keep warm. Dick solved this in a very simple manner by going into the woods and cutting down endless trees. It was hard work, and he must have had some help from our gardener, but I shall never forget the bliss of the radiators gradually warming for the first time and the whole house coming to life. This seemed truly to be the end of the war!

Katie kept the top of the house for her own use. This third floor was completely self-contained, and there was a separate staircase to the landing from the front door. The floor had five bedrooms and a delightful little kitchen and bathroom. It was very cosy, and she seemed content to be near us and yet completely independent. Indeed, it was a very happy time, for she and I were the greatest of friends and enjoyed each other's company immensely. A charming but rather eccentric lady who went by the name of Miss Barber came to look after Katie every day, and she was also a splendid cook. We would enjoy her delicious scones and rock cakes, which were passed down to us from the top floor.

The first Christmas at Gorse Hill was like a fairy tale. It was almost too wonderful to believe that we were actually celebrating the festival at home, after all those years of dreadful unreality. My parents were with us, and so was Uncle Fred. Dick's sister, Sue, and her little daughter, Elizabeth, came down from Shropshire, where she had gone after Henry's tragic disappearance and continued mysterious absence. Katie's brother, Uncle John, and his son, Michael, were also with us, and in spite of the fact that we were still severely rationed, we managed to prepare a bumper feast and a huge Christmas tree for the children, which Dick cut down himself. Neither of our brothers was present, though, as Mondy was not yet demobilised and Patrick – Dick's brother, who had been captured early in the war at St Nazaire – had either not yet returned to England or was spending Christmas with his wife, Nina, whose family lived in Oxford.

We spent the spring at Gorse Hill largely trying to get used to the idea of being at peace, and at the same time living under the very harsh conditions which were imposed upon us because of the scarcity of all commodities necessary to live comfortably, let alone gracefully. Most of our clothing coupons went towards keeping the rapidly-growing boys suitably clad, and food was very scarce and still strictly rationed. This was a real problem, as we were all beginning to yearn for good solid meals after the years of war. Living in the country, we were perhaps more fortunate than town-dwellers in that we occasionally dined on game or a rabbit, and we also had eggs, which were a blessing. We made sure that the boys had enough to eat, but both Dick and I were feeling the scarcity of food. I was certainly very run down, which may perhaps account for some of the rather strange events which I experienced while Dick was away in Malaya during the summer months.

There was also a servant problem. The gardener, Wright, lived on the estate with his family. He had been with the Corbetts for many years, and naturally resented my presence. I was very careful in handling this situation, and arranged with Katie that she should deal with him and the garden herself.

Dick and I decided that I should hire a married couple to live in as cook and houseman, and to this end I advertised the position. There was plenty of room for them, and we had many applicants for the job, but we couldn't find anyone suitable, and so we decided to invite a delightful elderly couple who lived nearby, the Munros, to come and work for us during the day. Mrs Munro was a charming woman, and I was very happy with her and her husband, whom we nicknamed the Admiral, as he had been in service on the royal yacht *Britannia*. He looked after the floors and the silver and kept the boilers going, and she helped me around the house. This was a happy arrangement while it lasted, but unfortunately the work was rather too much for them, and I soon had to consider finding another couple to live in the house.

Although I was quite accustomed to having domestic staff in my parents' home before the war, when we moved to Gorse Hill I seemed unable to get used to the idea of having strangers living in our home, perhaps because attitudes had changed completely during the war years, and we couldn't find a solution to this problem. The house was so large that help was certainly needed, especially with two small and lively boys to look after. We tried working with various couples, but it didn't work, and so for a whole year I managed with the Munros and odd bodies who came in to lend a hand while I looked after the boys and did all the cooking. As we were nearly always entertaining, it was certainly hard work. I didn't mind this, however, as the joy of living in our own home was a perpetual miracle. However, my health began to suffer and I often felt unwell.

My parents had finally decided to sell Oak Bank, although my mother was very sad indeed about this, as she would have loved to have kept the house to live in during holidays and weekends. Daddy was against this, though, as he felt that he would never have time to go there, and that it would be a large financial burden that would be little used, and so they moved to a beautiful and spacious flat in Portland Place, very near BBC

Broadcasting House, and also – most important of all – close to Regent's Park, where the boys could visit the zoo and feed the ducks in the lake on their frequent visits to London.

Dick's first visit to Malaya was in the spring of 1946, by which time Pompy was then five and a half years old and Roguey was just one and a half. The separation that I had been dreading so much finally had to be faced. I was very fearful because, although the Communist War was not yet raging, the situation was certainly unsettled, to put it mildly. Nevertheless, Dick had to go away and I had to accept it, and so off he went, and I was left as the *chatelaine* of Gorse Hill with my two boys, working hard to make our home more comfortable. We went to London on frequent visits to Portland Place, where we were always welcome. These helped me enormously, as at these times I could attend concerts and see my friends again, and the boys were blissfully happy with their grandparents, who adored them and did everything possible to make their visits enjoyable.

Dick wrote me long letters nearly every day, but communication wasn't as far-reaching as it is today and using the telephone was out of the question, and so there were endless periods without news. Travelling also took a long time. He would go over by flying boat, leaving from Bournemouth in a huge Sunderland plane, which he enjoyed because it was so spacious and comfortable. The journey would take almost a week, and they would make frequent stops to refuel. On this occasion, I remember that he flew directly to Singapore without visiting Colombo, as was usual.

It was at this time that I began to feel unwell, possibly because of my constant worrying about Dick, and also because of the long years of a restricted diet and now considerable overwork. Gorse Hill wasn't the sort of place that you could whiz over with a duster in a few minutes every morning. It really needed a lot of upkeep. This worried me, as it was such a beautiful house and I feared that it might deteriorate. We all loved it, but it was a dream that was beyond our ability to support. I knew that I would have to discuss this with Dick on his return, and I dreaded it, for he loved the place, which was his childhood home. However, it was a huge burden for a young couple to carry, and one that we couldn't really afford. I had to consider Dick's mother, too, who shared the house with us, but I knew that she had so much good sense and goodwill that she would understand it if we had to leave in order to find a house more suited to our financial means.

I remember walking with the boys one afternoon, pushing Roguey in his little pram, around the bottom of our hill towards Gwen du Maurier's woods, which touched on our garden, thinking how beautiful they were. Yet strangely, being so completely absorbed in the business of coping with a large house didn't suit my way of life. There were other things that I enjoyed much more. It was wonderful to have such a beautiful home, but it was also a burden, and one that was not the be all and end all of existence. Dick loved it, I knew, especially the land and the opportunities that it gave him to exercise, but I felt that, if we could find something smaller with a good piece of land and space in which to breathe, he would be just as happy, and we wouldn't be beset by such financial worry.

I remember that during this time I developed an awful cough which I couldn't shake off, and I asked the doctor to come and see me. He told me that I was very run down, and that I should have a good rest and look after myself. This was quite impossible, and in any case I didn't feel like resting. The problem wasn't the amount of work I had to do – this never worried me – but it seemed that we were working to little purpose, for I could see no solution to burdening ourselves with this unnecessarily extravagant way of living.

So many things had happened at Gorse Hill which, in a way, I couldn't understand. Apparently, when Dick's father, Eric Corbett, had first found the site, and before he had even purchased the land, there were rumours that there was a curse on the hill. This sounds quite ridiculous, and obviously he paid little attention to these stories, but I remembered that he died suddenly at the age of only 42. Then there were the dreadful things that had happened during the war, when the house was full of people being trained there to be parachuted into German-occupied Europe, as well as the extraordinary catastrophes when German planes were shot down over the hill on two separate raids, and the dead bodies of the crews were found hanging in the trees by the studio. I began to be filled with horror, and sometimes when I sat on the terrace in the sunshine I wondered why this house of all of the houses in the area should have been hit twice. On the second occasion, the fuselage of the plane fell onto the tennis court, which made the whole event horribly real.

As I have already explained, the design of the house was conventional. The living rooms all faced south, with a beautiful view and plenty of light, while the north side of the house – the side with the front door – was approached by a long drive and a circular court that always seemed gloomy, and I never liked this aspect. Also, the long corridors on all three floors, especially the one on the entrance floor, filled me with a strange unease. As I write, it sounds as though I was both neurotic and foolishly discontented at having been granted the realisation of a dream, but this wasn't so. I was very happy to be in this lovely home with Dick and the boys, and I would have given anything to have been able to relax and enjoy it. However, there was something about the place that made me uncomfortable and vaguely fearful.

There next occurred a series of very strange events which I had certainly never experienced before and which I hope will never occur again. I began to hear my name being called. I would be in a room, perhaps doing some housework, when I would suddenly hear "Isabella, Isabella" spoken in a peremptory tone. I would answer "Yes?", and then I would realise that there was no one in the house who could be calling me in this way. This happened over and over again, and I became quite frightened. There was an approachable and clever doctor in the neighbourhood called Dr Booker, and I asked him to come over and see me and told him of my strange experiences. He took them seriously, and didn't seem surprised by my strange story. "You have far too much to do," he told me, "and you're suffering from exhaustion as a result of all the years of war. You're also deeply concerned about your husband in Malaya. You can't go on like this." I answered that I had to go on until my husband came home.

This wasn't the end of the story, however. Strange things happened, which to this day I can't explain. As the evenings began to draw in, I would be sitting with Pompy and Roguey in front of the fire in the drawing room as dusk fell when suddenly the door of the drawing room would burst open violently, although there would be no one there. These incidents occurred on one or two occasions before Dick went to Malaya, and I can remember thinking that he might have come home unexpectedly early and was playing a trick on us. I would call out, "Dick, is that you? Stop playing silly games." There would be no answer, of course, as Dick wouldn't be home until much later. These occurrences would happen sometimes two or three times in an evening, and I became very frightened. I had to hide my fear from the boys, which wasn't easy, and I was reluctant to cause Katie any anxiety. I certainly didn't tell my parents, as they would have insisted on driving us back to London. In fact, I hinted of these things to Katie, and asked her if she had ever felt a strange atmosphere in the house. She answered me, quite crossly, that she had never had any strange feelings about Gorse Hill.

Later during this awful time while I was alone with the boys, there was another event which had nothing remotely to do with the supernatural but just human horror, although it was nearly as terrifying. Once again it began while I was alone in the drawing room in the evening. As September was now well advanced, it became dark early. I began to hear tapping on the windows. At first I thought that it was the wind blowing the branches of trees against the glass, but then I realised that there were no trees that near the house, and my heart caught. I called out, "Who's there?" No one answered. After this incident, I gave up sitting downstairs – it was too nerve-wracking – and I would go up to my room next to the boys and retire to bed early.

Then, one night, the *dénouement* of the horror occurred. Our very large bedroom was above the drawing room, and there were double doors to a little hall that opened onto the corridor. The boys' room was next to ours, but quite far away, as the corridor was a long one. On one night – it must have been very late – I heard knocking on the outer door. I knew that there was no one in our part of the house, as at that time I had no live-in staff and Katie had moved to the flat over the garage, which she did frequently. I was absolutely terrified. I switched on my bedside light, nearly knocking it over in my fright, and I ran to the little hall leading from the bedroom in order to get to the boys. I threw open the double doors which gave onto the corridor, and standing there was a tall man in dark trousers and a white shirt. I shrieked with terror, and he turned and ran downstairs. I didn't follow him but instead ran to the telephone in my bedroom and called the police, and then went and checked that the boys were still fast asleep. After that, I sat on the floor outside their door with Dick's shotgun on my lap, which I had been bringing upstairs with me every night. When I heard the police arriving, I rushed downstairs to let them in. I can still remember clearly my little dog, Wimpey, looking at me pathetically as though to say, "I did try to warn you, mistress." Indeed, it must have been his barking which woke me in the first place. He always slept in the kitchen by the Aga for the warmth, and was the first to be aware of the strange presence.

The police began their investigation immediately. They did indeed find

Isabella just before her first concert and tour, London, 1936

Isabella aged 2 with parents and baby Mondy, Milan, 1918

Isabella in the Jardini Publici, Milan, 1920

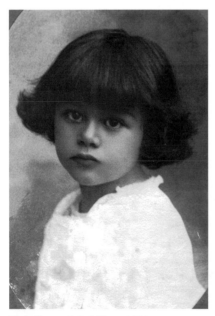

Isabella aged 5, Milan, 1921

Isabella with Uncle Fred, explaining the principle of a sundial, 1925

Signed photo of Edwin Fischer, inscribed: "To Isabella Valli with many thanks for kind help at our records of HMV. Edwin Fischer." 1931/2

Signed photograph of Artur Schnabel, 1932

Isabella aged 8 with her mother, Louise, and her brother, Mondy

The Chaliapins at Hendaye, 1931. Standing (l-r): Mme Chaliapin, Isabella, Mondy, Louise, Stella, Marina. Sitting (l-r): Chaliapin, Aunt Carrie, Camillo, Mme Chaliapin's mother

Isabella with Feodor Chaliapin at St Gilgen, 1936

Isabella aged about 16 in Uncle Fred's house

L-r: Coggie Margetson, Mausi Wagner and Stella Margetson, 1937

Isabella, wrapped up against the cold.
Winter, 1939

Dick at the time of his engagement to
Isabella, 1939

Uncle Fred's retirement banquet at the Savoy Hotel, 21 April 1939. Seated (l-r): Mrs Alfred Clark (wife of the chairman of EMI Industries), Fred Gaisberg, Sir Adrian Boult

Isabella at the time of her engagement to Dick, 1939

First and only holiday. Dick with Pompy and Roguey, Menaggio, July 1951

Isabella and Dick, 1939

The first orchestral session for Delysé, at the Conway Hall, London, 1954/5

Flying to Dublin to audition artists for the Envoy label. L-r: John McNally, Dermot O'Brien, Isabella, Dermot's manager, Harry Christmas and Ronnie Young

Isabella, Dermot O'Brien, Ronnie and Ian McNally recording the Irish sessions at IBC Studios, 1962. At the desk is Allen Stagg

that there had been an intruder, as there was food on the kitchen table and there were other signs of his occupancy. Imagine what a state of nerves I was in! I didn't know whether I should rouse Katie, but now that the police were present and the man had gone I decided that it was better to leave her in peace. When I told the police about the strange tapping on the windows, they weren't at all surprised, and explained that there was an escaped prisoner on the loose from a mental home nearby, and that they had been looking for him for weeks. When they investigated the grounds the next morning, they discovered that he had been hiding out in the bomb crater over the edge of the terrace not far from the drawing-room doors. They said that I should have called them when I had first heard these tapping sounds, but I said that I was afraid of being thought a hysterical woman. The police were so kind, and the nice sergeant refused to allow me to stay alone, and would come over and spend the night in the servants' hall until they caught the man and Dick came home, which was soon, thank God.

I felt sorry to think of all the sensational news with which he would be confronted, but in the event all of our troubles were set aside in the joy of his homecoming. As it was now the end of September, we invaded Gwen du Maurier's woods and gathered chestnuts and mushrooms, the sort which Dick loved to cook, which was an art that he had acquired during his holidays in Antibes. The relief of his presence was so wonderful that I soon forgot to worry about the mysteries that had taken place during his absence. We decided not to speak of them to anyone, as we couldn't face the arguments which would occur and our instant removal from Gorse Hill, upon which my parents would try to insist.

These weeks immediately after Dick's return were an unforgettably happy time. We would take the little boys with us for walks in the woods, although Roguey would be determined to push his pram rather than sit in it, which would delay our progress considerably. But who cared? We would laugh at his insistence on doing just what Pompy did, walking even when the going was rough. This happiness made up for the awful times I had endured during Dick's absence. Certainly the existence of the intruder was undeniable, but I couldn't decide if the strange voices that I had heard calling me and the other happenings were the result of weakness and worry. I believe that Gorse Hill was haunted, and indeed my mother always said that she was very uncomfortable there, but she had never said anything about it to me. A rather elderly couple whom we engaged after

Dick's return also said that they were unhappy in the house and felt that it had an uncomfortable aura.

At the backs of our minds, we knew that we would have to make some changes. Not only were we concerned about the financial problems, which could only increase, but as Pompy was now six years old he would shortly have to attend school, and neither of us would even consider sending him away to boarding school. We knew that soon we would have to deal with the problem.

In the meantime, we put our cares behind us as the second Christmas since the end of the war was drawing near, and we had agreed to spend it in London with my parents. It was a very happy occasion. My parents did everything they could think of to spoil us, and we all had a wonderful time, particularly as Dick was home safely. We relaxed and enjoyed every minute, sharing the boys' delight in the magic of Christmas.

When we returned home, the hill was covered in deep snow. Indeed, England was experiencing one of the coldest Christmases ever recorded. It was bitter, and Dick was hard-pressed to keep the huge house warm and stop the pipes from freezing. He accepted this challenge with enthusiasm, and I can see him now cutting down trees and, with the boys' help, pulling the logs to the house on their sleigh. The boys loved the weather, and Dick made a great snowman for their enjoyment. We were fortunate indeed in having the trees to cut, and I often wondered how people who depended on the meagre fuel ration issued by the government managed to keep warm. It was a hard winter but a very happy one for the boys, as they tobogganed tirelessly down the steep drive with Dick patiently pulling them up on the sledge after each descent.

From the beginning of 1947 we really began to feel that peace had returned. Most of our friends had been demobilised by then and were back at work in their pre-war jobs. Dick caught a train every morning for the City from Witley Station, and it seemed as though we were waking up after some awful dream to resume a normal life.

We had a very active social life at Gorse Hill, for many old friends of the Corbetts returned after their war service, and we were also visited by new friends that we had made during the war, and both my family and Dick's visited frequently. We had been able to find a rather elderly couple, Mr and Mrs May, who came to us as cook and houseman, which was of enormous help to me, as we were hosting dinner and cocktail parties nearly every weekend, with many guests attending. It also meant that we could leave the house in their care when we went to London to visit Portland Place.

The Queen's Hall had been completely destroyed by the bombing, and this was a severe loss indeed. "Tommy" Beecham staged his concerts at the Drury Lane theatre, and there was always the Albert Hall, at which I remember attending a Sibelius concert, but nothing could replace the loss of the Queen's Hall for acoustics, capacity and general atmosphere. To my mind, the halls that have been built since can't compare. The destruction of that hall was a mortal blow to the musical life of London.

In spite of this, it was wonderful to hear great music again, to gossip with musical friends and to visit the studios occasionally when invited by Uncle Fred, who still acted as a consultant. Aunt Carrie had returned to London from America after her long exile there during the war, and it was a joy to see her again after many years and to visit her and Uncle Fred at Crediton Hill and welcome them both to Gorse Hill, to which they were frequently invited. I was fortunate that there was great affection between Dick and all of my family, and also a friendship between Katie and my parents. This made our lives and those of the boys wonderfully peaceful and happy, and made our suffering after Dick's tragic and sudden death even more profound and poignant. Luckily, however, we were unable to look into the future.

In April, Aunt Birdie and Annette arrived from France. This was a moving occasion, as Katie and her sister had been separated throughout the war years and we had received no news of them. There was no doubt that they had gone through a dreadful time. Uncle Raoul had died, leaving his wife and daughters alone to face awful hardships, but I didn't ask for details as I felt that the experiences that they had endured were too painful for them to describe. After the war, Aunt Birdie, who had money in England, was able to buy a house in Kent and moved there some months after her arrival. Dick helped her considerably with the legal and financial affairs concerning this, which were extremely complicated, but he was happy to be of use to her. Until they had moved into their new home, Aunt Birdie and Annette had lived with Katie in her flat on the top floor of Gorse Hill.

Many friends came to stay for weekends, and we enjoyed all sorts of country activities, such as point-to-points and picnics. Lindsay Mackie, Dick's colleague at Thompson Alston, was a frequent visitor. He was a man of considerable culture and charm and also, at six feet seven, of immense height. He was also very handsome, and for a tall man he moved well, and he was an amusing and delightful companion. Leonard Figg, Sir Clifford's son, was another visitor of whom we were very fond, and the local people were also pleasant and hospitable. There were many dinner parties given by the Pleydell-Bouveries; the Jameses, who were architects and who had built a beautiful house nearby; and the Igoes, who were Irish and great fun. We would return this hospitality by hosting dinner parties ourselves when our friends visited from London. Amongst these were Bill Younger and his wife, known as Poo; Mondy and Catherine, of course; and Patrick and Nina. It was all unbelievably happy, and I remember thinking that, with Dick's visit to Malaya safely over, it was like living in a dream.

In July, Dick had to go on a business trip which pleased him very much: he had to visit the company's salmon fishing and canning plant in Vancouver, and he suggested that we should combine this with a holiday visit to the United States, where I would be able to see my American family again and introduce Dick to them for the first time. He would then carry on to Vancouver, and I would return to England on the *Queen Mary*. This would be the first time that I had ever left the boys, and it was a hard decision to make, but in spite of all of his travelling Dick had never been to the United States, and he was anxious to go there. I knew that the boys would be quite safe, well looked after and happy, as both Bam-Bam and Aunt Carrie would stay at Gorse Hill while we were away. The Mays were still there to look after the house as well, and so it was an opportunity that could not be missed.

We flew to America on 4 July, the first time that I'd left England since our marriage in 1939. The airport – Heathrow, I suppose – was nothing more than a small series of wooden huts. We flew in a Constellation, which was delightfully comfortable and roomy. On looking out of the windows at the four great propellers whirring away tirelessly, I thought of what those blades must have flown through during the war. Compared to flights today, it was a very slow and leisurely crossing of the Atlantic, but it seemed incredibly fast to me, as I had last travelled to America by sea.

First we landed at Shannon, where everyone disembarked and the plane was refuelled for the long Atlantic flight, and we explored the airport and bought some Irish whisky as a gift. It seemed such an adventure, and to be on holiday together was a dream which during the war I could never have imagined would come true. On the following morning, we landed at

Gander, in Newfoundland, where we refuelled once again before taking off for the bumpy flight down the east coast of America to New York, where Sue and John Tarrant met us and drove us to their home in Newhaven, Connecticut. Dick and Sue were overjoyed to see each other, as he was devoted to his young sister and hoped that she had at last found happiness in her second marriage. She had gone through such terrible times of uncertainty when Henry was posted as missing, when no one had known if he were dead or alive, that one longed to hear that she was enjoying peace at last. In fact, it wasn't until some 40 years later, when their daughter, Elizabeth, and I paid a strange and moving visit to a quiet grave in a Belgian churchyard, that Elizabeth finally accepted the reality of her father's death.

At the time of our visit to Newhaven, however, we tried to put thoughts of Henry's death behind us and wish a happy marriage for Sue and John Tarrant. She'd had a dreadful tussle with her mother, who couldn't accept that she wanted to marry again, and indeed it was only Dick and me who supported her. It was a sad family affair, and neither she nor her mother ever mended the breach in their relationship. Sue was therefore very happy to see us, and welcomed us into her home. She was a wonderful cook, and produced the most delicious meals, which tasted like the nectar of the gods after the long years of dreary fare that we'd had to endure during the war.

Our next trip was to Washington, DC, where we stayed with my cousin Isabel, one of the twins, who was now married to Maurice Hawes, whom she had met whilst staying with us in London. Maurice was the nephew of the American president of the Coty company, who was known as Uncle Ben. We were all very fond of Maurice, who was not only charming but also a very cultured man and a graduate of Cambridge. There had also been opposition to this marriage, unbelievable though it may seem, as Maurice was half Jewish, and poor Isabel had to fight before she finally succeeded in marrying him. It caused quite a family split, as we backed Maurice, and Isabel's parents blamed us bitterly. When will people ever realise that it's useless to oppose two people when they're in love and determined to marry?

Louise, Isabel's twin, who hadn't married but had seemed to reach a happy alternative arrangement with an Italian man, also arrived in Washington, and we had a lot of fun in the beautiful city, visiting its art galleries and sailing and fishing in Chesapeake Bay. Dick had always been fascinated by American history, and our library was stocked with many books on the subject, so he was deeply interested in everything that he saw and heard. We visited Congress and the Senate, and were present when General Marshall testified at a very critical meeting of a foreign affairs committee. I remember standing next to him in the lift when the session was over and thinking that he was a most impressive man, and how much the whole world would owe to his plan.

Our presence at this event was made possible by my cousin, Warren, the son of Rudolf Forster, who served as an executive clerk at the White House for 46 years. He was a highly respected figure and a personal friend of many of the presidents under whom he served. On Uncle Rudolf's death, President Roosevelt posthumously awarded him the Medal of Merit, and he was the first recipient of the award since it had been created by Congress in 1942. I hadn't seen Warren since I'd been a very young girl, and in my memory he was still the handsome big cousin who had descended on our home in Milan with the two St Bernard puppies that he bought in Switzerland to take back to America. I also remembered that I had been told that he was the twelfth strongest man in America – a legendary figure, in fact!

We ended our holiday by spending two days in New York, which was great fun, and after this Dick accompanied me to the *Queen Mary*, on which I was to sail back to England. He walked me to my delightful cabin and told me to enjoy myself and try to behave, and then left to take the train all the way across the United States and Canada to Vancouver. I know that we both enjoyed our respective journeys immensely, and I trust that we *both* behaved ourselves! When Dick got back to England some three weeks after my return, he was filled with admiration for Vancouver and frightened the life out of me by wanting to pack up everything and move us all out there.

The boys were overjoyed to see me, and Bam-Bam and Aunt Carrie told me that they had been very good and helpful, although I think that my mother and my aunt were glad to return to their homes. They had been very kind, looking after the boys so that Dick and I could spend a carefree time in the States, and we were deeply grateful to them. My mother warned me that she thought that the Mays would soon be handing in their notice. Apparently they didn't like the atmosphere of the house, which they found to be "spooky", so I was again faced with the memory of the strange happenings that I had experienced during Dick's absence in Malaya. My mother told me that she had also been uncomfortable, and that she had felt quite nervous at times. As I had never told her of my previous experiences, I was forced to reconsider the whole matter. The Mays indeed gave notice, and left quite soon after Dick's return. I was grateful that they had been decent enough to remain during our holiday, as I couldn't have gone away otherwise, but they were too old to cope with our hectic life and our rather irregular style of living, and so it was probably for the best.

The next couple who moved into the house to help us with our domestic arrangements were Polish. This was quite a new sort of venture. The husband was or had been a major in the Polish army, fighting with the Allies, and his wife was apparently the daughter of an eminent judge who had been imprisoned by the Russians. They had a twelve-year-old son, a nice boy who attended the local village school in Witley, and we hoped that, after so many awful experiences, they would appreciate living in a good home, which they did. Unfortunately, they took advantage of us by inviting other members of their family and friends, in considerable numbers, to visit them. The wife was a very nice woman and an excellent cook, and the major tried to carry out his duties efficiently, but it didn't really work.

The crisis came one weekend, just after lunch, when I had to speak to the wife about some arrangements. I went into the servants' sitting room and found the huge table occupied by twelve people, all eating vast quantities of food. They had excellent manners, and all stood to be introduced. One was a general in the Polish army, and the couple's daughter was also there with her boyfriend. I went to look for Dick and said, "This can't go on. We're running a hotel here for the Poles. There are twelve of them lunching in the kitchen. It can't go on. We shall be broke!" Dick agreed with me instantly, thank God, so there was no conflict between us.

We decided on the spot that we would have to find a much smaller house which wouldn't be the colossal financial burden that Gorse Hill had become. It was a sad decision, especially for Dick, who loved the place so much, as indeed we all did, but it was foolish for him to have to work so hard just to keep this enormous house running, so it was agreed that I would begin to look for a smaller house with plenty of land. As Pompy was now approaching his seventh year, he had to start serious school, and as there was nothing of the right kind in the district this was another reason to move. To this end, I set off on my quest. We decided to say nothing to Katie until our plans approached fruition, but we believed that, in her heart of hearts, she was also feeling the burden of keeping her part of the house and grounds in proper condition.

Fate was on our side, however, for it was shortly after we had made our decision that I saw a completely renovated 17th-century cottage advertised in the Cranleigh local newspaper, with a three-quarter-acre garden as well as a two-acre field, situated on the outskirts of a beautiful village on the Surrey/Sussex border. I decided on the spot to drive over and have a look at it.

I fell in love with Old Pound Cottage on sight. The owner, Mr Bagley, who had obviously bought it as an investment, had done a good job of rescuing the enchanting old house from decay. It was in perfect architectural order, and he hadn't destroyed any of the period features, although it was very small – indeed, the whole house could have fitted comfortably into the drawing room of Gorse Hill – but as far as I was concerned this was to its advantage. The sitting room was quite a good size, with a huge open fireplace and with two little seats inside the hearth, and I thought to myself how the boys would love them! There was also a charming dining room, which had obviously been added later, and on top of this was a bedroom with windows on either side, which would be perfect for the boys.

Every other room in the cottage was from the original period of its construction. The main bedroom, which was over the sitting room, remained untouched, with exposed beams, and the owner had very cleverly converted the room above the kitchen into an excellent bathroom. The garden was laid out beautifully, with many fruit trees – many of them very old, including a quince – and a small, round pond. At the farthest extreme of the garden there was an old barn, which was accessed by a drive, and beyond the barn was the two-acre field. A sturdy garage had been built onto the side of the cottage, and a huge old hazelnut tree hung over the gate, while pink roses climbed up the wall over the front door. However, Mr Bagley had furnished the cottage in a dreadful Tudor style, and we were told that if we purchased the cottage we would have to buy this as well. I cared nothing about the furniture, because I had fallen madly in love with Old Pound Cottage.

Before I left, I explored Alfold village, which only heightened my enthusiasm, for it was quite delightful, with a fine old inn on a green which was surrounded by timbered houses. The only possible snag was that it was fairly close to Dunsfold Aerodrome, which was one of the largest fighter stations, but I knew that there would be little objection to this as both Dick and the boys were plane crazy, which was hardly surprising after the war.

I could hardly wait for Dick to return home from work that evening so that I could tell him of my discovery, and on the very next weekend the boys, Dick and I drove over to Alfold to meet Mr Bagley at Old Pound Cottage. I needn't have feared that Dick might not have shared my enthusiasm, for he was also instantly enraptured by the charm of the place, and was pleased with the amount of open space which surrounded it, which would give him ample freedom, and the garden would also keep him very busy. He saw at once, as I did, that we could run the whole place ourselves and never need to depend on outside help. (Actually, we did find a treasure to help me, but I will speak of her later.)

The boys were mad with excitement when they rushed into the cottage and discovered the little seats inside the old fireplace. It was love at first sight, as far as they were concerned, and they never changed their minds. We made the decision to purchase that very day, and paid a deposit on the house. We had only one thing to worry us, and that was breaking the news to Katie. However, she took it wonderfully well, and didn't seem very surprised. I think that she had realised for a long time that Gorse Hill was too much to cope with under the changed conditions of life.

We wondered whether the boys would feel cramped in the small cottage, as they had much less space than they'd had at Gorse Hill, with only one small room in which to sleep and keep their toys and other possessions. I thought that, as they had so much space outside – as well as the huge barn, in which they kept their bicycle and tricycle – this made up for the lack of room inside the cottage. In any case, the close proximity to Dick and me gave them the security which children crave. They seemed to be supremely content and happy with their bedroom, which was built relatively recently and therefore bright and cheerful, without any heavy oak beams darkening it.

Our bedroom was part of the original building, above the sitting room. It was heavily timbered with oak beams and still had the original windows. It was a good-sized room for a cottage, and our furniture fitted into it comfortably once the removal men had succeeded in manoeuvring it up the narrow staircase that rose from the stone-paved hall. We were very pleased with the result, for the room looked charming. There was another room across the little passage from our bedroom and the boys' room in which we placed a bed for visitors, and where Dick kept his clothes. There was a basin and running water in there, and our visitors always seemed to be very happy. As I write this, it sounds as though the cottage was very cramped, but actually it wasn't, as it had been tastefully and skilfully modernised while keeping most of the original features, such as floors and beams, intact.

In spite of the cottage's smallness, we managed to entertain many visitors. Children loved to stay with us, as there seemed to be something peculiarly appealing to them in the cosiness and security of the old place. Stewart and Mary Crawford's eldest son, Mark, who was about ten months older than Pompy, was a frequent visitor, as was "Skimper" Hoare-Ruthven, Pamela's youngest boy, whose usual habitat was Windsor Castle. One of my most vivid – and now poignant – memories is of the three little boys, Pompy, Roguey and Skimper, sitting on the bed in a line as though they were in the cockpit of a fighter plane, with Dick at the end of the bed as the pilot, carrying out all sorts of complicated flying manoeuvres. As I watched them and listened to their delighted laughter, I remembered the terrible loss that Skimper had suffered with the death of his father, Patrick Hoare-Ruthven, in North Africa, and thought how blessed it was for us to have come through the war without a similar loss. Luckily for our peace of mind, we had no idea what fate had in store for us.

Pamela Hoare-Ruthven was one of Dick's closest friends. He had known her long before the war and her marriage, for her family lived very near Gorse Hill. She was of Protestant Irish stock, and was a delightful product of those fantastic people. Her marriage shortly before the war was of short duration, alas, for Patrick was killed in the fighting in North Africa.

There was one delightful occasion when our two boys were invited to a Christmas party at Windsor Castle, of which Pamela's father-in-law, the Earl of Gowrie, was the governor. When Millie, our faithful "treasure", who was also a passionate Royalist, heard of this, she insisted on accompanying us, to "help with the boys". I knew that she would never forgive me if we left her behind, so she went with us, and behaved impeccably, as I knew that she would. She was a great success at the party, and Lady Gowrie – who was a warm-hearted and delightful human being – took to her at once, and commandeered her assistance in looking after the children. It was a great party and much enjoyed by everyone there, especially Millie! The Gowries were delightful hosts, and knew just how to put everyone at their ease, a trait I have noticed in many who have personally served the royal family.

Pamela would sometimes come and visit us at Old Pound Cottage, always dropping in unexpectedly. I remember that on one weekend she arrived with her father-in-law, Lord Gowrie, as we were repainting the windows on the front of the house and Dick was hanging onto a ladder, no doubt covered in paint. I invited Lord Gowrie into the cottage and gave him a tour of the place, and I well remember his remark on going into the sitting room when he saw its size. "I've never seen so much in so small a room. Even the grand piano is there!"

"Well, we don't all live in castles," I replied, which amused him. He was delighted with our old cottage, and thought it enchanting. Pamela then persuaded us to allow Pompy to spend a weekend at Windsor Castle as the guest of her elder boy, Grey, which didn't please Pompy at all, as he had never met Grey and he dreaded the idea of staying away from home with relative strangers. It must indeed have been something of an ordeal, for he spent the night in Grey's room, which was in the Norman Tower, and he told us afterwards that he was frightened because it seemed to be haunted. Luckily, there was a very kind nanny there who comforted him and came to his rescue.

We had many good friends in Alfold and the surrounding villages. Our next door neighbour, Ivy Fleming, curiously enough turned out to be related to Helen Holland, one of the Corbetts' oldest friends, and so we started off very well, for Ivy was an attractive woman who knew everyone in the area. Her cottage, The Pound, was larger than ours and certainly a more untouched period piece. It was very beautiful but also a little spooky, and the boys never liked visiting there. She didn't seem to mind the atmosphere at all, but her second son, John, refused to sleep in the old house when he came to visit her and would camp in the garden. The house had a huge living room with a great open fireplace, furnished as a dining room, but Ivy hardly used it and lived in a charming little white-panelled parlour. I felt that there was a ghost present at the top of the staircase, and Ivy agreed that she always felt something strange about that particular spot, but she didn't care because she was quite fearless. She was a warm and loveable neighbour, and we became very intimate friends during the years that I and my family spent at Old Pound Cottage.

Douglas and Elspeth Riley-Smith, who lived in a converted mill in a nearby village, were also great friends. They were a most hospitable and amusing couple, with a large complement of children, who were all given exotic names, and many dogs, who were called Number One Friend, Number Two Friend, *et cetera ad infinitum*. Douglas – who had been a member of Footlights while at Cambridge – collected glassware, much of which he found in Alfold, as the area went back to the early days of glass-blowing. Elspeth, meanwhile, was a very pretty woman and wrote seriously as a poet. They were just eccentric enough to be most amusing company, and we enjoyed visiting them immensely.

One of the main reasons for moving from Gorse Hill to a smaller house was that there were no day schools near Witley, and Dick and I were both determined not to send Pompy away when he reached the age of eight. So one of our first tasks on moving to Old Pound Cottage was to arrange for him to attend a very highly recommended pre-prep school in Cranleigh, our local market town, for which a car collected the local children every morning and brought them home in the afternoon. I can't say that this plan met with much enthusiasm from Pompy, however, as he was so happy at home that he could see little reason in having to be educated. To this day, I can see his little face looking at me tragically from the car in which he was incarcerated with about three other children, waving to me forlornly as he was driven away to prison. However, it was a good little school, and by the time he went on to the Arnold House prep school in London he was well prepared. This routine lasted for a year. Dick would take a bus for Cranleigh Station, where he would catch a train for London, and Pompy would leave for school. Meanwhile, Roguey, who was then only three years old, stayed with me in a blissful untutored state. As happy as this was, I'm sure that he would rather have been with his big brother, even if it had meant going to school.

Our first year at Old Pound Cottage was wonderfully carefree. The burden of running Gorse Hill was gone, and we were able to enjoy life without the constant worry of living beyond our means. We were visited by old friends and made many new ones in the neighbourhood, and we were fortunate enough to have acquired the help of dear Millie, who came every day to see what she could do for the "little lady", as she called me (largely because she was nearly six feet tall). She was a Covey, one of a family of farming stock who had lived in the village for centuries. Jack, her brother, was a wild fellow, but there was good Norman blood there, for

Millie's behaviour was always beyond reproach, and she knew just how to behave at all times. We all adored her, and she was an integral part of our life in the cottage.

Our only concern was the effect that our decision to move might have had on Katie. When I think back, I realise how brave and unselfish she had been during our last days at Gorse Hill, for she was left to cope with the selling and closing down of her home. However, I think that she had realised for a long time that living in the large house was impractical, not only for us but for her as well, and she faced up to face the situation bravely.

9 The Happy Years

I remember this next period of my life as being the halcyon years. We enjoyed our country life to the full. It was an immensely sociable time, for not only were we visited by our friends and families, who somehow managed to squeeze into our small cottage, but there were also parties at weekends in our friends' homes as well as in ours. Millie was always much in demand when it was our turn to entertain, and in fact our guests always enquired if Millie was on the scene when they arrived, for with her great height, tawny red hair and wild eyes she certainly added colour to the proceedings. I can see her now, our little dining room packed with guests, fighting her way through the crowd on her knees with plates or bottles grasped in her hands. Her farming upbringing wouldn't allow her to tolerate the waste of our field, and so she insisted that we kept chickens and ducks as a source of food. Of course, these birds became our pets, especially the baby ducks, and the boys insisted that we took them with us in a cardboard box whenever we went out in the car. Millie also involved us in the breeding of budgerigars, and these beautiful creatures lived in a large cage in a small shed. I remember once that we summoned the village policeman to help in rescuing an escaped yellow budgie, and he cycled madly after the bird as it flew from tree to tree across the village. Those were mad, happy days, and I look back on them with nostalgia and joy.

By September 1948, we had carried out the second part of our plan and found a maisonette to rent in London, at 58 Wellington Road, St John's Wood, situated just a few minutes away from Arnold House, the prep school at which Pompy had been entered. It was a highly respected institution, well known, and successful in the high number of boys who were accepted to go on from there to public schools.

Our lifestyle accordingly changed considerably. We would leave London on Friday afternoons, when Dick returned from the City, and drive down to Old Pound Cottage, in great excitement and anticipation, to find

Millie waiting for us with a warm welcome and a huge supper. We usually returned to London on Sunday evenings and dined at Portland Place with "Bam-Bam" and "Pa". It was a bold plan, requiring quite a lot of organisation on my part, but it was worth it, as it suited everyone. Dick enjoyed his country life at the weekends and during the school holidays, and was spared the tiring train journey from the country to the City every day, while the boys were able to attend a fine school and still live at home. I also had the pleasure of living something of the life to which I had been accustomed, and of hearing great music again, as well as that of renewing contacts in the musical world. I also had the joy of seeing much of my parents, as well as and Uncle Fred and Aunt Carrie.

It was fortunate that Dick shared my hatred of boarding schools. He had been brought up in the traditional English fashion of being sent away to prep school at the age of eight and then had gone on to Eton. He had loathed leaving home, and had been miserably unhappy at his prep school, and indeed didn't enjoy Eton, where he was never in very good health. He finished his pre-university education at a school in Switzerland, where he'd had a wonderful time and learned to speak excellent French. There was no quarrel between us as to whether the boys should be sent away, so he indulged both himself and me by taking on the burden of running two homes. It couldn't have been otherwise.

58 Wellington Road was a typical St John's Wood house. It was built in the early years of the 19th century, and had the spaciousness typical of that period of architecture. We had a good-sized sitting room, kitchen and bathroom on the first floor of the maisonette, and at the top of a very steep and dangerous staircase were two large bedrooms, one occupied by the boys and the other by us. The house had been badly damaged by a large bomb that had fallen very close during the war, and it was in a poor state. All of the floors slanted in a perilous fashion, and for this reason we were able to negotiate a very reasonable rent. The neighbourhood was pleasant, though, as we were very close to Arnold House School and almost next door to the local underground station, which was very convenient for Dick. The only disadvantage was that, as Wellington Road was the main highway leading north-west from the centre of London, it was noisy during the rush hours, but that didn't worry us much, as the place had so many other advantages. We were situated between my parents' home in Portland Place and the place where Mondy and Catherine lived, as they had acquired a maisonette in

Hampstead just a little further on from us, off the Finchley Road. This was convenient for Mondy, who was by this time working for my father in the Coty organisation. His office was in Stratford Place, off Oxford Street, and therefore within easy reach by public transport. As I write this, I realise that, in those years, we were unconsciously struggling to fit into the life that we had known before the war, and we were swarming like disturbed bees, desperately trying to settle again into our hive.

When Roguey was about five years old, we decided that he should attend a small school within easy walking distance, very near Arnold House, so that both boys could go off to school together. This was the plan, anyway, but unfortunately it didn't work. When I took Roguey to the school on his first morning and he saw that there were little girls among the pupils, he absolutely refused to stay there. He made such a terrible commotion – much to my embarrassment – that the teacher, who was a nice girl, assured me that she thought that he would settle down once I had left him. I tried to do this, with a heavy heart, but at noon I rushed back to fetch him and found a most pathetic and obstinate little bundle waiting for me. The teacher said that she hoped that he would accept the situation eventually, but Dick and I decided that it was better not to create a drama, and instead decided to keep him at home until he was old enough to enter the pre-prep school for boys at Arnold House, at the age of six. When the time eventually came, he set off happily with Pompy, dressed in his Arnold House uniform. His pride had been seriously offended when he had been left at a school with little girls, for he wanted to be like Pompy in everything. So this miniature drama was happily overcome!

For some time, I had been feeling a strong desire to resume my work in music. My menfolk deserted me during the day, as Dick worked in the City and the boys were both at school. I didn't wish to lead the sort of life then considered the norm for a married woman, comprising housework and shopping, followed by lunch meetings with various women friends. I refused to drift into this routine, for my life before the war had been so occupied by my work in music that I was aware that I had to resume at least some of the activities to which I had given so much of my youth. Of course, I knew that I couldn't go back to the life of a professional pianist, which involved hours of practice and constant travelling. In any case, I had absolutely no desire to be away from my beloved little family, so my mind turned to my preoccupation with the art of recording, in which I had always been intensely interested since childhood, and in which Uncle Fred had taken such pains to train me from an early age.

Before speaking of this to anyone else, I discussed it with Dick, who was instantly sympathetic. He was intelligent enough to know that I needed such an interest in my life, and was relieved that the project I had in mind could be undertaken from home. It was also something in which he could take a personal interest and share with me. Thus encouraged, I bearded Uncle Fred in his den (actually his bedroom), where the great man now spent much of his day, as his health was failing, alas, and told him of my plan. To my intense relief, he encouraged me and offered to help in any way that he could to start the ball rolling. We spent many happy hours together, planning how to start the operation with the least risk and the greatest chance of success. How well I remember those happy repertoire meetings in his home in Crediton Hill, in which we dreamed and planned our recording programme. I like to think that it gave him some interest in the last period of his life. Because he would never grow old in mind and spirit, he was able to encourage me to dream of following in his footsteps, however humbly.

Those three years that Dick, the boys and I spent together in our ramshackle old flat in St John's Wood were very happy. We were close to family and friends and able to take part in the cultural life of London. The boys were busily engaged in school life, and many model planes were hung from the ceiling of their huge bedroom on the top floor of the flat, painstakingly constructed by Pompy from balsa wood, thin paper and a lot of glue. There was also an extensive railway system, which covered the entire floor. It was very dangerous to enter there, and I had long given up any attempts at keeping it clean. Our bedroom – which also sloped perilously – was comfortable, if not beautiful, but we were happy there, and we knew that, at the end of each week, on Friday afternoons, we could pile into our car and drive down to our beloved Old Pound Cottage in Alfold.

We were visited frequently by friends and family from abroad. Louise Maurer was one of my twin cousins, and had served in some capacity with the American forces in Italy and had grown very fond of that country, and she was now staying with Aunt Carrie and Uncle Fred. She spent a lot of time with us, captivating the boys, who found her rather eccentric charm entirely to their satisfaction, and they came to call her "Loopy Lou". Then Mausi appeared on the scene, probably on her way back from America, where she had spent the latter years of the war. Needless to say, my dear mother spent much time with us, struggling up the dangerous stairs to play endless games with the boys or have wonderful "chats", during which they acted out daring adventures. She was so gifted in her handling of children, and the boys adored her. There is no doubt in my mind that, even if my marriage to Dick hadn't been as blissfully happy as it turned out to be, my parents would still have derived the utmost satisfaction from their relationship with the boys.

When we left Gorse Hill to move into the cottage at the end of 1947, Katie had stayed back at the house for a short while in order to sell the property and to put her affairs in order. It must have been a hard time for the poor woman, as her plans for settling back into her old home – about which she must have dreamt during the war years -- faded away, and yet she never complained or appeared to blame me in any way for having found life at Gorse Hill impossible. Nor did she ever hint that I had persuaded Dick to leave it for the cottage. Katie and I had such a wonderful relationship that nothing could shake the solid foundation of our understanding of each other.

Gorse Hill didn't remain on the market for very long, and in the meantime Katie's adventurous and romantic nature had spurred her into falling in love with the most beautiful old house not far from Old Pound Cottage. Lying deep in the woodlands, it had originally been a hunting lodge, and had been owned by the diarist John Evelyn, a friend of Samuel Pepys. Pollingfold was one of the most romantic dwellings imaginable. It was timbered with exposed beams, built on three floors, and nearly all of the windows contained the original glass. The front door was slightly below garden level and built of solid oak, through which one entered into a fairly large, stone-paved hall. The staircase, rising from the hallway, was of polished oak, and the stairs were wide and shallow. There was a huge window halfway up, and so plenty of light fell onto both the hall below and the broad landing, from which one entered a fine, long sitting room with a huge open fireplace at one end and a large casement window overlooking the gardens at the other. There was also a dining room and kitchen on this floor. The house had been rearranged to suit modern living, but it had been redesigned with such taste and skill that one didn't feel that the beautiful building had been desecrated in any way. The gardens had also been laid out tastefully and kept in splendid order. In fact, it was a small architectural jewel. In spite of the fact that Dick told his mother that it was totally unsuitable for a woman of her age to live in alone, and that it would cost far too much to maintain, Katie was determined to buy it.

She took Old Lizzie with her as a companion, and all of her grandchildren spent many happy days with her in the romantic old lodge. There was something about the place that appealed to them, and the atmosphere in Pollingfold – which in some old houses could be awe-inspiring – was completely happy and reassuring. I well remember many occasions when I watched our boys and Sue's daughter, Elizabeth, when she was on a visit from America, playing croquet or cricket on the lawn and hearing their happy laughter. It was a paradise for children.

However, Dick had been right when he had advised Katie to resist buying the old house, for she soon discovered that it needed constant care and a great deal of money to keep it in a habitable condition. There was no mains electricity, and the old oil-powered generator had to be kept in running condition and constantly supplied. Then she also had to contribute her share for the upkeep of the very long drive, which was costly, and pay the gardener's wages, who was needed nearly every day and all day. Dick was forever being summoned to her rescue when the generator refused to start, and Katie eventually had to face up to the fact that it was in a shocking state of repair and would have to be replaced. Katie loved the place so much that we never dreamed of persuading her to think of leaving it, but when she was faced with a colossal estimate for her share in the upkeep of the drive she finally agreed that she had to give up her dream of spending the rest of her life in Pollingfold. There was a family conference, and she decided to move to Oxford to be near Patrick, who was then a don at Balliol. I felt so sorry for her, for I knew that the beauty of Pollingfold had appealed to her artistic nature, and that even the joy of being near Patrick wouldn't quite make up for its loss. She found a flat in a house in North Oxford, which she made just as charming, but it wasn't the same as being surrounded by the beauty of Pollingfold.

10 Death In Malaya

In spite of the happiness of our lives during these early years after the war, there was a cloud of dread over us which grew darker and more menacing every day. The situation in Malaya was worsening, and every day there was more news of the bitter war waged by the Chinese communists and of savage attacks on our planters. The tragic seriousness of the situation was brought home to us on the early BBC news one morning in the late autumn of 1951, when it was announced that the Chinese had assassinated General Templar, commander-in-chief in Malaya.

I shall never forget hearing this news, nor the look on Dick's face, nor the terrible premonition which briefly overcame us as we sat at the breakfast table with the boys. Dick and I just looked at each other wordlessly, as we didn't wish to disturb the boys before they left for school. It was a moment written forever on my memory. Of course, I tried to persuade Dick to put off his next tour, which was now imminent, until the war quietened down in Malaya, but I knew that this was of no avail. He felt that it was his duty to see for himself how his planters were coping with the dreadful situation, and I knew that it was useless to try and dissuade him.

In order to lift the feeling of dread with which I was tormented, Dick suggested that I joined him in Ceylon after his visit to Malaya. I had never been to the Far East, and I must admit that I had little interest in doing so, but because much of Dick's life was involved with that part of the world I felt that I should agree to this plan. As far as the care of the boys was concerned, it was a suitable time, as Dick was leaving for Malaya at the beginning of November and I would join him at the end of the month in Colombo. Meanwhile, the boys would be able to stay with my parents in Portland Place, from where Waylett could easily take them to school and pick them up again later, and I knew that I would have nothing to fear concerning their care. I felt that, by making a holiday of the end of Dick's tour, it would somehow lighten the atmosphere, so I went ahead and had all of the necessary shots and bought lightweight clothes, of which my wardrobe was noticeably lacking. When Dick's company, Thompson Alston, sent me my air tickets and the itinerary, I remember placing them in a drawer in our desk, and in my heart of hearts there was a terrible premonition that they would never be used.

Dick and I tried to be cheerful so that the boys wouldn't be too worried about his imminent departure, but the news from Malaya was worse every day, and stopping myself from begging Dick not to go wasn't easy. One of his partners, Lindsay Mackie, offered to take his place, as he was unmarried and had no wife and children to consider, but Dick was adamant, and I knew that it was useless to try and dissuade him any further. My parents were also very unhappy, and I know that my father spoke to Dick and tactfully tried to suggest that he postponed his trip, but to no avail. It was almost as though Dick had made up his mind to undertake a trial, like Tamino in *Die Zauberflöte*, in an attempt to prove something to himself. He felt that it was his duty to go. It could even have been that he was under orders from the government. I shall never know.

On 6 November 1951, I drove him to Victoria to catch the coach for the airport. It was pouring with rain, and as we parted he joked, "Look after the boys and the car," as we had only just acquired a bright red Riley.

"I think you care more about leaving the car than leaving me!" I told him.

"Of course," he answered, and these were the last words that we ever exchanged. It's impossible to describe the dreadful sense of anguish that I felt as I left him, but I knew that I had to pull myself together to face the boys, and so I drove back to them, alone – had I known it – for ever.

On 13 November (14 November, Malaya time), six days after Dick's departure, the phone rang at about eight o'clock in the morning. It was answered by Maria, the daughter of Mummy's Italian housekeeper, who had been staying with us in our flat. She couldn't understand the English voice, and called me to the telephone. "I think he said he was a newspaper," she said. For one terrible moment my heart stopped beating.

When I asked the man who he was, he said, "This is *The Daily Mirror*. Can you confirm the news of your husband's murder in Malaya?"

"How dare you! *How dare you?*" I cried, and slammed down the receiver.

From then on, it was chaos. I phoned Lindsay Mackie at the company's London office, who received the news with horror, as the company hadn't yet been informed by the War Office. From that moment, he took charge of everything that followed. Exactly how *The Daily Mirror* had received the news before anyone else was never explained, but the question of why the telephone call was made to me before official information was received was asked in the House of Commons.

Roguey was upstairs in bed, quite ill with scarlet fever, and Pompy had already gone to school. My mother came over at once, and Lindsay phoned to warn me that the story was splashed all over the newspaper billboards in the streets. I was afraid that someone from Arnold House might have seen one in St John's Wood tube station, and that the information would reach Pompy before he came home. I rang Mr Smart, the headmaster, to warn him, as I had decided to leave Pompy at school until his normal time to return in the afternoon, when I would break the news to him and Roguey together. To this day, I remember those two little boys looking at me with large eyes full of incomprehension as I tried to explain to them that their Daddy had been killed and would never come home again. It was terrible, and I could find no way to comfort them except to hold them close.

My mother and father came to me, begging me to leave the flat and come home with them, but I refused. I clung to the idea of carrying on and trying to make life as normal as possible for the boys. I insisted that we should go down to Old Pound Cottage for the weekend, for I knew that the dear old place would give them more comfort than anything else possibly could, so we drove away from London on that Friday in the new car and were greeted by Millie, who of course had heard the news. In her arms she held an adorable puppy, a Cairn terrier, which had been sent from Scotland and brought to the cottage so that Millie could present him to the boys on our arrival. It was a wonderful, kindly, imaginative gift from Elspeth and Douglas Riley-Smith, and one which neither the boys nor I would ever forget. His name, Millie told us, was Ian, and when he was in the boys' arms their joy knew no bounds. It saved both them and myself from the terrible moment of returning to the cottage without Dick, and I knew that the puppy would do more than anything else to comfort the boys and assuage their grief. Ian travelled with us back and forth from the cottage to London, and became a brother to the boys and almost a third son for me. He was so intelligent and sensitive that we knew that he had been sent to us for a purpose. Although he loved games, and at times could be as excited as the boys, he was quiet by nature and always behaved like a perfect gentleman.

Dick's death received considerable press coverage. The war in Malaya was a matter of great public concern at the time, and Dick had been well known and highly respected in the City, as well as being a director of a major East India company and chairman of the Rubber Growers' Council. A memorial service was held in one of the great city churches. I didn't take the boys with me, as I feared that it would have been too much for them to endure, and I was accompanied instead by Dick's younger sister, Susan. The church was packed to capacity, and Patrick, Dick's younger brother, gave the most moving eulogy. It was very beautiful, but I hardly heard anything as I was hanging onto my self-control and longing for the ordeal to end. I wondered afterwards if I should have taken the boys with me, but I felt that it would have been too much to ask of them. Perhaps that was wrong, for I fear that there may have been times since then when they have wondered if their father's death had really happened.

I received many letters, which I never had the courage to read until quite recently, when I began to write these memoirs. Dick was buried immediately after his death in Ipoh at the same time as the manager of the estate, CW Dicks. The details of the ceremony were sent to me, and I learned that the two men had been given a full military funeral. As I received the concessions that I was due, as the widow of a serving officer killed in action, I began to wonder whether Dick's mission had been entirely concerned with his business, or whether he had also been involved with work for the government.

The three of us carried on with the routine of life that Dick and I had planned. The boys continued to attend Arnold House School, and were both doing well. Every Friday afternoon we would set off for the cottage, where Millie would greet us with a warm welcome and an excellent supper. Ian, the puppy, was at the age when both of his ears stood up straight and perky above his intelligent little face, and he was a constant source of comfort and amusement to us all.

Because of the proximity of Old Pound Cottage to RAF Dunsfold, the boys were constantly on the alert to catch the sound of planes approaching, and they seemed to be able to hear them from great distance. As soon as they heard one, there was a wild rush into the garden, down to the field and the old barn, where they would climb up a ladder onto the roof to watch the plane approach and land. All of this excitement was accompanied by the wild barking of Ian, who could also hear the approach of fighter planes from a long distance, and would rush after the boys, only to be thwarted by the ladder.

Our friends continued to heap invitations upon us so that we didn't feel lonely. Ivy Fleming, who lived next door, had been devoted to Dick, and the Riley-Smiths never failed to stop at Old Pound Cottage whenever they were passing to ask if we needed any help and to see how Ian was faring. Lindsay Bradlay and her husband, Jim, who had suffered grievously as a Japanese prisoner of war, also seemed unable to do enough for us. There were also many others who helped, including Marjorie Naumann, whose only son, Anthony, had been blinded at the age of 21, a few days before the end of hostilities in Europe. I had met her brother, Aubrey Wallich, for the first time some years previously, when he had come to the cottage to attend one of our wild cocktail parties. He was an eminent figure in Malaya, and Dick knew him well. I can remember that, on that occasion, Pompy and Roguey bombarded him with little apples from their bedroom window, an incident that he never forgot. But, in spite of their apparent lack of hospitality, it didn't prevent Aubrey from being brave enough to offer to share his life with us when he retired from Malaya at a later date.

We faced the first Christmas without Dick with dread. The boys and I stayed at the flat in Wellington Road and spent Christmas Day at Portland Place with my parents, who lavished loving care and generosity on the boys to try and make them less conscious of Dick's absence, and in some measure they succeeded in this. The celebration was an ordeal, however, for not only was Dick not with us but Uncle Fred's genial presence was also missing. I can't remember if Aunt Carrie was there, although I believe that by that time she had already gone back to Washington. We had all dreaded the occasion, but the Christmas atmosphere comforted us and gave the boys some happiness.

About two days before Christmas, a strange incident occurred which seemed to be a message from Dick, telling me that I should pull myself together and gather strength. I was driving down Avenue Road, coming to the entrance to Regent's Park, when a police officer stepped out from a side street and ordered me to stop. I was driving fairly fast, certainly exceeding the speed limit, and my heart sank as I was signalled to pull in. I remember thinking, What now? What's going to happen to me next? To my astonishment, when the officer walked up to the car, I recognised him instantly as Bruce Nicholson, a boy with whom I had been to kindergarten. I had seen him casually on a few occasions, years before the war, for he lived in the same street as Aunt Carrie and Uncle Fred, and we had perhaps exchanged a few childish words, although I hadn't seen or thought of him since. He recognised me at once, and greeted me warmly, but admonished me for speeding and gave me a warning; much to my relief, he didn't charge me on this occasion. We chatted for a while, and I told him of my two sons, but said nothing of Dick's death. He must have seen something in my face, however, because he said, "Isabella, I don't know what's happened to you, but be careful when you drive. Think of the boys." It was very strange, meeting this man after all those years and under such circumstances. It made me remember the promise that I'd made to Dick as we'd parted, and I made sure that I drove with care after this rather bizarre meeting.

1951 proved to be a most appalling year for all of our families. As well as Dick's death, we also experienced a number of other tragedies. Mark Crawford, the eldest son of Stewart and Mary Crawford, died suddenly at his boarding school, aged only twelve years. The grief suffered by his parents and his brother and sister, and indeed by us all, at the loss of such a young life can only be imagined.

On 2 September of that awful year, my family and I suffered deep sorrow in the death of my beloved uncle, Fred Gaisberg, at the age of 78. Although he hadn't been well for some time, and we had been expecting this, I felt as though a foundation of my life had been removed. We had been such close companions and shared so many interests, even to the very last days of his life, when we had been busily involved in discussing recording repertoire. He never seemed to grow old, and his death was very hard to accept. He had many friends and had been a great force in the world of music, and I was sure that it would be a long time before those with whom he had worked so hard and so brilliantly throughout his life would accept that he was no longer there to advise and help them. There were many articles written about him at the time of his death, praising the pioneering work he had done for the recording industry and his remarkable talent as an impresario. Hardly any of the writers failed to pay tribute to his kindness and generosity. Uncle Fred's death was felt deeply by my family, and the loss of his comforting presence became even more acute after Dick's terrible death some weeks later.

It's almost impossible to accept that, on 2 February 1952, barely three months later, my cousin Leo Brugnatelli died in Milan from tuberculosis, which had been aggravated by his service during the war in the Italian Army, fighting in Greece. He had been 25 years old, and his death represented the loss not only of a potentially brilliant writer and lawyer but also of a most lovable human being.

As I write of these losses, I can only sum them up by thinking that the Grim Reaper had been very busy in our family during that terrible year. Looking back on those days, I can never say enough in praise of Katie's wonderful selflessness in the face of the grief that she suffered with the loss of Dick, her eldest son, and of her grandson, Mark, and the courage and fortitude that she showed in subduing her own feelings so that she could be of the utmost assistance to those others who were bereaved. When Katie gave her love, she gave it unquestioningly, and she supported me in my grief and in all decisions and plans for the future. I shall never forget her generous spirit, nor feel that she is ever very far from me.

In the months that followed, I tried to immerse myself in some of the activities of my former life by attending concerts and meeting many of my old schoolfriends. Coggie Margetson and Gildie Crawford did all that they could to help, and Mondy came around every evening on his way home from the office for a drink and a chat with the boys, trying to fill the void of Dick's absence. Lindsay Mackie took me out to dinner and the theatre occasionally, and also helped me immensely by advising me on my financial affairs. He helped me to set up a trust fund for the boys, so that their education was taken care of until they graduated from university. This removed a weight from my shoulders, and I was very grateful to him for his guidance and help.

Although I was keeping myself occupied with looking after the boys, running the two houses and sorting out my financial affairs, I was determined to begin working again. I knew that I had to revive my great interest in music, which had been paramount in my life before my marriage and the war. I also felt that, when the time came, it was essential for the boys to be free to lead their own lives. I decided that the best way to achieve this would be to resume my previous activities in a way that wouldn't interfere with my caring for them, and so I had to work from home, and it had to be some kind of work in which the boys could take an interest and, at times, share.

As these thoughts passed through my mind, I realised that I had to move slowly and cautiously (which is not really in my nature), as I could no longer ask for guidance from Uncle Fred nor count on Dick's encouragement and good business sense. I made no move, therefore, but often spoke of my thoughts with my father and dreamed of ways to start recording a catalogue. I followed my instincts, which told me that something would happen, or that someone would appear who would show me a way in which I could benefit from the training that I had received from Uncle Fred in my early days. It seemed that all of those years in which he had patiently taken me with him to concerts, meeting great artists and watching him working with them in the recording studios, had had a purpose which might now be fulfilled.

In the meantime, the life which I had shared with Dick went on quietly while I waited for something to occur which would reveal the path I was to follow.

11 *The Great Philharmonia Adventure*

After the terrible disaster of Dick's death in November 1951, the boys and I continued to live in the house in Wellington Road during the week and would go down to our little cottage for the weekends, although we thought of Old Pound Cottage as our real home. Dick had loved it, as did Pompy and Roguey, and we only lived in London during the week so that the boys could attend Arnold House School.

In the afternoons, I would cross the busy Wellington Road to fetch Roguey, who was then only seven years old. On one afternoon in early May 1952, I was on my way to the school when I heard somebody call out "Isabella!" I looked, and there was Walter Legge, whom I hadn't seen for many years. We were only able to talk for a brief while, as I was in my car and he was walking on his way to the EMI studios in Abbey Road. He knew that I had lost my husband, of course, and asked me what I was doing now. I told him that I was trying to make life as normal as possible for the boys and myself. Then, quite out of the blue, he asked me if I would like a job, and equally impulsively I answered that I would love to work in music again. He explained that Jane Withers, the manager of Philharmonia, Walter's own orchestra, had been taken seriously ill, and that she would have to go into a nursing home very shortly. This left Walter in a pretty desperate situation, as the orchestra was shortly due to start on its first European tour since the war, with Herbert von Karajan as conductor. He asked me if I would consider taking over as orchestral manager.

What an extraordinary proposition, after just a few minutes of conversation in the street! I explained that I couldn't make a decision instantly, as I had the boys to consider, and that I would also have to discuss it with my mother to see if she was willing to look after them during my absence. "Well, we're in the midst of sessions at the Kingsway Hall," he said. "Come along tomorrow morning and talk it over with me and meet von Karajan."

On the following morning, I parked the car and walked down Kingsway to the hall, where the session was due to begin at ten o'clock. My thoughts were in a turmoil. I wondered if my life was once again to take a momentous turn, and whether, if I made a decision, it would be the right one.

The orchestra was tuning up when I got to the Kingsway Hall, so I sat at the back of the stalls to listen, and I assumed that Walter was with von Karajan in the control room. The session began with von Karajan rehearsing Richard Strauss's great tone poem *Don Juan*, which was to be included in the programme of the tour. It was very exciting to hear this music again, especially as the orchestra sounded in splendid form. Philharmonia comprised the finest British instrumentalists, whom I was sure Walter had been dreaming of including in his own orchestra as soon as the war had come to an end. As I listened, I thought of how wonderful it would be to become involved with this talented group of people, and how I would find it difficult to refuse Walter's offer, if he decided to make one, and presumably if von Karajan approved.

During the first break, Walter came to find me and took me to the control room to meet the great man, who was polite but showed little interest, as he was engrossed in the session. Walter and I briefly discussed the forthcoming tour, and he then asked me if I thought that I could take Jane Withers's place as orchestral manager. I gave the only possible answer that I could at that time – that I would do my best to help them out of their present difficulty, but that Walter had to understand that I'd never done anything like this before. Walter seemed confident that I had the necessary qualifications, however: I was skilled with languages, I was a musician, and above all I was Fred Gaisberg's niece. Because I'd so often been my uncle's companion at recording sessions and other great musical events before the war, he felt certain that I'd acquired sufficient experience in handling artists, all of which would help me in dealing with the orchestra.

I knew that Walter could be impulsive when it came to making decisions, as I'm sure von Karajan did as well. The conductor showed no such enthusiasm, but I soon learned that this was just his way. What he didn't know, but what he perhaps suspected, was that Walter was showing me sympathy and understanding during a tragic time in my life by giving me the opportunity to immerse myself in a task which could only be of profound interest to me. We chatted for a while, and then it was decided that Jane would accompany the orchestra for the first series of concerts in Paris and Switzerland and that I would join them in Milan on 19 May, after her departure.

Meanwhile, I had to make arrangements for the two boys to stay with my parents in their flat in Portland Place, from which they could easily be delivered and collected from school. Although I knew that they would be very happy with my mother and father, it was our first separation since Dick's death, and so it was possible that it would cause them some anxiety. After thinking about it, I decided to go ahead and seize the opportunity which had so unexpectedly presented itself, in the hope that it would open a door that would lead to a fascinating future.

I looked forward immensely to the train journey across France and the Alps and into Italy. I was highly excited at the prospect of visiting my birthplace, Milan, and hopefully seeing my family there after all the years of war. I arrived on the morning of 19 May, and as the train drew into the station I saw Uncle Leo smiling and waving to me. It was a moving moment to see his handsome bearded face again, and I only wished that I could have had more time to spend with him, but I could do little more than arrange to see my family as soon as I discovered what lay before me. As Jane Withers was waiting for me to turn up so that she could leave for London, I had to rush off to the Hotel American, where the orchestra was billeted.

As I entered the hotel and went to the reception to register, I noticed a group of people standing together watching me. One of them, a tall handsome fellow whom I recognised immediately as the cellist David Ffrangçon-Thomas, walked over and said, "Are you really Isabella Valli, Fred Gaisberg's niece? We were told that you'd be coming to look after us. We've heard so many strange stories that we weren't sure if we should believe this one. We're so relieved and happy to see you." It was reassuring to be greeted so warmly, and it gave me courage to cope with what I gathered, after a long talk with David, was going to be a difficult and delicate operation. He explained that they had already given a number of concerts, starting in Paris and, I believe, in Berne and Basle, and ending in Turin on the very night before I joined them. Toscanini, who was in Milan, had sent members of the orchestra of La Scala, as well as his great friend and colleague the distinguished conductor de Sebata, to hear them in Turin, and so the orchestra had already endured a considerable travelling schedule, not to mention the strain of playing a heavy programme of particularly difficult and exhausting music. The programmes that they played were selected from the following repertoire: Handel's *Water Music*, arranged by Harty; Stravinsky's *Jeu de Cartes*; Tchaikovsky's fifth symphony; Mozart's divertimento in B flat, K 286; Brahms's second symphony; and Richard Strauss's tone poem *Don Juan*.

Members of the orchestra approached me in small groups, rather like lost children, and voiced their relief at seeing me, especially as Jane Withers was leaving for London almost immediately. I could well understand the reason for their unease, as this was their first post-war tour of Europe, which was still dominated by political problems and power blocs, as we were shortly to discover when we reached Vienna. The musicians also felt that they lacked leadership, as Walter was preoccupied in looking after von Karajan and Elisabeth Schwarzkopf, who was accompanying him for part of the tour. Apparently, the orchestra were travelling on their own, which made them feel neglected. This was exaggerated but understandable, under the difficult circumstances, and they implored me to act as liaison between them and management. I soon discovered what a difficult task this would be, as Walter disappeared whenever any difficulty or drama appeared on the horizon. Luckily, von Karajan's personal manager, Mattone, was very efficient and proved to be most helpful.

It was quite extraordinary to find myself in Milan again and involved in such an unexpected adventure. The concerts were scheduled to take place in La Scala, the great opera house that held so many associations for me. I thought of Uncle Fred's recordings of the great artists who performed there in the early days of the gramophone, to say nothing of his determination to record the voice of the fabulous young tenor Enrico Caruso, after hearing him sing in *Germania* at La Scala in 1902. Uncle Fred had decided to finance the recording himself, against the orders of the London directors, and achieved such success that the recording contributed largely to Caruso's engagement at the Metropolitan in New York, thus launching his memorable career.

I have a much more personal memory of my mother, who had made her debut at La Scala in 1912 as leading flower maiden in *Parsifal*, in the Italian première of Wagner's great opera, under the direction of Tullio Serafin, when my father occupied the same seat for every performance because he was so deeply in love with the young American singer.

All in all, it was a great thrill to visit La Scala for the first time. I wasn't disappointed, either, for indeed it is a most brilliant and beautiful opera house. The orchestral quarters are luxurious and efficient. Both the management and the orchestra greeted us warmly and enthusiastically, and they did everything they could to make us as comfortable as possible. However, in spite of their kindness, we would experience a number of scenes caused largely by lack of direction from Philharmonia's management, which brought out the worst in the more temperamental members of the orchestra.

After Jane's departure for London, I was left alone to deal with the situation, which at times became so fraught that it was farcical. In a letter to Aubrey Wallich, I gave a pretty vivid description of some of the events that occurred shortly after my arrival in Milan:

20 MAY, MILANO

This tour is a nightmare of bad organisation, maybe because Jane was so ill during the days of preparation. Walter is full of idealistic dreams about the future but leaves the handling of this very awkward tour to inexperienced incompetents. I was livid with Walter yesterday but won my battle by insisting that either he or von K's manager, Mattone, come with me on the trip to Vienna tonight. I refused to take sole responsibility.

You should have seen me last night in the Scala orchestra room, coping with the men of our crowd and the men of the Scala orchestra, who were there to hear gossip and to give advice. Our librarian, Clem, was stretched out on the floor in a faint, his assistant, Miss Arditi, having hysterics, Jane Withers looking like a ghost, the second trombone stretched out on a chair having hurt his leg, the second flute missing, and von K shouting for them to come on the platform. In the meantime, when I peeped out to see the house, Walter was seated comfortably in the front waiting for the concert to start. In all honesty, of course, one has to remember that Walter had his hands full coping with von Karajan and matters of policy. [Here I dare not quote from my letter.]

What a crazy affair! But the concert was a sensation, and the Scala was wonderful. There was a magnificent party afterwards for everyone. Most lavish and beautifully done. Speeches

etc…That was fine, and the orchestra loved it. Wonderful result. I
hear that Toscanini, who was present, has agreed to conduct us
later in the year in London. Great!

One of the objectives of the tour had been to persuade Toscanini to attend
the concert, and hopefully to get him to agree to conduct the orchestra
later in London, and as you can see this objective was achieved. Because
of the line-up of the orchestra, this was not surprising. It was indeed a star
cast, with such musicians as Dennis Brain, Max Salpeter, Gareth Morris,
Sidney Sutcliffe, Reginald Kell, Raymond Clark, Herbert Downes, the
concert-master Manoug Parikian and many other famous names. It was
an orchestra to dream of; I wasn't surprised that Toscanini wanted to
conduct it. When this was agreed, all of our tribulations were forgotten
and jubilation reigned. The artistic success of the concert, and the
tremendously warm reception accorded by the Milanese public, together
with the brilliant generosity of the reception after the concert, did much
to boost the flagging morale of the orchestra. Walter and von Karajan
must have also felt greatly encouraged and elated by snagging Toscanini.
This was an undoubted triumph.

Immediately after the last concert at La Scala, we gathered together the
musicians, the instruments, the music and the personal luggage and were
driven to the station in three coaches that waited for us outside the artists'
entrance of the opera house. There were also crowds of well-wishers
gathered there to bid us farewell, including members of the house
orchestra. We departed in a cloud of warmth and glory.

Unfortunately, we weren't able to enjoy this happy atmosphere for very
long. When we arrived at the station, we were conducted to our special
train, which was due to leave for Vienna at 12.15am, only to find that there
were no sleeping cars. I was afraid that the orchestra would riot, as they
had been assured of these arrangements and were absolutely furious at
being let down. I was thankful that I had insisted that Mattone
accompanied us, for I needed his help at this point. As usual, the women
of the orchestra came to my rescue and persuaded the men to board the
train and settle down for the long night ahead.

I was in a compartment with David Ffrangçon-Thomas, Osian Ellis and
Marie Goosens, and we talked through most of the night. I heard about
Wales for the first time, its history, poetry and music. This was all

completely new to me, and I had to confess my ignorance about Wales and that I'd never been there. The two Welshmen were profoundly shocked, and I encountered for the first time their passion when discussing their language, history and culture. When I told them that I was planning to start my own record company, and that I was looking for original and inexpensive repertoire, we became excited with the thought that a beautifully-arranged programme of Welsh folk music could be just what I needed for my first recording. David and Osian told me that they were giving a recital at the Wigmore Hall shortly after our return to London, and I decided that I would go along to hear them. It sounded fascinating. Looking back, I can't help but think how strange it was that I experienced my first contact with Wales – which proved to have so strong an influence in my life – on a train in the night, somewhere in the middle of Europe.

We arrived at the Austrian border at about six o'clock in the morning. We were now entering the Russian zone, and it wasn't a very prepossessing sight. Armed soldiers in long grey coats were lined up along the platform, and as we stopped they entered the train and began examining our papers. Some of our men were rather worried, including David Ffrangçon-Thomas, who had fought as a paratrooper in eastern Europe and had come up against the Russians on a number of occasions. He feared that he might be *persona non grata*, but luckily there was nothing wrong with his papers. The Russians came right through the train, examining all of our passports, and scrutinised the passage where the instruments were stored – which was poor Clem's department – particularly closely. We were very happy when they gave us clearance and we were free to proceed to Vienna. Once again, I was thankful to have had Mattone with us, for he proved to be very helpful in dealing with the Russians.

We arrived in Vienna at around noon after a very tiring journey. It wasn't surprising that the orchestra was in a difficult mood, as the hotels in Vienna were in bad state after the war, and certainly didn't present a very prepossessing appearance. We were booked into two of them, the Wymberger and the Terminus, in which the main part of the band was supposed to stay. The Terminus certainly looked very unattractive at first sight, and a number of the men refused to stay there. I offered to stay there with them, and Walter, summoned by the uprising, took the rest to the Wymberger, which in their rebellious mood they insisted was a better hotel. Meanwhile, about 20 of them, including the women, remained with me.

The trouble wasn't over yet. After viewing their rooms, the men of the party decided that they wouldn't stay in the Terminus at all, and tried to force their way out of the hotel. Believe it or not, I had to stand with my back to the door and threaten that they would have to physically remove me in order to get out. I'm glad to say that they refrained from doing this; if they'd forced their way out, goodness knows what would have happened, for I knew that there was no more room in the Wymberger. It's hard to believe that this really happened, but musicians can behave like babies, and these had endured a lot of unnecessary discomfort. Actually, the Terminus's management staff was very kind to us, and did their best to make us comfortable. It became quite a home from home.

After the orchestra members had settled into the hotels, we were instructed to make for the Musikverein Salle, where the concerts were to take place, as von Karajan wished to see the orchestra, and as the hall was nearby we walked there. In order to reach the Musikverein, we had to pass the Russian Army's headquarters, which were situated in a magnificent square, with armed soldiers all along the pavement outside the building. At every street corner there was a jeep in which four Russian soldiers were seated holding machine guns – a sinister sight indeed. They sat there quietly, and appeared not to notice us at all. I felt like an old hen with her chicks as I told the orchestra to walk past quickly and not to look at the Russians! I was so afraid that their British sense of humour would get us into trouble.

We eventually reached our destination safely, for which I was absolutely thankful, to find Walter and von Karajan anxiously awaiting us. After a short seating rehearsal, we all went back to our hotels for a rest and a meal, which was much needed, as we had our first concert that night. We knew that it was going to be an ordeal to face not only the Vienna Philharmonic Orchestra, who would all be present, but also the critical Viennese public, who were jealous of their own great orchestra's reputation.

There was to be no rest for me that afternoon, however, as I was faced with a number of serious problems. First of all, I had to get hold of our agent, who so far had paid us no attention at all. I needed to know whether he had arranged for the train from Munich to Hamburg to have sleeping cars, which I was told was his responsibility. I was sure that there would be a serious situation if the orchestra had to repeat the ordeal that they had undergone on the journey from Milan to Vienna. I eventually found Dr

Gamsjaeger, after some difficulty, and he assured me that the arrangement was all in order.

A much greater problem was that of getting the grey cards from him for every member of the party. Without these cards, the Russians wouldn't allow us to leave their zone. He told me that they hadn't arrived yet, but called me later in the evening to tell me that the cards had been received. However, I was horrified – but not particularly surprised – to hear that seven cards were missing, including mine, the tuba player's, the trombonists' and the second harpist's, and that two others were on the list of missing persons.

I couldn't get any help from anyone. No Gamsjaeger, no Mattone, no Walter and no von Karajan – they had all vanished. At about six o'clock in the evening, I telephoned the British ambassador, Sir Harold Caccia, to be told by his wife that he was in the bath prior to getting dressed for the concert. "Get him out at once!", I cried in despair. She was nice to me when I explained my desperate situation, and suggested that I found her husband during the interval of the concert, when we could discuss how arrangements could be made to help me. Sir Harold was very kind, and it was decided that he would contact the American ambassador, whom he felt sure would agree to fly the seven of us who were without cards to Linz, the next concert destination. At the same time, the first secretary of the legation was working on the Russians to see if he could extract the cards in time for the missing cardholders to depart with the orchestra in the coaches. Alas, things didn't work out that easily.

Meanwhile, I had to forget about these relatively minor worries and concentrate on the concert that evening, which proved to be a great artistic success. The orchestra and von Karajan were magnificent, in spite of their tiredness and the underlying animosity which had been evident at the Musikverein. I think that they were angered by this attitude, and they rose to the occasion by playing like gods. I was very proud of them.

Here, I have to mention the attitude of the Musikverein, the Vienna Philharmonic Orchestra, and even the agent, Dr Gamsjaeger. They certainly didn't give us the warm welcome that the orchestra and management at La Scala gave us on our arrival there. There were reasons for this, however, and Walter and von Karajan should have anticipated their attitude. First of all, von Karajan had been one of their principal conductors during the war years, and here he was with a British orchestra and Walter Legge, the representative of a British record company, attempting to establish himself with the controlling powers. Under these conditions, it was asking a lot to expect a warm welcome from an organisation with the history and tradition of the Musikverein. In one of my letters to London, I wrote, "We have had a fabulous artistic success here, but we have been treated really badly by the Vienna Musikverein, who have shown a complete lack of co-operation, even to the point of our agent refusing to speak to us. Elisabeth Schwarzkopf walks about in tears and swearing vengeance on all Viennese musicians and critics."

In my capacity as nanny to the orchestra, which is what I felt myself to be during the Vienna episode, I warned them not to leave anything of value unattended anywhere or at any time, especially their instruments. Unfortunately, Peter Mountain, a young first violinist, left his violin on the table in the orchestra room for a few minutes, and when he returned, the instrument – a Stradivarius, no less – was gone. The first that I heard of it was a tremendous outburst of hysterical excitement as Peter came rushing to me with the awful news. We made an instant search but could find it nowhere. The thief must have had his eye on it and whipped it away at the first available opportunity. It was a dreadful, depressing occurrence, and added to my difficulties, as I had to find another fiddle for Peter to use at the concert that night. It was no easy task to find an instrument even remotely approaching the quality of his Strad. I telephoned the police immediately after the theft, and the head of the Vienna police himself came to meet Peter and me at our hotel. He was most kind and helpful, but said that it was stupid to leave anything valuable unattended in Vienna because it was such a short distance from so many borders, and valuables could be smuggled out of the country practically within minutes. As far as I know, the instrument was never found, and for the rest of the tour we had to find Peter a different instrument for every performance.

This occurred in the afternoon of our first concert in Vienna. My thoughts were now concentrated on making the performance as fine as possible and rounding up the orchestra to ensure that they all arrived at the Musikverein in good order. This they did, bless them, and they gave a truly great performance. It was a grand event indeed, and was attended by many in the diplomatic corps, including the Russian, French and US ambassadors. There must have been a reception after the concert, but I was too agitated and exhausted to attend. I'd managed to speak with Sir

Harold Caccia, the British ambassador, during the interval of the concert, and before going to sleep that night I prayed that he would be able to obtain those all-important grey cards from the Russians so that the seven of us could get out of the Russian zone along with the rest of the orchestra.

When I returned to my room the following morning, after I'd taken a short walk in an attempt to calm my troubled nerves, the phone was ringing. It was the nice young attaché from the embassy who had been entrusted to look after me calling to give me some bad news. So far the Russians wouldn't budge, as it appeared that the seven missing names hadn't applied for grey cards from the Russian embassy in London, and therefore they weren't on the Russian list in Vienna. I despaired at the thought of being left behind in Vienna, but worst of all was the fact that the musicians with me were vital to the performance in Linz. The man from the embassy said that I wasn't to worry, though, for he would stick to the Russian office dealing with the matter like glue, if necessary spending all day and night there until he got the cards. I fear that the poor young man must have been used to these dramas, as the Russians seemed intent on making life as difficult as possible for everyone. I consoled myself by thinking that, if I had to let the coaches go to Linz without us on the following morning, the seven of us cardless ones would be flown out by the Americans.

The second concert was also applauded enthusiastically by the audience. The house was completely sold out for two nights running. In spite of this, however, we received indifferent reviews from the critics. Walter took this unfair treatment philosophically, as did von Karajan, although Elisabeth was furious. I remember that she left us after the Vienna concerts to carry out her own engagements.

My troubles weren't over. In the middle of the night, I awoke to hear the wind howling and sheets of rain beating against the window. With such weather in the mountains there could be no rescue by the US Air Force the following morning.

At a very early hour, my young attaché phoned to say that he hadn't yet got my cards, and that I should make sure that the main part of the orchestra got on the coaches bound for Linz and that I should then keep my little troupe with me at our hotel and await events. He told me to be of good cheer, as he felt sure that the Russians were just playing with him, and that the cards would turn up in time for us to catch the one o'clock train, the last which could get us to Linz in time for the concert that night.

We sat there with our luggage and instruments waiting for a problematical rescue. Well, our diplomat *did* succeed and he *did* keep his word. We were sitting there on our luggage when suddenly we heard police sirens approaching the hotel. We grabbed our bags and rushed outside to find our friend from the embassy with a coach and a police escort ready to rush us to the station in time to catch the one o'clock train. What joy, relief and gratitude we felt towards him and our embassy! What would we have done without their help? We arrived in Linz at about six o'clock to find that the rest of the orchestra were already there and getting dressed for the concert, which was due to start at eight o'clock. I was greeted sourly by von Karajan, who was alone now that Walter and Clem had gone on to Munich to prepare for the next concert. Because Clem was absent, I had to be sure that everyone was present, as some, like Dennis Brain, had travelled in their own cars. I also had to perform one or two other tasks, such as checking that the music stands were correctly placed on the platform and that the music was in the right order. As expected, Clem had organised everything most efficiently before his departure.

I was quite nervous, as this was the first time that I'd been left alone to manage a concert. The musicians were very helpful, though, and walked onto the stage to take their positions looking relaxed and immaculate, as though they'd driven to Linz from Vienna in Rolls Royces rather than in coaches. So far so good. The maestro then approached the stage entrance, with his overcoat draped over his shoulders, and I prepared for the little ceremony of accepting his coat and handing him his baton, which was usually carried out by Clem. I don't know if it was due to the shock of seeing me instead of Clem, but to my surprise he dropped the coat on the ground and snatched the baton from my hand without a word of acknowledgement. I said nothing, but I didn't pick up his coat! He walked onto the platform to tumultuous applause, however, and conducted marvellously.

Perhaps this incident made too strong an impression on me. I wasn't used to such behaviour and I have never encountered it since. I've never been able to understand why there was this antipathy towards me. There was no history of ill feeling between von Karajan and myself, as I had met him for the first time only when Walter introduced us during the recording session in the Kingsway Hall. After this little episode, however, I retired to the front of the house and gloried in the beautiful performance. On thinking it over, I decided that von Karajan, too, was suffering from this long and arduous tour, and that the whole incident should be forgotten.

We set off for Munich early the next morning. As a treat, Walter had laid on a coach for anyone who would like an excursion through the Salzkammergut. As I had many happy memories of holidays in that beautiful part of Europe, I decided to accept his offer, and about a dozen others joined our party, including Marie Goosens and Marie Wilson, both of whom were a great help to me throughout the tour. The main part of the orchestra would meanwhile go by train to Munich, breaking up the journey in Salzburg so that they could visit Mozart's birthplace if they wished, and would then join us on the platform of Salzburg Station to continue the train journey to Munich. I bade farewell to the train party, and implored them not to let me down in Salzburg and to turn up in time for the train to Munich.

The coach journey was a bit disappointing, as it poured with rain the whole day, as it often does in that part of the world. As a result, we all felt rather dispirited, and most of my fellow travellers fell into a gentle doze. I suddenly remembered that I'd been given a bottle of whiskey before leaving London in case of emergencies. I decided to call this an emergency and, as I was sitting alone at the back of the coach and the others seemed to be either asleep or looking out of the windows, I thought that I'd take a quick beneficial nip while no one was looking. As luck would have it, one of them turned around and caught me in the act. There followed loud applause and requests to join the party. From then on, everything went very happily, and we arrived in Salzburg feeling remarkably benign. It's amazing how a drink can soften the atmosphere. My little party was delighted, and I'm sure that the story was circulated later in the day.

When we arrived in Salzburg, we really didn't have any time for sightseeing, and I was growing nervous wondering if I was going to be able to gather the rest of the orchestra together at the station in time to board the Munich train. My troupe and I waited and waited. Time was getting critically short, and there was no sign of the musicians or their instruments. I could almost swear that I heard the train puffing its way towards us. Finally, I decided that I and my party would go on to Munich without them and leave them to make their way as best they could, although I knew how unpopular I would be if I arrived without the orchestra. They eventually turned up, of course, in the nick of time, strolling onto the platform nonchalantly just as the train arrived. A wild scramble ensued, and then off we went to Munich. I decided to behave in an equally casual fashion so that they wouldn't have the satisfaction of knowing how worried I'd been!

It was cold and pouring with rain when we reached Munich, where we were deposited at our hotel and told by the agent, Herr Wedder, that we were expected at the concert hall, the Deutsches Museum, the following morning at ten o'clock, and that three coaches would come to the hotel to pick us up at 9.30am, two coaches for the musicians and one for Clem and the baggage, including the instruments. We were also informed that we would have to take our concert clothes with us, as we would be changing into them at the hall before the concert and then back into travelling clothes afterwards, because we were going directly from the concert to the station to board the special train for the long journey to Hamburg.

On the following morning, we were all waiting outside the hotel with instruments and luggage piled on the pavement when the coaches arrived. Half of the orchestra got onto the first coach with me while the second coach took the other half and Clem got into the third with the instruments and luggage. Off we went to the hall, the musicians waving to each other and in splendid form. I should have been suspicious. When my coach arrived at the hall, closely followed by Clem, who began to unload the instruments, I walked into the hall to find Walter and von Karajan waiting for us. They greeted us and everything seemed very pleasant – unbelievably pleasant. I remember that I'd tied a veil around my head, covering my eyes, to stop the wind from blowing my hair in my face. Walter was amused by this, and called me Mata Hari.

We waited and waited for the arrival of the second coach. There was no sign of it. Von Karajan was getting more and more angry, as he couldn't start the rehearsal with only half an orchestra. He turned on me and shouted, "What have you done? Where's the rest of the orchestra? Why didn't you stay with them?"

"Only half of us could go into each coach," I told him. "I went with one half and the other half was told to go straight to the concert hall." I told him that I could do no more than that, as I could only ride in one coach at a time. Nothing would appease his wrath, though, and in this instance I was entirely in agreement with him.

Finally, the rest of the orchestra turned up, looking very shamefaced but laughing, although they weren't laughing by the time von Karajan had finished with them. It appeared that they had decided to take the opportunity to go on a *rundfarht* (sightseeing tour) of Munich. Oh dear. What a start to the day!

We disappeared after the rehearsal, and were told to do whatever we wished until it was time to prepare for the concert, where we played to a wildly enthusiastic audience. In spite of the heavy rain, there appeared to be thousands of people outside the hall, milling around the orchestra both before and after the concert, when we had to force our way through the crowds to board the three coaches which were waiting to take us straight to the station. When I finally reached the station, it was after eleven o'clock and the train was due to leave at midnight.

I found the train waiting for us on the platform, its wagon-lits already lit up. As far as I could see, there were no problems. The orchestra had been told to be there at 11.45pm, so while I was waiting for them I thought that, as I'd had nothing to eat for hours, I would go to the little café in the station for some coffee and a bite. There was nothing for the musicians to do but walk onto the train, and so I sat there quietly, enjoying my little rest until it was time to walk along the platform and find a berth for myself.

To my horror, as I approached the train I heard such a noise and commotion that it sounded as if the whole train was about to shake itself to pieces and explode. I climbed on board to find a battle raging. People were shouting, "Where's my wagon-lit?" "There's nowhere for me to sleep!" "There aren't enough berths on the train!" They were behaving very badly. Apparently, a number of them had arrived early, gone into their compartments and locked their doors, hoping that they could remain alone. I understood that they were all very tired, but this was stupid behaviour, as they had been told that there was one berth for every member of the orchestra and no more. I argued with them. I walked up and down the train and implored any occupant who was alone in a compartment to open up and admit someone without a berth, with no success. The doors remained resolutely shut.

In the midst of this bedlam, von Karajan walked onto the train. This could only be described as a nightmare. Luckily, the conductor, who was looking very elegant, was in a benign mood after the tremendous success of the concert, and he came to my rescue by shouting in a stentorian voice, "Come out of the compartments and show yourselves. There is a berth for everyone, if you will only behave like adults." This calmed them down, and order was restored.

Next came the problem of where I was to sleep. "I'm so tired I don't mind who I share a compartment with," I said. Many offers were laughingly made, and the fraught atmosphere dissipated as quickly as it had come. Finally, one of the women emerged, looking rather shamefaced, and said that there was a free berth in her compartment. By this time, the train had pulled out the station and we were on our way. Von Karajan said goodnight, and asked me to come and see him at eight o'clock the next morning.

At the appointed time, I duly went to see von Karajan, who had two compartments joined together. He had his papers out on the table and he was sitting curled up in a corner in black satin pyjamas, looking like a large black cat. He asked me to sit down. When I sat down he looked up from his papers, smiled, and said, "Well, won't you come a little nearer? I'm not going to bite you."

I wasn't at all amused by his patronising manner, and replied, "Thank you, but I'm very comfortable here. Would you mind giving me your orders?" I absolutely refused to soften in any way. He explained his wishes, I thanked him very much and took my departure. I refused utterly to succumb to his unexpected display of charm. We simply didn't understand one another. Our relationship couldn't be called a success.

We arrived in Hamburg quite early on the morning of 27 May and we were free until that afternoon, when we had to prepare for the concert that evening at the Musikhalle. Most of the orchestra went off to explore the city, and I had a good walk on my own. They promised to be back at the hotel on time, and they kept their word.

One rather amusing thing happened quite late that afternoon. I came down from my room in the hotel where we were all staying to hear dance music being played. I peeped round a door to see a *thé dansant* (tea dance) in progress in this wreck of a hotel. There were solemn German men sitting at little tables drinking tea and then getting to their feet to cross to a table, where unattended ladies were also drinking tea, and the men would then bow stiffly and ask them to dance. It was somehow a very funny sight. At that moment, the viola player Joe Loban, who was a very jolly fellow, saw me and asked, "What are you looking at?"

"A tea dance in progress," I answered.

"Come on," he said. "Let's have a go."

While we were involved in this caper, some other members of the orchestra, who had also been attracted by the music, looked in and saw us. Of course, this caused considerable hilarity, and the gossip went around the orchestra. For the rest of the tour, Joe was known as "gigolo Joe". This little episode pleased everyone, and morale was considerably lifted.

After the concert, there was a shock awaiting us. We learned that we weren't going to be able to travel to Berlin by train, as had been planned, as the Russians had ordered a blockade of Berlin. This was a serious blow, as Berlin was the culmination of the tour, and the concert there was the real purpose behind our endeavours on behalf of von Karajan. Because he had remained in Germany throughout the war, and had continued to work there as a conductor, he'd had to re-establish himself with the Allied powers – particularly in Berlin – at the head of a British orchestra. This was also vitally important for EMI, who at Walter's instigation had backed the whole tour very heavily indeed.

There was no way of getting into Berlin except by plane. We had to charter three aircraft and spend one more night in Hamburg, and I dread to think what that must have cost. On the following morning, three aircraft were readied for departure, one for Clem and the large instruments and two more to carry the orchestra. A number of the musicians were unhappy about flying, and they also didn't like being separated from their double basses, harps and timpani, all of which were with Clem. In the end, though, the flight was uneventful. The greatest excitement was in landing at Tempelhof Airport, right in the heart of the city. That was a frightening experience, but a very impressive one at that, and one which I have never forgotten.

On leaving Tempelhof, we went straight to our hotel, the Steinplatz, which we had to enter by walking down a tunnel of what appeared to be rubble supported by heavy wooden beams. We wondered where we would find ourselves this time! We needn't have worried, though, for once inside we found warmth, light and a gracious welcome. This hotel was in the tradition for which Germany was famous before the war. The food was very good, the table furnishings of the highest quality and the beds comfortable, all of which put us in the best possible humour to face the rehearsal and the last and most important concert of the tour.

The Titania Palace was the only hall of any size left standing in Berlin. It had originally been a sports stadium, I believe, and it was huge. The acoustics weren't that good, but we had to make the best of it. We knew that the Berliners were very interested in hearing the British orchestra, especially under the direction of the great Herbert von Karajan. It was certainly a challenge that we were willing to meet, and the orchestra was on its toes to show what it could do.

That morning, a complete run-through of the programme was staged, ending with Richard Strauss's fabulously exciting tone poem *Don Juan*, and von Karajan conducted without a break. During the rehearsal, Walter and I sat in the empty auditorium, listening spellbound whilst von Karajan whipped the orchestra into a state of bewildering inspiration. It was almost as though he was demanding that they throw away any memory of the hardships and discomforts that they had had to endure on the tour and to concentrate with him in giving every inch of themselves to making great music.

At the end of the rehearsal, Walter turned to me and said, "Well, Isabella. It was worth it all, wasn't it?"

I wondered how von Karajan and the orchestra could possibly reach such heights again that evening, whether they could bring themselves to boiling point once again. I needn't have worried, though, for the superb performance – which brought the packed house to a state of almost frightening enthusiasm – must have delighted both von Karajan and the orchestra. There was no doubt that the concert was an outstanding success for von Karajan, Philharmonia and Walter Legge. It fully justified the enormous investment of both money and energy that had been required to carry this great artistic venture to a successful conclusion.

When we reached the Hook of Holland that evening, we were thankful to board the ship which was to take us across the North Sea to England and our families. I was longing to see my two sons again, and when I arrived at my parents' flat on the following morning I was greeted by a rapturous welcome from the boys and Ian, our little terrier. My father and mother were also deeply relieved to have me back safely. Everything had been fine in my absence, and I was grateful to them for having allowed me the freedom to accept the offer from Walter and to go on the great Philharmonia adventure. My family and friends were longing to hear my story, but I begged them to give me twelve hours, at least, in which to sleep and recover. I certainly dined out for a long time on the story of my odyssey!

12 *The Birth Of Delysé*

During the weeks that followed, I had to decide if I wanted to join Philharmonia on a permanent basis, sharing the job of orchestral manager with Jane Withers, who had fortunately recovered from her illness. On 24 July, Walter wrote me a long letter in which he asked me to consider whether or not the demanding work with the orchestra would interfere too much with the time and care which he felt that I should wish to devote to my boys. Much as I was attracted to the idea of working with this great orchestra, the content of his letter only added weight to the decision to which I was now becoming more and more inclined, that I would be much happier setting up my own record label and company and working as a freelance producer.

Walter would have been very surprised had he known that I'd already been invited by Mr Mittel, one of the senior directors of EMI, to join the company as a classical producer, and that I had declined the offer. I must confess that I was sorely tempted by the prospect of working in the studios where Uncle Fred had produced so many of his great recordings, and where I had spent many magical hours in my youth, but I decided to follow my instincts to work as an independent, which would enable me to base myself at home and have the freedom to organise my timetable so that the boys wouldn't be neglected and our happy routine of weekends in the country wouldn't be upset. I realised that this decision would undoubtedly involve financial risk, but as I had set aside a trust fund to pay for the boys' education I decided to take the plunge and register the company, which I did on 28 July 1954 in the name of Isabella Wallich, trading as the Elyse Recording Company at 58 Wellington Road, London NW8. My father and I chose this name for no other reason than because we thought that it sounded international and elegant.

I reassured myself by remembering that I'd discussed things with Uncle Fred shortly before his death, and that somewhat to my amazement he had been both sympathetic and encouraging. He understood me very well, and had realised that it was necessary for me to work in music in one way or another. After all, he had fostered this side of my development from my early childhood. During the last few months of his life, he gave me a lot of advice, which I have never forgotten, even if, alas, I've not always followed it. He told me that I should try to find any unusual musical material that had been neglected by the major companies, so that I wouldn't appear to be setting up as a rival to them and so that I could even benefit from taking advantage of their distribution organisations, as I would be filling in gaps in their own catalogues. It was for this reason that I chose to start my recording catalogue with Welsh music, which was attractive, unknown and inexpensive to record. While I stuck to this formula, I was very successful indeed; it was only when I grew more ambitious, and deviated from the plan to record a more conventional repertoire, that my financial troubles began. Later, during my career as a producer involved in monumental productions, such as Mahler's eighth symphony, I would think, What would uncle say to me now? I dared not answer!

Through Walter Legge, I had the privilege of becoming involved in another great musical event. While we had been on tour, he had told me in strictest confidence that he hoped to bring about a recording of *Tristan Und Isolde* with Philharmonia, with the great Norwegian soprano Kirsten Flagstad in the role of Isolde and Wilhelm Furtwängler as conductor. This was a truly monumental project, and he asked me if I would be willing to help by looking after Furtwängler during the sessions. Of course, I agreed.

There were, however, grave difficulties to be overcome. Von Karajan was under the impression that he would be conducting the Bayreuth performance of the opera for EMI, which was no doubt a project that he had often discussed with Walter. In the meantime, EMI as a company had committed itself to record the opera with Furtwängler. Walter had apparently ignored this decision, and continued to back von Karajan's claim, thus bitterly antagonising Furtwängler. The company's decision prevailed, and Walter was forced to accept it, having by now aroused the anger of both conductors. Furtwängler was incensed by Walter's backing of von Karajan, and declared that, if Walter ended up producing the recording, he would refuse to conduct. Kirsten Flagstad supported Walter, however, and declared that, unless he produced, she wouldn't agree to participate in the recording. It was a stalemate.

The temptation to record *Tristan* was too great, however, and

Furtwängler finally agreed, as did Kirsten, which is where I came into the picture. Walter asked me to act as a sort of buffer between him and Furtwängler, to look after the great man and to make him as comfortable and as happy as possible. The fact that I was Fred Gaisberg's niece would help in this, as Furtwängler and Uncle Fred had got along well together before the war. I don't know what was actually said to Furtwängler, but he agreed to conduct the recording with Walter as producer.

The sessions at the Kingsway Hall proved to be a veritable feast of music-making. Not only did the two great artists give inspired performances, almost as though they were making up for their experiences during the war years, but Furtwängler wrung superb playing from the orchestra. During the sessions, Walter and Kirsten would arrive in a car to pick me up from our flat in Wellington Road. (At the time, Kirsten was staying with Walter and Elizabeth in their house, just around the corner from our flat.) Walter would be tense and anxious about the day's work which lay before him, while Kirsten would sit calmly and unmoved, as though she was going to attend a mothers' meeting rather than about to perform some of the most passionate love music ever written. As it turned out, the sessions went smoothly and successfully. As well as Kirsten, Walter had also engaged Suthaus as Tristan, Blanche Thebom as Brangäne and Dietrich Fischer-Dieskau as Kurwenal.

I had long admired Furtwängler, the greatest of all Wagner conductors of the period, and to hear him working again in such intimate conditions was a unique privilege. He and his young wife, Elizabeth, behaved charmingly to me, and I like to think that my presence helped to keep the atmosphere relaxed. There was only one fairly anxious moment, when Furtwängler emerged from the control room and stormed out of the hall into the street, ripping his raincoat, which had caught on the door handle, and disappeared. The little scene was watched with amazement and some amusement by the orchestra, and signalled the end of the session for the day. Our great conductor was later found striding around the outer circle of Regent's Park, presumably walking off the tension caused by the difficult and highly charged emotions that the great work engendered. Other than this happily insignificant incident, the sessions passed off successfully and in a relaxed atmosphere, for which Walter and I were truly thankful. I considered it to be music-making at its greatest, and I felt privileged to have been present.

Shortly after I had registered my record company, it was discovered that there was a Swiss record company with the similar name of Elite, so I was obliged to modify the name of Elyse by adding a D to the beginning and an accent at the end. This was satisfactory to all parties, and I was then free to begin trading as Delysé. I set up my office in the sitting room of the flat and engaged the services of a pleasant and capable lady called Mrs Talbot.

It was now time to make up my mind about what my first recording would be, and on what principle I would build my catalogue. The material had to be unusual and inexpensive to record. I cast my mind back to the long and uncomfortable journey through the night between Milan and Vienna during the Philharmonia tour, when I travelled in the company of David Ffrangçon-Thomas and Osian Ellis, and how they whiled away the weary hours by painting a vivid picture of the magic of Welsh poetry and music. I had never been to Wales and knew nothing of Welsh culture, but I remembered how impressed I had been by what they told me. A recital that they had staged in the Wigmore Hall, which I attended some months after our return from the tour, had impressed me immensely. The first part of the programme had consisted of folk music played by David on the cello, accompanied by Osian on the harp, while the second part had been devoted to Osian singing to his own accompaniment. This concert was my introduction to Penillion, that strange, other-worldly poetic and musical idiom known only in Wales, and I remember thinking at the time that its poignant intimacy would make it perfect recording material.

I decided that this beautiful performance should open the Delysé catalogue. It was indeed a good idea, for release number EC 3133, *Welsh Folk Music*, was a success with both the critics and with the public, and brought me to the attention of Sir Edward Lewis, chairman of Decca, who instructed his distribution company, Selecta, to place an order for 250 copies. It was my first order, and I had it framed to hang on the wall of my office, where it remained for many years

As I was cautiously shaping my career as an independent recording producer during the latter part of 1953 and 1954, I had also embarked on a great change in my personal life, which was of the utmost importance to me and to the boys. Aubrey Wallich, who was a distinguished figure in Malaya, having been a member of the legislative council of the federation, had known Dick well. He had returned to England shortly after Dick's death to join the board of his company in London, and by a strange coincidence, his sister, Marjorie Naumann, lived very near us in the country, and it was through her that I saw much of Aubrey, who became a close friend. He showed us a great deal of kindness by organising many imaginative expeditions for the boys, which I could never have attempted to undertake on my own. Not only was Aubrey a man of fine intellect but he was also a keen sportsman. He loved horses, and introduced us to the pleasure of attending some of the great race meetings, such as Goodwood, which wasn't far away from the cottage, and in this way brought a completely new interest into our country lives. He was also a gallant soldier, and had won the Military Cross during the First World War before he had reached his 20th birthday. Much to Pompy's delight, he had also been a pilot in the Malayan Auxiliary Air Force, and had flown the last plane out of Malaya during the Japanese advance in 1942. As he was well known in the aircraft industry, he was able to get tickets for the Farnborough Air Show, which was a great thrill for the boys.

Aubrey was 20 years older than I, and some members of the family feared that the difference in ages was too great, but I valued his companionship and hoped that he would enjoy acquiring a ready-made family after his long years as a bachelor. It was a risk, but I felt that his kindness and strength of character could only be a benefit to us all, and so it was decided. We were married at my parents' home in All Souls, Langham Place, in March 1954. All of my family was there, as well as many of the Corbetts, including dear Katie, who gave me strong support in taking this step. In fact, she and Aubrey became firm friends, which was a blessing to us all.

I had made up my mind about my first recording, and brought it to a successful launch in my programme of releases. I could have placed the technical side of the operation into the hands of either Decca or EMI, but I decided against this because I wanted to be in complete control and entirely responsible for the atmosphere which I wanted to achieve. I didn't want a studio sound, and so I had to find a decent recording venue, which is a difficult task in London, as most halls there are plagued by extraneous noise from excessive traffic and the network of underground railways. However, after a conversation with Coggie Margetson I was fortunate enough to be introduced to an excellent young sound engineer called Raymond Lavy, whom she had employed to transfer from tape to disc some recordings that she had made for her private collection. He not only acted as my engineer but he also recommended that I use the Conway Hall in Red Lion Square for my sessions. He said that it was amazingly quiet, as it was well away from the traffic of Kingsway, and there was no underground nearby. On visiting the hall, I decided that the sound was just what I wanted, and in fact it became the venue of nearly all of my early Delysé recordings.

Many meetings with David and Osian followed, at which we discussed the projected programme. If the recordings proved to be a success, the artists would introduce me to many gifted artists from Wales, which would delight them and please me, for it was the sort of idea that no one else had considered, because it was such specialist material. I also needed their help on the musical side of the project, as well as the expertise of a fluent Welsh speaker. By this time, I knew enough about the passion felt by the Welsh to realise that I had to incorporate an expert linguist on my team.

The answer lay in the memory of a rather adventurous expedition I had undertaken to South Wales on my own, some weeks earlier, on David's suggestion, to hear the first concert of the newly-formed Orchestra of Wales, who were to play at a concert in Maesteg, a mining town between Cardiff and Swansea. David had said that I would be very interested in this, and that I would meet many fascinating people, and so off I went. I drove for what seemed like an eternity, up and up into the hills in the pitch dark trying to find the place, which became more and more elusive. I felt sure that I was lost and that I would never be found again. Suddenly, just as I was beginning to despair, through the driving rain I saw lights and people, and I realised that I'd arrived. I was warmly greeted by the orchestra manager, who led me into a packed hall, where the orchestra was already seated, waiting for the appearance of their conductor, Kenneth Loveland, an excellent musician with whom I would work in later years.

As I watched the proceedings, I saw a very determined plump lady walk briskly across the front of the hall and whisper to David Ffrangçon-Thomas, who was leading the cellos. He pointed to me and she turned and waved. This was my first sighting of Matti Prichard, who was to become invaluable to me both as a Welsh-speaking specialist and as a brilliant newspaper woman, and she would eventually manage all of Delysé's promotion and contacts with the press in a most astonishingly successful way. Of much greater importance, she also became one of my closest friends. Her husband, Caradog, was considered to be the most eminent living poet writing in the Welsh language. I was fortunate, indeed, as far as the creation of the Welsh catalogue was concerned, for in the future it would be in her safe hands.

On a warm summer's day in July 1954, the Delysé operation moved into the Conway Hall, Red Lion Square, some hours before the artists were due to arrive. The crew, who were there to set up the Levers-Rich equipment that I had purchased second hand, consisted of a very nervous and excited producer, myself and an equally agitated Raymond Lavy. We placed the equipment in the control room and set up the EMI microphones in the hall, and after this there was nothing left to do but to await the arrival of the artists and to pray that nothing would go seriously wrong. In fact, a disaster had already been narrowly averted when, during a previous inspection of the hall, we'd heard the unmistakable sound of a printing press from the building next door, about which we hadn't been warned. Luckily, we were able to arrange our sessions to take place when the presses weren't in use, although it gave me something to think about when it came to arranging future sessions.

My two boys were desolated, because they were both at school when the recordings took place – Pompy at Westminster and Roguey at Arnold House – and couldn't be excused, but I remember them arriving at the end of the day, breathless with excitement and anxiety, followed closely by Aubrey, straight from his office in the City. By that time, we knew that we'd made a successful recording. David and Osian gave superb performances, which Raymond and I were able to capture after the initial trial playbacks and a few adjustments to the microphones, so that we could report that we'd recorded the whole programme without any apparent or unforeseen problems. There was some musical editing to be done, which took place in our home in Wellington Road that evening, and I was grateful to Raymond for his part in this operation, which he carried out very skilfully. By the time it was all over and the master tape was ready to go to Decca for processing, we were all very proud of ourselves.

When I look back on the early Delysé recording sessions at the Conway Hall, I'm astounded by my innocent courage and by the results which we achieved, both artistically and technically, considering the primitiveness of our equipment. The excellence of the artists was unquestioned, and the inspiration and enthusiasm felt by all was truly extraordinary. It must have been the combination of all of these factors that produced the unusual and attractive quality of those early records.

The success of this first venture caused great interest in both Wales and amongst the Welsh people living in England, for not only did the recording receive excellent reviews in the local newspapers but the critics in the English press were also enthusiastic, which encouraged me greatly.

Following this triumph, I decided to begin my second venture, which of course had to be Welsh if I were to take advantage of my initial success. I went to Cardiff to hear a young tenor by the name of Brychan Powell, who had been recommended to me by David, and also to meet many of the Welsh-speaking intelligentsia, who were showing considerable interest in my ambition to create a catalogue of Welsh music and musicians. Amongst these was Hywel Davies, one of the most attractive and fascinating men I have ever known. He became a close friend, and in his position as controller of BBC Wales he was not only able to give me some excellent advice on my choice of repertoire and artists but also valuable help in promoting the Delysé label. Another "golden tongue" whom I met in Cardiff was the famous broadcaster Wynford Vaughan Thomas, who assisted me generously in publicising my recordings. It's difficult to describe the magic of these two men's conversation. I had never heard anything like it before, and indeed have heard similar only very rarely since, if ever.

My second recording session followed shortly after this, again in the Conway Hall. This was a far more ambitious venture, as I had decided to accompany Brychan Powell in performing some traditional Welsh songs with a small orchestra. David Ffrangçon-Thomas was engaged to conduct, and he was also responsible for the delightful orchestral arrangements. Once again, Raymond Lavy was engaged as the engineer, and once again he and I met many hours before the sessions to set up the microphones in the hall and the dear old Levers-Rich in the control room.

This occasion was more complicated and dangerous, and it nearly became a disaster. At a very early stage during the first session, probably when we were just about to record the first take after experimenting with the balance, Raymond said to me, "I think that the spindle the tape plate is fixed on is slipping. I can't control the speed." Imagine my horror when I looked into the hall and saw the orchestra sitting ready in position and Brychan standing nervously before his microphone, ready to begin. I was almost paralysed with fear, but for the first (and not the last) time my instant reaction was, Don't say a word. Let them go on rehearsing while you decide what to do. I told Raymond to phone the manufacturer and ask them if they could rush a replacement spindle to us, but they were too far away, and in any case it would taken ages to reach us. Meanwhile, the session had to go on.

"There's only one thing you can do," said Raymond. "You'll have to keep a finger on the top of the spindle and hold it down in the cup loosely enough to allow it to turn but firmly enough to keep it in position." So this is what I did for the whole of that first session. I stood by the machine for nearly three hours, with my finger almost worn to the bone, until a representative of Levers-Rich arrived breathlessly with a replacement spindle. Raymond and I never let on to the artists what had taken place in the control room and how close they had been to expending so much effort for so little result.

In spite of this near disaster, however, we achieved a delightful recording, and I learned my second very valuable lesson: never risk going into a session without being absolutely sure that the equipment is in first-class condition. Mind you, I've seen terrible things go unexpectedly wrong even in the studios of major companies!

By the autumn of 1954, I had two Welsh recordings on my list: *Welsh Folk Music* (EC 3133) and *Songs From Wales* (EC 3134). During the months leading up to Christmas, I concentrated on getting to know the dealers and fixing up a system of distribution throughout the United Kingdom as well as in countries where there were pockets of Welsh exiles. In Canada, I had found a very excellent distributor in St Clair Low, of Toronto. There was also a large Welsh population in Patagonia and in the United States, where distribution was undertaken by EMI, and it was amazing how much interest my first two recordings generated in those territories. Matti Prichard told me that I had to attend the National Eisteddfod, which took place at the end of August every year, alternatively in North and then in South Wales, where she said I would get to know many people important in the cultural life of the country and also hear interesting artists and choirs. I looked forward to this event with immense interest.

In the meantime, with Aubrey's help, I was getting the business side of Delysé into shape. His experience was invaluable, for not only was he happy to advise me but he also enjoyed the selling expeditions, when he would set off bravely in his car with a suitcase full of sample records with which to approach dealers all over the country. His charm earned him considerable orders, and I was very grateful for his help. I think that he quite enjoyed the experience, which was certainly a change from his previous activities in life.

The time was approaching for me to begin my next recording, and once again I decided to use the Conway Hall and engage Raymond Lavy as the engineer. The only thing Welsh about this new project was that it featured Welsh artists, but the programme was European. David Ffrangçon-Thomas had spoken to me about the excellent small orchestra that Leslie Bridgewater had put together during the war to broadcast Viennese music in weekly programmes. These broadcasts were of a fine musical quality, and very popular. David suggested that they would make an attractive recording, and might indeed become a series. I thought that this was a good idea, for with such instrumentalists few musicians were needed to make a fine sound. As it turned out, *Music From Vienna* (EK 2123), played by the Leslie Bridgewater Orchestra and conducted by David Ffrangçon-Thomas, was recorded most successfully, although as far as sales were concerned it was less successful, and convinced me that, for the time being at least, I shouldn't venture into the general catalogue, which was the province of the major recording companies.

On his return from Malaya in 1952, Aubrey had brought with him two Dalmatian dogs, Sally and Susan, her daughter, while Ian made the third member of the family. We were therefore very short of space, both in London and in the country, and so we decided to move from the flat in Wellington Road to a charming Regency house nearby in Clifton Hill, St John's Wood. It was very well suited to our activities, for the large ground floor consisted of two rooms (which became my offices) as well as a large, old kitchen, a bedroom and a bathroom. We lived on the two upper floors, which were entered by the front door. These consisted of a charming drawing room and a large dining room with a lift going down to the kitchen (with which the boys played many pranks), as well as a study for Aubrey which was fitted with large windows that looked out onto the garden. We needed this generous amount of space, as there was much entertaining to be done, both for Delysé and for Aubrey's contacts from Malaya.

We also agreed to sell Old Pound Cottage to Katie, who had long expressed a wish to live there if we ever decided to leave. This was a happy arrangement, for in this way we felt that the dear old place remained in the family, at least for a while longer. We then bought a very ancient house called Ludgates, parts of which dated back to the 14th century. It was situated in Nutbourne, a village near Pulborough. The old part of the house consisted of a large drawing room with open fireplaces at either end, which was in fact too old for modern living. All of our activities took place in the new wing, where there was a charming sun room and a large dining room and kitchen. When we had guests over to stay, they described the bedrooms in the old house as "creepy", and said they would prefer not to repeat the experience! The boys had a playroom in the old wing, which they rarely used, for they also objected to the atmosphere.

The grounds were beautiful, though, and gave Aubrey and the boys plenty of scope in which to indulge in country pursuits. Aubrey tried to get them interested in horses, but he wasn't very successful. He also thought that it would be a good idea to set up some laying batteries for hens so that we could earn something from the land. This didn't prosper, though, as the hens refused to lay in sufficient quantity, and to my horror both Aubrey and the boys caught fleas! I had never been very enthusiastic about this idea, anyway, and felt that the hens were taking their revenge on us for keeping them locked up in such horrible captivity. The only real enthusiast was the terrier, Ian, who spent days and nights chasing the rats that were attracted to the eggs, and actually killed a record number of 30 in one day!

Back at the studio, I followed the Viennese recording by plunging into much deeper musical waters. I think that my upbringing as Uncle Fred's niece, hearing great music performed by great artists during my youth, must have stirred my blood and influenced the choice I made for my next project. I had been impressed with Brychan Powell upon hearing him sing with the Welsh National Opera, and I had also enjoyed working with him on his first recordings of Welsh songs. It seemed to me that his voice was of a high enough quality to tackle a serious operatic programme, which might gain the notice of the general music public as well as the critics. Perhaps memories of my uncle's discovery of Caruso stirred the impresario in me. At any rate I made up my mind to invest in Brychan Powell's future, and I asked David to act as fixer and to hire the necessary orchestral musicians. I had heard that Vilem Tausky had fled to England during the war and, knowing that he was a fine and experienced opera conductor, I engaged him for the sessions, which were once again to take place at the Conway Hall.

We chose an interesting and highly demanding programme, and it was indeed a heavy burden of responsibility that I placed on Brychan's young shoulders. It included the arias 'Una Furtiva Lagrima', 'Tombe Degli Avi Miei' and 'Tu, Che A Dio Spiegasti, l'Ali' by Donizetti, and the programme was completed with three beautiful arias by Giordano: 'Un Di Par Azzuro Spazzio', 'Comme Un Bel Di Maggio' and 'Amor, Ti Vieta Di Non Amar'.

Brychan sang admirably, and rose to the occasion like a seasoned trooper, while Vilem Tausky was very helpful and generous in his support. Everything went according to plan, and we even completed the sessions in the time required by union rules.

This recording was a bold venture, and to my relief and some amazement the critics gave us consistently serious reviews. They seemed to sense that I was trying to do something worthwhile, and with the memory of Uncle Fred's achievements perhaps still fairly fresh in their minds they decided that I might be worth encouraging. For whatever reason, they showed me considerable kindness.

I met many fine artists during this period, including Helga Mott, a gifted lieder singer of the Elena Gerhardt school. She was of German birth, and the wife of Englishman Tom Mott. They were the most charming and delightful couple, and their hospitality was boundless. They gave many parties in their home in Onslow Square, which contained an enormous studio with a stage at one end. If we were lucky, the guests would be entertained by Helga, who would sing nostalgic Viennese songs in dialect when in the mood. Her parties were attended by many interesting people, such as David Cecil and Rupert Bruce-Lockhart, as well as many famous actors, politicians, and diplomats. The Motts and Aubrey and I became very good friends, and enjoyed many delightful meals together. I made two beautiful recordings with Helga, the first in 1958, once again at the Conway Hall, for which Erik Werba came over to accompany her. The programme included many songs by Richard Strauss, which suited Helga admirably, and also Schubert's 'Der Hirt Aus Dem Felsen', in which the solo clarinettist was Jack Brymer. The sessions proved to be a delight, for not only was it a joy to work with such gifted artists but also by this time I felt completely at home in the Conway Hall.

It might appear that I had abandoned my decision to capture the Welsh record market. This was not so, however, for, while I was to some extent indulging my musical tastes in finding interesting and gifted artists to record in a general classical repertoire, I was steadily learning more and more about Wales and the various aspects of their musical and literary culture. To this end, I was greatly helped by being able to attend many of the National Eisteddfods, where I heard some quite outstandingly gifted performers and, most interesting to me, the beautiful singing of the choirs, which I determined to record.

One of the most important things that I learned was the vast difference in the language and musical culture of North and South Wales. This knowledge mattered enormously when choosing the choirs and the solo artists to interpret works that sprang from the two regions. In fact, I would have been unable to create the Welsh catalogue with sufficient respect for the language (of which I was ignorant) without the help of Matti Prichard's almost fanatical guidance. She truly loved the culture, and wouldn't have allowed me to make any mistakes.

Hywel Davies had spoken to me of a completely authentic choir, The Cor Godre Aran, whose members lived on the shores of the beautiful Lake Bala, in North Wales. He told me that, if I really wanted to capture the atmosphere of that region, I could do no better than to record this group. Their conductor, Tom Jones, was a man of considerable experience and knowledge, and Hywel advised me to go to the Merioneth village of Llanuwchllyn in order to meet him and listen to the choir in its own ambience. Hywel was so enthusiastic in this that he even offered to meet me there so that he could introduce us, and he was as good as his word.

We arrived at the sleepy old village, after I had driven across from London and Hywel from Cardiff, to hear a wonderfully curious and moving performance of this strange Penillion music, of which Tom Jones was a master. The choir consisted of local farmers, a schoolmaster and perhaps a doctor, and they performed as only those with Welsh blood in their veins can. It was a marvellous experience, and I was immensely interested. I decided on the spot that I would make a recording of them. Tom Jones offered to bring the choir to London, but I refused, and told him that we should make the recording there, in its own atmosphere, for I knew that this would make all the difference to the quality of the sound. There was a delightful little hotel in the town, and the food there was excellent. I enjoyed some delicious Welsh lamb, which I felt sure that the technical team would appreciate.

Music From The Welsh Mountains (EC 3137) became my next recording, with which I was extremely pleased. It received splendid reviews, mainly from the Welsh critics, and it placed me highly in the estimations of Welsh-speaking populations all over the world. I knew that Uncle Fred would have been pleased!

The next addition to the Welsh catalogue was another recording of a male voice choir. It couldn't have been more different to The Cor Godre Aran, even though The Rhos Choir – a choir composed entirely of miners – also came from North Wales. I'd heard them sing at the National Eisteddfod, and I'd been very impressed by the quality of their voices. Shortly after this, I drove up to Rhosllannerchrugog to hear them again, and found them at rehearsal in the hall of the chapel. Rhos was a straggling village of what appeared to be somewhat dreary little houses, but after the hospitality I received from one of the members of the choir, when his wife invited me to spend the night in their home, I realised that, although the outside of the houses appeared rather sad, inside it was all warmth and comfort. I couldn't have received a kinder welcome, nor enjoyed more generous hospitality anywhere in the world.

The men appeared to be rather aloof and on their guard, but as soon as they had been singing for a while, and I demonstrated my pleasure in the performance, the atmosphere changed and they became enthusiastic about the project. I discussed the programme with their conductor, Edward Jones, and the excellent organist, John Tudor Davies, and we decided that we would open the recording with the Welsh national anthem, 'Hen Wlad Fy Nhadau', and that we would include many popular hymns, all sung in Welsh.

I was deeply impressed with the beauty of the men's voices, and particularly with the passion that they put into the words. They sounded quite different to The Cor Godre Aran, who had felt equally strongly about the language but who had seemed more concerned with its intellectual importance. It was decided that The Rhos Choir would come to London for the sessions, which I would arrange to take place in the church in Hamilton Terrace, St John's Wood, which was near my home and which I knew had a good organ. This event nearly ended in disaster, and would have been cancelled had it not been for the bravery of the choir, who were determined not to let me down. The sessions were scheduled to take place on a Saturday afternoon, when the men were free from their work in the mines, but we had forgotten that this was also the date of the rugby final between England and Wales at Twickenham!

On the appointed day, the Delysé team were all set up and awaiting the arrival of the coach. We were to start the sessions at 2.30pm, and we'd hoped that they would arrive early so that they could settle down and get used to the surroundings before we began. When it got to 2.15pm, Matti

Prichard said, "They have to pass the very doors of Twickenham. They'll never be able to resist going in to watch the match – no Welshman could!"

What had actually happened was even more dramatic, however, for the coach had run out of petrol just a few minutes from the entrance to the famous stadium, and they'd sat there waiting while more petrol was brought from the nearest garage in the midst of the crowds and excitement. Luckily for me, they withstood temptation and proceeded gallantly on with their journey. They were full of apologies at being late, but I was so relieved to see them that I could only give them a warm greeting. When I saw that a number of them had their arms in slings, and that one was even on crutches, I could hardly express my gratitude that they had undertaken the journey. It turned out that there had been an accident in the mine on the previous day, and it was a miracle that they had escaped injuries that would have made the journey to London quite impossible.

All of this excitement gave the recording a special atmosphere. The men sang superbly, and the recording enjoyed a considerable success. The critics were enthusiastic, too, and the record sold well all over the world. In fact, it was such a success that I invited the choir to come back to London a year later, when I recorded a second programme. The title of the first was *Music From The Welsh Mines* (DS 6042), and the second was entitled *Songs Of Peace And Goodwill* (DS 6047).

My recordings were now being issued in stereo, and for some time the technical work had been in the hands of Allen Stagg and his team at IBC Studios, which I thought of as a school, with Allen as the devoted and capable headmaster. Indeed, I wasn't far wrong, for in later years, whenever I was in search of a good sound engineer, either at the great studios of EMI and Decca or in the smaller and more specialised institutions, I was bound to find one of Allen's protégés there in a responsible position.

My activities in creating a Welsh catalogue were becoming well known to the "exiles" from Wales living in London, who were interested and very supportive, and so I decided to give their own choir, The London Welsh Youth Choir, the chance to show what they could do. I remembered something that Uncle Fred had said to me, on the top deck of a London bus, when I was still a little girl: "If you place a fine tenor – preferably a famous one, of course – in front of a microphone backed only by a choir and and organ, and they sing popular religious songs, you can't fail to make a recording which would not only give immense pleasure to a large section of the public but would also prove to be financially successful." To this end, I followed my uncle's advice and my own gut instinct, and invited Brychan Powell – in whose beautiful Welsh voice I already had confidence – to sing with The London Welsh Youth Choir in a programme of popular religious music, accompanied by Cyril Anthony at the organ and conducted by Kenneth Thomas. We selected the beautiful and well-loved church of St Peters in Eaton Square as the recording venue, and after Allen Stagg and I had assured ourselves of its immunity from extraneous noise and the excellence of its acoustics I decided to go ahead and prepare for the sessions.

Before the sessions actually took place, however, there were a number of rehearsals with Brychan and the choir in the hall of the London Welsh Association in Grey's Inn Road, so we were well prepared for the great moment when the equipment was transferred from IBC Studios to the church and the young artists arrived to give their best. As it turned out, everything went smoothly under Kenneth's expert direction. Brychan was in good voice, and obviously enjoyed working with his young compatriots. If Uncle Fred's advice didn't bring quite the financial success for which I'd hoped, DS 6041 did well enough. It received some very good reviews, and filled an honourable place in the Delysé catalogue.

On looking back, I can't imagine how I survived all of this work. I couldn't have done so without Aubrey's help, and indeed at the end of 1957 I had to undergo a serious operation, from which it took me some time to recover. Nevertheless, in the two years that followed, I not only recorded both the band and the choir of the Welsh Guards but I also decided to create a label to record light music, which I named Envoy. By this time, however, it was necessary for me to engage more staff, and in 1959 we moved to offices in a fine building owned by the Methodist mission in Marylebone Road, where I was lucky enough to draw an experienced team into the Delysé/Envoy organisation.

In 1958, Pompy had reached his 18th year, and it was time for him to go to Oxford. I remember so well the day that we all accompanied him to Christ Church and settled him into his rooms in Tom Quad, which he shared with a boy from Eton. Pompy had done wonderfully well during his last year at Westminster, and much to the amazement of the teaching staff (but not mine, for I knew how brilliant he was, in his quiet way) he had won a scholarship to Christ Church. I shall never forget how proud I was when the headmaster of Westminster School telephoned to give me the news, and the tremendous excitement that followed when the family heard of his success. Roguey was now 13 and head boy of his prep school, Arnold House, and had just gained his entrance to Westminster. I was proud of them both, and I couldn't help but think how dreadful it was that Dick wasn't with us to share in their success.

My staff now included of a young man called Tony Turney, who was a help to Aubrey, since he was quite experienced on the sales side of the record industry, and I was also fortunate enough to persuade Mabel Tobin, Walter Legge's sister, to act as my personal assistant. She was a knowledgeable musician, and she had also been brought up in the ways of the recording world. I was also fortunate enough to acquire the services of an accountant called Mr Kaye, who had worked for the retailers Marks & Spencer and was bored with his early retirement. He threw himself enthusiastically into the hurly burly of Delysé. Chris Lennox, who had been in charge of the packing and despatch department of Thompson, Diamond and Butcher, the largest independent distributor in the industry, joined Delysé in the same capacity. He was a tower of strength, with a wonderful Cockney wit and funny little superstitions, which I imagine he must have learned from his service at sea during the war. He became deeply distressed if he ever heard me whistling, and would rush from his packing room and implore me to stop at once, as apparently this manifestation of cheer brought bad luck in the navy. I was indeed fortunate to have been surrounded and helped by such a devoted team.

In September 1960, tragedy struck again in my life when Aubrey died of cancer after suffering for many months from a dreadful illness, which he fought valiantly to overcome. I could hardly believe that such an apparently strong and healthy man could succumb so quickly to the terrible disease. It was an horrific blow to the boys and to me, and for a while I was in a state of shock. Luckily, the pressure of my work was a great help to me, and by now I was so deeply involved in every aspect of the company that there was no alternative but to carry on.

During the last two years of Aubrey's life, we had sold Ludgates, which had turned out to be far too much to handle along with all of our other commitments, and we had bought a much smaller house called Kings Holden just above Pulborough itself. A short time after Aubrey's death, the boys and I decided that, with all the activities in which I was involved, and with Pompy now at Oxford and therefore at home so seldom, it would be better to sell this house as well. We could thus concentrate our lives in our home at Clifton Hill, London, as Roguey was still at Westminster, and I was deeply concerned with my ever-growing company.

There was a very popular television programme shown once a week on the National Network called *The Land Of Song*, produced by TWW, the Welsh television company based in Cardiff, and was presented in Welsh. The star of the show was Ivor Emmanuel, one of the most popular singers of the day, and he was supported by the voices of about 70 children. Ivor had everything it takes to make a star: he was very handsome, tall and dark, with fine and interesting features, and above all he possessed a magnificent baritone voice. He had already established a successful career in musical comedy, and nothing need have stopped him from performing in opera if he had wanted to do so, although apparently he preferred to concentrate on the lighter side of the performing arts. When I first heard about him and saw this superb television show, I decided that I had to persuade TWW to grant me the recording rights at all costs.

Here at last was the golden opportunity that would develop logically from the seeds that I had sown with the recordings of my Welsh catalogue. Curiously enough, no other company had seen the potential in using the show as a recording venture, maybe because they feared that it was too regional in character. However, it was right up my street, and I was determined to approach TWW.

To this end, I arranged for a meeting with Norman Whitehead, their musical director, and went straight to their offices in Cardiff, where I was greeted by Norman and Frank Brown, a director of the company that was in charge of the administration of the show. The meeting went very smoothly; I didn't need to sell the idea, for they knew Delysé well and admired what I had already achieved in sponsoring Welsh music and artists, and more importantly they were also aware that I knew how to promote the product in this specialised field. Everything was settled at this first meeting, and I returned to London triumphantly with the draft of a contract which would enable me to record enough material for two EPs or one LP, whichever I considered to be the most marketable. I was thrilled, for I knew that this was the financial break that I'd been seeking.

The production and administrative responsibilities concerned with this project were quite an undertaking. First of all, I discussed the engineering aspects with Allen Stagg, for we would need to find a hall in which we could accommodate 70 children and an orchestra of about 30 musicians, and which would allow Ivor plenty of space in which to project his fine voice. We could have used IBC's large studios, but both Allen and I were keen to avoid obtaining something that sounded as if it had been recorded in a studio, particularly as the songs were so largely concerned with the Welsh countryside; we wanted the children's fresh young voices to sound as if they were singing in the open air. So once again I returned to the Conway Hall, which had many excellent features as a recording venue, and I gave the green light to organise the transportation of the children from Cardiff to London. TWW kindly took this particular burden from my shoulders, and in fact they couldn't have been more helpful.

After this, we had to provide good food and accommodation for the children, as we wanted them to be comfortable and happy, and my staff all set about their respective tasks with enormous enthusiasm, for interest in the operation was great. I had already received many requests from the major distributors, such as Decca and EMI, who wanted to obtain the sole distribution rights. This I refused, for I wanted everyone to have the chance to sell as many records as possible. I knew that I had a winner – always providing that no stroke of ill luck befell the actual sessions.

In the event, everything went splendidly well. The children regarded the whole operation as an outing, but the experience that they had gained in the television studios had turned them into little professionals, and they performed with zeal and enthusiasm. The fact that we had chosen to record the most popular numbers in the shows meant that the children knew them inside out, so there were no problems with the performance, and Ivor Emmanuel's genial personality was very helpful, as the children obviously worshipped him. Norman Whitehead was much liked and respected, which helped enormously when it came to getting everything onto tape in the allotted time. This was important, as we still had to abide by union rules, even though the whole event had the atmosphere of a school outing. The children were trained to be entirely professional, however, and so the sessions proceeded like clockwork, and were some of the easiest and certainly most pleasant that I had produced thus far.

As I had hoped and predicted, the success of the recording was phenomenal. The publicity that we received from TWW couldn't fail to promote the two 7" EPs, which like the TV show were both entitled *The*

Land Of Song. In fact, when the release date was reached and we arrived at the office, we couldn't get into the doors because there were so many letters containing orders lying on the floor. It was indeed a wonderful sight, and we could hardly contain our elation and delight. This was my first big hit, and I must say that I was very proud of it. There is no doubt that *The Land Of Song* brought me luck, for the enormous exposure that the two EPs enjoyed – stemming largely from the popularity of the weekly TV show – meant that the sales of the records continued to flourish, and the Delysé bank account began to look very healthy. (It's amazing how this state of affairs gives one confidence!) After this coup, I was approached by many well-known artists, and in fact my recording programme became exceedingly interesting, not only from a financial point of view but also in terms of programme material. I could now afford to record some material in which I had long been interested.

Some little while after Aubrey's death, a likeable young agent whom I had met telephoned and asked if I would be interested in hearing a young guitarist from Australia, whom he considered to be outstandingly talented. His name was John Williams, and he was just 16 years old. Would I care to hear him? "I certainly would," I replied. "Bring him along to Clifton Hill to play for me."

This dark, pleasant-looking youth arrived, and after a few minutes of general conversation he told me that he had played for Segovia. My curiosity was aroused when his agent interposed by saying that the maestro had described John as "a prince amongst guitarists", and I couldn't wait to hear him. I asked if he needed a more suitable seat than my piano chair, and he endeared himself to me immediately by answering that any old seat would do. In fact, he said that he wouldn't mind just perching on the arm of the settee! His modesty and simplicity of manner were intriguing, and I begged him to begin. I didn't need to hear very much to know that I was indeed in the presence of a master. He played with the complete dedication and confidence of many great artists, and when he had finished I said that I would be happy to record him as soon as he wished.

I told Allen that I would be needing the studio for some sessions as soon as possible, and he said, "Which choir is it this time?"

"Nothing could be more different. I propose to place a young man with a guitar in front of the microphone, and I promise you that we'll hear the performance of a great musician."

Allen was very excited at the prospect, for I knew that it wasn't easy to make a successful guitar recording, as one has to compromise between achieving the warmth and immediacy of the sound without also recording the noise of the performer's hand sliding along the fingerboard. It was an interesting challenge for him, and he looked forward to it eagerly.

Once we had achieved the sound that we all wanted, the sessions couldn't have been easier, for John played with the command and assurance of someone with great talent. We recorded a Bach suite that had originally been composed for the cello and had been transcribed for guitar by John Duarte, as well as a group of pieces by Spanish and South American composers, including Villa-Lobos's beautiful first étude. This latter was the hit of the record, and was often chosen to be played on BBC programmes. We presented this 12" record in a simple sleeve in a beautiful shade of green with just the words *John Williams* in bold black print, followed by the words *Guitar Recital*. This wonderful record gave me immense pleasure, and it was one of which I was extremely proud. It was so successful that we decided to record a second volume a short time later. These recordings were issued under licence throughout the world, and were on sale for many years. John William's reputation grew rapidly, and he became such a prominent international artist that there was no difficulty in finding markets for the release and distribution of his records.

I had recently met David Hughes, a singer of popular ballads and light songs who also starred in his own television series of spectacular musical shows. On watching these shows, I had often thought that he had an outstanding tenor voice, and so, when Matti Prichard – who knew him well – told me that he was desperately anxious to break away from his present activities and to study and concentrate on making a career in opera, I agreed to meet him. When I remembered that he was also very good looking, and had been dubbed in his TV promotion as "Mr Heart-throb", I was rather dubious, but nevertheless Matti arranged for him and his accompanist to come to her house and perform for me.

When I met this very serious and charming young man, he told me with great sincerity that he was determined to break into the world of opera, and after I had heard his voice I was impressed. However, I warned him that, in the world of opera, he would probably have to wait a long time before he would even begin to make the sort of money that he was earning at present, and he told me that both he and his wife, Anne, were quite prepared for this. I was captivated by his modesty, which was extraordinary when one considered his already successful career and the adulation of his fans.

I grew very fond of David and Anne and their little family, and I often paid them visits in Elstree, where they had a charming house. It was there that I met Ronnie Young, who was a great friend of David's and a man on whom he relied very much for advice and guidance, both in his personal and his professional affairs. Ronnie held a degree in psychiatry, but didn't wish to practise and at the time was rather at a loose end. When David informed him of Aubrey's unexpected and sudden death, and he found out that I was looking for someone to help on the business and administrative side of the company, he asked me if I would consider taking him on at Delysé as general manager. As at that time he was uncertain of his own plans, we decided to give the idea a try, for if he were successful I would then have more freedom to concentrate on the musical and creative side of my work. It was a fortunate decision, for Ronnie turned out to be very helpful and was a good friend to both me and the boys.

I told David that I would be ready to make a recording in about six months' time, if he was prepared to take singing lessons and to work hard on the programme that I considered to be most suitable for his light tenor voice. He was overjoyed, and stuck to his part of the bargain by working nearly every day with his voice coach and coming to Clifton Hill two or three times a week to rehearse the programme. The songs I asked him to sing were love songs from the 17th, 18th and 19th centuries by Paisiello, Caccini, Purcell and Arne. As I had foreseen, they suited his voice admirably, and the sessions at the Conway Hall took place in the happiest possible way. I had decided to use a small orchestra to accompany David. Robert Docker arranged the music and conducted a group of fine session musicians and, as always, Allen Stagg was in charge of the technical side of things.

When the technical work was completed, I presented the LP in a beautiful cover which was illustrated with a reproduction of a famous painting by Fragonard entitled 'The Swing', while the record itself was called *Love Songs Sung By David Hughes* (DS 6062). It achieved the success for which I had hoped; not only were the critics very kind in their reviews but the publicity David enjoyed as a well-known pop star was exceedingly helpful, and Delysé shared in the glory.

Shortly after the record's release, I organised a concert for David at

Fenton House to which I also invited Sandor Gorlinsky, the most important impresario in London at the time, particularly in the management of operatic singers. Gorlinsky was interested enough to send a copy of David's record to Glyndebourne, and David was immediately invited to attend an audition there. As a result, they gave him the score of Mozart's *Idomeneo* and told him to study the title role, on condition that he promised to give up immediately singing in the style by which he had been earning his living! David didn't hesitate to agree to this, as he was so thrilled to think that his dream of appearing on the operatic stage might be realised. His success gave me great satisfaction, and made all the hard work and financial risk worthwhile. His operatic career went from strength to strength, and as his voice developed he was soon singing leading tenor roles at Glyndebourne, the Coliseum, and eventually at Covent Garden. It was a proud and rewarding occasion when Matti, Ronnie Young and I went to Covent Garden a few years later to hear him sing the role of Cassio in Verdi's *Otello*.

Alas, David's story had a tragic end, for he died suddenly from a massive heart attack during the first interval of *Madame Butterfly* at the Coliseum, where he was singing the role of Pinkerton. It was a terrible shock to his poor wife, Anne, who had been in the theatre at the time, and to his friends and the public. Apparently he had known that he was in danger and that he should really have given up singing very demanding roles, but he simply couldn't bear to think of continuing life without the joy of fulfilling his ambition as an artist. It was a tragically premature end to a man who was willing to sacrifice so much for his career.

I then went on to record two great Welsh artists, both baritones and both named Evans, although their voices were utterly dissimilar in quality and style, and their careers followed completely different directions. Geraint Evans had already achieved international fame by singing baritone roles that demanded great dramatic vocal talent, including Verdi's *Falstaff*, in major operatic houses around the world, and had also appeared in many of Mozart's operas at Glyndebourne, Vienna and Salzburg under the batons of some of the world's most eminent conductors. Through my work with Welsh music and artists, we had met on many occasions and liked each other, and I told him that I would dearly love to record his voice, but confessed that I wasn't yet able to involve myself in the huge cost of an operatic venture. He told me that I should let him know if I came up with an idea that would be acceptable to us both, and that we would then see what could be done.

During a recent visit to Cardiff, I had gone to Llandaff Cathedral to see Epstein's famous statue 'Christ In Majesty', which had been erected after the war. I was enormously impressed by both it and the dramatic beauty of the cathedral. The thought flashed through my mind while I was there that this would be the ideal setting to record a programme with Geraint Evans, if I could only persuade him to sing some well-known oratorio arias, which I knew he had loved since his young days in the Welsh valleys. If only he could find the time, I was sure he would be happy to do this, as it wouldn't interfere with the operatic recordings that he was making for the major companies in any way. I phoned him and put the proposition to him, and he accepted enthusiastically at once, as long as he could spare the time from his heavy schedule of engagements.

Geraint was singing Leporello in *Don Giovanni* in Salzburg during the summer of 1961. He told me that he could get away for two days after one of the performances if he flew over to Cardiff on the early-morning plane, which would allow us one session during that afternoon and two more on the following day before he had to take the evening plane back to Salzburg. It would be a tight schedule in every way, for I had to engage the BBC Welsh Orchestra as well as three choirs – The Shelly Singers, The Lyrian Singers and The Glendower Singers – and the services of the conductor, Mansel Thomas. All had to be paid, whether the sessions took place or not, so it was a great risk to take, given that Geraint's presence relied entirely on the plane being able to take off. As the weather is often very bad in Salzburg, this possibility had to be considered!

They say that fortune favours the brave, and I was indeed very fortunate, for Geraint turned up in time for the sessions and in fine form. I was touched when he told me that he had returned from the opera house in Salzburg very late on the previous night, and that, as he had to leave at around four o'clock the following morning in order to board his plane, he had decided to sleep on a deck chair in the garden of his digs, covered only by his overcoat and his umbrella, so that he wouldn't disturb the rest of the household. I could only thank God that it hadn't rained, and wondered how many other artists of his international renown would have gone to such lengths to avoid disappointing me.

Geraint's arrival was, as always, very dramatic. While I was anxiously waiting for him and the orchestra and choirs were rehearsing, he suddenly emerged from behind one of the great columns of the cathedral, with his overcoat slung over his shoulders as though he were making one of his unique stage entrances. I was so relieved, as were the orchestra and choirs, who all gave him a great ovation of welcome. From that moment, I knew that, barring any unexpected disasters, it was going to be a great recording session.

Geraint knew all of the oratorio arias that we were recording that day from his childhood; they were in his blood, and he sang them superbly. I think that he felt inspired by the beauty of the cathedral, as indeed we all were, and he particularly enjoyed singing with his own people, which in his busy life he rarely had the opportunity to do. Mansel Thomas conducted the great favourites from *Elijah* with skill and sympathy, and we managed to get through the programme in the allotted time, including 'Lord God Of Abraham', 'Cast Thy Burden', 'Is Not His Word Like A Fire?' and others, which gave Geraint enormous scope for his sense of drama. It was indeed a most memorable session, and I was deeply touched by Geraint's generosity and enthusiasm in making the great effort of coming to Cardiff during his heavy season in Salzburg and of giving so much of himself in such a wonderful performance.

On the record's release, the critics were ecstatic. *Gramophone* wrote, "How strange that it should take one of the smaller record companies to produce the first solo recital to be made by one of the few really international singers these islands have produced since the war. Geraint Evans is in demand at La Scala, the Vienna State Opera, San Francisco and Salzburg, but not apparently by our leading record manufacturers. This recital of oratorio arias is one of the finest discs of its kind ever heard. The choral singing is splendid...the attack is crisp and the words wonderfully clear under the stylish direction of Mansel Thomas. The recording made in Llandaff Cathedral is superbly spacious, rich, with a tremendous sense of presence, and the music surges off the disc with terrific impact." Meanwhile, *The Popular Press* reported that "the sacred music record of Geraint Evans in Llandaff Cathedral has already sold more than 10,000 copies".

I now come to the third exciting voice I recorded at that time. Although Meredydd was also an Evans, he couldn't have been more different from Geraint, with the exception that they both had beautiful baritone voices.

Geraint had been born in the mining area of South Wales, while Meredydd came from the rural north. When I attended the National Eisteddfod of that year, Matti Prichard insisted that I should hear Meredydd singing in one of the informal gatherings which took place at night after the official ceremonies had ended. She explained that he was a tutor at Bangor University and an authority on the Welsh language, and when she told me that he had a fine voice, and that he devoted much of his time to the collection and performance of traditional Welsh songs, I decided to go with her to hear him at a country inn after we had closed our Delysé stand on the eisteddfod field.

We arrived quite late in the evening and went upstairs above the bar to find a large gathering waiting for Meredydd to start singing, and he soon began with an extraordinarily beautiful song that had been handed down from generation to generation. (He sang many of these, sometimes alone or with harp accompaniment.) Suddenly, without any visible signal from him, he was joined by a group of friends. When I asked Matti who they were, she told me that one was a carpenter, one a quarryman, another an insurance agent...in fact, they were just men who lived in the area and who enjoyed spending much of their leisure time singing together.

I can't begin to describe how fascinated I was by Meredydd's personality and by his beautiful voice, as well as the atmosphere created by him and his friends in the performance of these haunting traditional folk songs. I decided on the spot that a recording of these talented people could only be a success, and I asked Meredydd if he would be interested in coming to London to make a recording, if he and his friends could find time to do so. He said that he was certain that they would be thrilled by the prospect. It was thus arranged that Meredydd should come to London for a meeting so that we could discuss the best way to produce such an unusual recording programme.

On my return to London, I considered the matter carefully and chose a programme that I hoped would appeal to Meredydd. This was not an easy task, because above all I didn't want to interfere with the intimacy of the performance, but I knew that I would have to create a production that would also attract a more sophisticated – and possibly international – public.

I was in a state of some trepidation, fearing that Meredydd might feel that my ideas would destroy the character of the music, but to my relief he accepted my suggestions with enthusiasm. When I told him that I would like to engage the great harpist Maria Korchinska to accompany him in some of his songs, feeling that, as a Russian, she would have an instinctive feeling for his own folk music, he was enough of a professional to be delighted. He also agreed that I should invite Robert Docker to write some arrangements for a small group of musicians who would accompany The Tryfan Octet in those songs in which they joined Meredydd. He suggested that I might like to feature his American-born wife, Phyllis Kinney, who was also steeped in the tradition of Welsh folk music. I thought that this was an excellent idea, as it would lighten an otherwise very masculine recording.

I then set about organising the sessions, discussing the technical aspects with Allen Stagg and hiring studio one at IBC for two days. I also obtained from Meredydd the manuscript of the songs, which Robert Docker was to arrange, and engaged the services of Maria Korchinska, who was delighted with the idea, as I'd thought that she would be. I knew that these folk songs would appeal to her Russian soul, and that she and Meredydd would get on splendidly. Meanwhile, I left it to Robert Docker to choose the musicians who would be best suited to this rather special session.

After a few weeks, we all met at IBC Studios in Portland Place. The contingent from North Wales arrived on the night before the session, so they were well rested and there was no danger of late arrivals. Robert Docker conducted his small group of excellent musicians in the attractive arrangements that he had written most competently, as usual, and was sympathetic and helpful to Meredydd and The Tryfan Octet. We were able to get through all of the numbers in which the orchestra and the group were involved in one day, as I had planned, so that we could concentrate entirely on songs with Meredydd, Phyllis and Korchinska on the second.

It wasn't wishful thinking that led me to believe that this was an inspired recording. From the moment that I'd first heard Meredydd, during my visit to North Wales, I knew that, if I could capture the atmosphere of dedication and love which he and his friends generated in the singing of their folk music, I couldn't fail to produce a recording of unique quality.

To our delight, we received favourable and enthusiastic reviews, as well as an international award for "a recording of unusual merit". It's only because the critic of *Gramophone* magazine summed up my intentions in the opening words of his review that I dare to quote them: "There is an intimacy about this record which adds greatly to its charm. The atmosphere is very much that of a group of friends singing and playing for their own enjoyment and nothing else." The reviewer went on, "It may seem odd [that]...for the harpist Delysé went to Russia, but in the event they couldn't have done better, for Maria Korchinska is obviously in complete sympathy with her colleagues. Moreover, there is an affinity between the singing of Mr Evans and Russian singers in that both possess the gift of living their songs, brief and undramatic as many of them are." He finished his article with the following words: "Delysé have issued a number of Welsh records, but this, I think, is the most desirable of them all."

After this, I gave myself my own personal and private accolade, saying to myself that Uncle Fred would have been pleased with me.

The success of my recent recordings for the Delysé label encouraged me greatly, and I was happy with the way in which things were progressing. Not only was I pleased with the warmth in which my last efforts were received but I was also glad that the catalogue was now beginning to prove financially successful, and that my distribution system was efficiently established, not only in the United Kingdom but also in the Dominions and America.

It was at this time that I decided to create and market the Envoy label, on which I planned to issue music that could not be described as classical. The label would feature popular groups, both Welsh and English, as well as military bands, in which I was now becoming interested, including recordings of the Welsh Guards, the Lifeguards, and the Royal Horse Guards.

At the end of 1962, I wanted to make a number of Irish recordings, which I believed could be very successful, as they would fill a gap which existed in the catalogues of most record companies. I had discovered that there was a demand for such recordings in both the UK and America, and that there was very little of any quality to fill it. To this end, I approached Harry Christmas, who had known Uncle Fred and whom I had met on a number of occasions. At that time, he was managing director of EMI in Ireland, and he enthusiastically agreed to help me make contact with the Irish scene. With his help, I pulled off a real coup by setting up a recording programme on an exclusive basis with one of Ireland's most popular radio and TV artists, Dermot O'Brien, along with his Clubmen. They had just returned from a highly successful tour of the United States, where they were as well known and popular as they were in their native country. Dermot had just finalised a contract for a 20-week season on Eirean radio and television, so signing him to my Envoy label was a feather in my cap.

These arrangements involved a lot of travelling between England and Eire, and Ronnie Young's presence and skill in dealing with people proved helpful and at times reassuring. I planned to bring Dermot and his band to London in order to record a number of LPs, but first I wanted to watch them at work and feel the atmosphere in which they performed, and so Ronnie and I took some pretty wild drives to remote villages where Dermot and his band were appearing at popular church dances, an important part of Irish social life. It was tremendous fun, but also very exhausting. Nevertheless, the recordings I made with Dermot proved highly successful for all concerned for many years to come.

My activities in Ireland also suited Harry Christmas well, for his company wasn't very generous in allocating funds for recording purposes. His function in Ireland was to manage and promote the EMI catalogues, rather than to dabble in A&R. However, Harry found himself very short of material which he felt was much in demand – that is, recordings of native Irish music made by the Irish for the Irish. That said, he had succeeded in obtaining finance to record the most popular show band in Dublin at the time, with which he had negotiated an exclusive contract. When I came along and recorded Dermot O'Brien, Harry was delighted, for it meant that, after concluding a distribution and marketing deal with me, he could control the recordings made by the two most popular show bands in Ireland.

My activities didn't end with the six LPs that I recorded with Dermot in London. Allen Stagg brought equipment over to Dublin, and we also recorded The Guinness Choir in a programme of traditional Irish airs, for which I had engaged Arthur Wilkinson to write the orchestral arrangements. At the same time, I seized the opportunity to hear a number of popular ballad singers, and also recorded a few for my Envoy label. Two of the most talented of these singers were John McNally and Liam DeValley, who were not only outstanding in the art of Irish ballad singing but also very pleasant and attractive men.

My activities in Ireland as a producer received quite considerable notice from the Irish press. A number of record companies asked me to produce for them on a freelance basis, but I was much too busy building my own catalogue to accept these offers. I did, however, agree to produce two recordings for a company called Claddagh, which promoted serious music by Irish composers, and as the sessions were to take place in London at

EMI Studios I was able to carry out these commissions without too much inconvenience. One of these recordings was a string quartet by Frederick May, for which the very fine Aeolian Quartet was engaged, and the other was an orchestral work by Sean O'Riarda called *Vertical Man*, which was performed by the London Philharmonic Orchestra, who were conducted, strangely enough, by an Italian, Carlo Franci. I found these sessions most refreshing, as for once I wasn't responsible for the financial arrangements!

Far more interesting than these, however, were the sessions I undertook to produce for Harry Christmas and EMI. To this end, I flew to Belfast to record the Belfast Symphony Orchestra, conducted by Havelock Nelson, their permanent conductor, with the soloist Veronica Dunne, a fine Irish soprano of the Italian school who was then living in Dublin. Havelock Nelson was a charming man and an excellent conductor, and the orchestra played well. Harry was a generous host, and arranged for Veronica and me to stay in a delightful country house hotel just outside Belfast, which I later heard had been destroyed by bombs. I liked Belfast very much and found the people kind and pleasant, although I remember driving along the infamous Shanklin Road in Harry's car, with its Dublin number plates, and saying to him, "I don't like the feel of this at all. Terrible trouble is brewing." This was, after all, the beginning of the present troubles.

Harry laughed at me and said, "Oh, it's nothing. It'll all blow over."

I didn't agree, though, and I was thankful to get away when the sessions were completed. It was a shame. They were such lovely people, and yet such terrible times lay before them.

13 *Trains, Boats And Wales*

My life from 1961 onwards can best be described as adventurous. I had been inspired to open new recording vistas, such as the Irish catalogue, which was shortly followed by the creation of a collection of children's recordings. This venture later proved successful, as I decided to concentrate entirely on the reading of well-known children's stories – a sensible idea, as the initial costs of achieving this were low. However, everything depended on the choice of the stories and on the person reading them. I was determined that the success should lie in the performance of the reader, and that there should be no artificial sound effects or disturbing background music involved.

The creation of the children's catalogue proved to be a lucrative source of income to Delysé over the years. I remembered that, when my two boys had been very young, they had enjoyed the series of railway stories written by that extraordinary clergyman the Reverend W Awdrey. The stories seemed to pour from his pen in an unending flow, and they had loved them so much! I therefore contacted the publishers of the stories, Edmund Ward, and suggested to them that the stories would make wonderful records. They were impressed, and agreed to allow me to proceed with the idea if I could find the right person to read them. I discussed this once again with my two boys, and we decided without any argument that there was only one person in the world to do this: Johnny Morris. We had watched him, enthralled, on his television series, talking to strange animals in zoos and having extraordinary conversations with them in their own language, and so I decided that, if I could persuade this brilliant artist with a genius for mimicry to make train noises instead of animal sounds, Delysé would be onto another winner and would give pleasure to thousands of children.

When I telephoned Johnny to see if I could interest him in the idea, his wife, Eileen, answered the phone. She said that Johnny was away, and when I explained why I wanted to speak to him she seemed quite unimpressed but said that she would ask him to contact me. I was rather discouraged by her attitude, and feared that she might influence him against my suggestion. When we finally did speak to one another, Johnny seemed amazed, and said that he couldn't imagine making train noises. I assured him that I was certain that he could mimic any sort of noise in the world. Because he was such a kind man, and could tell how enthusiastic I was, he agreed to give it a try. I sent him some of the little books and he said, in typical fashion, that he would have a go.

I organised the studio for what turned out to be the easiest and certainly one of the most amusing sessions I had ever experienced. I explained to Johnny that there would be no background music or effects because I knew that children hated the story to be interrupted, so it was up to Johnny to create a voice for each engine character, as well as the Fat Controller, and also the sounds of whistles, hisses of escaping steam and bangs expected from the trains of that period. Johnny protested that he had never made such noises before, but I just placed him in front of a microphone, made him as comfortable as possible and listened.

As I expected, he was fantastic. In a few minutes, he created a distinctive voice personality for each engine, and he made the most realistic train noises. I think that he really enjoyed himself, as we in the control room certainly did. I was confident that my hunch to persuade Johnny to record these wonderful little stories was absolutely right.

The project proved to be highly successful. We turned out the little EPs in a cover illustrated with the same picture as the one used in the book, and each disc had a different story on each side. They looked attractive on display in the shops, and were irresistible to both parents and children, for not only was Johnny's name a great draw but also, at eight shillings and sixpence, the records were marketed at a price which was within the range of most young families. In the long years of friendship which I later enjoyed with Johnny and Eileen, they frequently confessed their amazement at the success of these little records. This release proved to be the beginning of the important Delysé children's catalogue, which became famous throughout the English-speaking world and for which we went on to record many of Johnny's own stories about Lorenzo the llama – a most endearing little creature who enchanted generations of children – and whimsical stories entitled *Big Top Berty*, *Ferry Boat Fred*, *Tarzan And The Hapes* and others.

As a result of this success, other publishers of children's books approached me, interested in having some of their own famous stories recorded, and so it was that the series went on to include *Alice In Wonderland*, read by David Davis of BBC fame; Edward Lear's *Nonsense Poems*; and also the 'Little Red Fox' and 'Snug And Serena' stories, which were read by Marjorie Westbury. These artists were the most popular personalities on BBC children's programmes at that time, and this made the records immensely successful.

Many other famous stories read by well-known actors were also added to the Delysé children's catalogue, and these contributed considerably to the earning power of the company. In fact, I continued to market the EPs – which were distributed by EMI, Selecta and two other major distributors – throughout the '60s. As is always the way, success created imitation and competition, and EMI soon decided to start their own children's label which, although failing to destroy my success, certainly diluted my position in this field of activity to some extent.

In the meantime, the boys had grown up. Pompy had been at Oxford for three years and had graduated in 1962 to embark on a career in the aircraft industry, while Roguey had completed his time at Westminster and was about to go up to Christ Church to follow in his brother's footsteps. Both boys had done brilliantly by gaining scholarships to Oxford, and I was very happy and proud of their success.

During Pompy's period at Oxford, I had made frequent visits to see if all was well with him, and sometimes attended the Sunday service at Christ Church Cathedral. The music and the choral singing there was impressive, and I said to Pompy in fun that it might be a good idea to bring the equipment to Oxford and to make a recording while he was there as a student. I was only half joking, but he took it seriously and said, "Oxford is always news, and any interesting and attractively-presented publication, whether a book or a record, stands a good chance of selling, if mainly to tourists."

After giving the idea some further thought, I arranged for a meeting with Dr Sidney Watson, the conductor of the choir, who had rooms in Tom Quad. He proved to be very receptive, and agreed to the idea quite enthusiastically. While discussing a possible programme with him, he spoke of John Webster, the organist of University College, whom he described as "one of the most brilliant organists in the world, and an authority on music of the Baroque period". He also told me that the instrument on which he played in the University College Chapel was one of the finest of its period in England. As I was going to the expense of bringing the engineers and the equipment to Oxford, it certainly seemed sensible to make two recordings rather than just one.

It was very kind of Dr Watson to tell me about John Webster, and indeed the doctor was most helpful throughout the sessions. I took the opportunity of meeting Mr Webster on this visit, and found him to be a delightful man. He was fanatically enthusiastic about his work, and we spent a very happy time discussing the recording programme, which we decided would consist of six of Bach's chorale preludes and a prelude and fugue in F minor, as well as a number of works by English composers of the same period.

I arrived with Allen Stagg and the engineers some weeks later and set up the equipment in the vestry of Christ Church Cathedral, which made a very good control room. Pompy greeted us with great excitement and helped the engineers with their preparations. He had been really looking forward to this event, news of which had spread throughout the college.

Had I known of the naughty prank concocted by him and some of his friends, I wouldn't have settled down to the sessions with such calm concentration and enjoyment. I later learned that Pompy and his friends had climbed the steeple of the cathedral to watch the session from the roof! Luckily, they weren't discovered, and got away without disaster either to themselves, the cathedral or the sessions. Nor were they ever found out, for if they had been they would have been severely punished and "sent down". We in the control room knew nothing of this, however, and we were able to record the *Vittoria Mass*, 'Simile Est Regnum Coelorum' and a number of items by Byrd in perfect peace.

The sessions at University College took place on the following day, when we completed the planned programme of the Bach chorales and the English works without any problems. In fact, John Webster's love of the music and the joy which he so obviously felt in playing was an inspiration. It was indeed a privilege to work with such a fine artist. Although I felt almost sure that we would get exceptional reviews, I hoped for John's sake that this would be so. I needn't have feared, though, for both of the recordings were highly praised and achieved very satisfactory sales. I would have liked to have recorded the complete set of chorales with John at a later date, but alas he died quite suddenly. This was a great loss to the world of church music, in which he was a superb exponent, and his death was a dreadful shock to his many friends. He was a very special human being, and I'm very thankful to have had the opportunity of making at least one recording of this fine musician.

In 1963, our home life saw many changes and some adventures. I made a decision that was to influence the boys forever, as well as possibly some of their children: I bought a boat! I did this mainly because I was concerned about Roguey's health. He had worked tremendously hard during his last year at Westminster in order to gain his entrance to Christ Church. It was in his nature to give himself completely when a target had to be met, and certain symptoms that were apparent in his behaviour made me fear that he had put too much strain on his system. I consulted Ronnie Young (who was, after all, a psychiatrist and knew Roguey well), and he came up with the suggestion that I buy a boat. I must admit that the idea seemed completely bizarre at the time, but Ronnie argued that it would be of immense benefit not only to Roguey but also to the rest of the family. The idea seemed quite far-fetched, as we'd never had any interest in sailing, and indeed the boys didn't really care about sport of any kind. In this respect, maybe there was something to consider in Ronnie's idea; perhaps there had been something seriously lacking in their lives.

In the meantime, it was decided that the boys should make a coast-to-coast trip of America and meet members of the family there and drive through the Arizona Desert before finally returning on the *Queen Elizabeth*. I saw them off on this adventure with some trepidation but also with confidence, for I knew that they could be trusted not to get involved in any silly misadventures.

I had never spoken to the boys about the boat project, but during their absence Ronnie and I travelled to many yacht harbours during the weekends, even venturing as far as Scotland in our search for a suitable craft. It all seemed very discouraging, for the boats were either too expensive, too large, too small or totally unsuitable in some other way. We finally descended on Moody's Boatyard on the River Hamble, near Southampton, and viewed many yachts, both sail and motor powered, with the usual lack of success. Then the proprietor, Eric Moody, suggested that we might like to take a look at an old twin-diesel boat named *Marguerite II*, which he said was a bargain. Her owner, an elderly MP, had built her in 1927, and had kept her in excellent condition. Mr Moody told us that she was a vessel of great charm and character, and that she had taken part in the Dunkirk operation. She was 50 feet long and rather narrow, and her wooden hull was black, while she was painted a horrible creamy yellow below. In spite of this, though, I could see the beauty and elegance of her lines, and I fell in love with her on the spot. As I had recently sold our house in Pulborough (which we rarely visited), I felt that, at £4,700, she wasn't too expensive, and that the adventure and excitement that she would bring into our lives would be worth the financial outlay.

I kept her a secret from the boys until their return from America, for I wanted to surprise them. In fact, they were so overcome with amazement that they refused to believe me when I told them of the purchase that I had made. I told them to jump into Pompy's Lotus Élan – which he had just bought with his first years' earnings from his job at Vickers – and drive down to Moody's yard on the Hamble, where they would find out if my story was true. I followed with Ronnie Young in my estate car, laden with provisions. This was the first of many such happy journeys.

I found the boys in a state bordering on euphoria. They had been too excited to await our arrival, and had made enquiries in the yard as to whether a Mrs Wallich had purchased a boat called *Marguerite*. On being told that this was indeed so, they had rushed down to the water and climbed on board. I shall never forget the excitement when we first boarded her. We explored every inch of her below, from her large saloon to the aft cabin with its own washroom (which was to be mine), and thence through a narrow passageway on the port side which led past the engine casings to the spacious galley, where I would spend much of my time. Beyond this was the forward cabin, which the boys would occupy, with their own narrow washroom in the bows. We decided to paint her hull and the cabins below white. I was already measuring the portholes for curtain material and the long comfortable seat – which could be converted into a double bunk, running along the length of the port side of the saloon – for covers!

Maggie, as she soon became known, was a dream and a joy. We loved her dearly, and spent many wonderful weekends and holidays aboard her. We also had many adventures and many scares on her, for she was not an easy boat to handle, especially when we tried to moor her between pylons. I had many anxious moments watching the boys struggling desperately to tie her to a buoy with a heavy rope in a leaky dinghy and a swirling current.

We all had our official positions as crew: Ronnie was the skipper, Pompy was in charge of the engines and Roguey was the navigator, while I was a combination of purser and cook. We had to make many improvements in the interests of comfort and, more importantly, safety, such as changing all of the heavy old ropes with light, modern replacements and completely overhauling the engines.

This proved particularly necessary for, as we grew more experienced, we became more adventurous and sailed further and further, finally setting off for our very first crossing of the Channel to France, aiming to make our landfall at Le Havre. As navigator, this was Roguey's responsibility, and he made a wonderful job of it, for as we approached the French coast, after a beautiful crossing, we realised with tremendous relief that he had steered us perfectly. It's impossible to describe the excitement that we all felt when we made it, and we showered congratulations on our able navigator. Pompy, too, won great praise, for the engines – which he had tended with loving and anxious care – took us unfalteringly across the Channel in 18 hours. It seemed a very long way to sail, and indeed it was for such a small vessel, but we made it to France without any anxious incidents.

We were very proud of ourselves as we tied up alongside the quay in the French port and took our papers to Passport Control and the Customs office. We felt that everyone was looking at *Maggie* with great admiration and at us, the owners of such a beautiful old craft, with envy. Indeed, she was very impressive, and attracted a lot of attention wherever we berthed on our long cruise up the Seine to Paris, via Rouen. Once at the capital, we finally brought her into the harbour of the yacht club just below the Place de la Concorde. How proud we were of our achievement, and of our dear *Maggie*, as the almost constant crowd of onlookers gathered around to admire her and watch our activities on board. We felt like animals in a zoo! Ronnie Young had been so right in advising the ownership of a boat as being the almost infallible cure for all psychological problems. By the time one has exhausted oneself physically with all the chores necessary to look after her and braved the hazards of the sea, there simply isn't time to think about oneself at all.

From 1963, when I first bought *Maggie*, until 1968, I took every opportunity to escape to her, away from my hectic life. I savoured every moment that I spent sailing with the boys, for I was conscious that it could only last a short while, as they would soon be off to lead their own lives. Indeed this is what happened, for in 1968 Pompy decided to leave England and emigrated to the United States in pursuit of work. Roguey, meanwhile, later married Jeannie Collar, who had been a fellow student at Oxford, and they acquired their own sailing boat, *Cottontail*, which they built themselves in Moody's yard. *Maggie* would thus be without a crew, for Ronnie later decided to join his brother in the Caribbean. It was certainly a wrench, but life had to go on, and mine was full of interest and activity. *Maggie* was later sold to an engineer with a large family who lived on the west coast of Ireland, and I was sure that she would be well looked after and much loved.

The introduction of *Maggie* into our lives wasn't the only auspicious event that occurred in 1963, for I also embarked on what can only be described as a mammoth recording project. Because of the number of Welsh recordings I had included in the Delysé catalogue, I had received a lot of help and encouragement from the warm-hearted people of the principality, and so I wanted to do something in return. In a moment of rashness, I hired the Albert Hall and invited a number of famous actors and musicians, with whom I had become friendly, to participate in a concert to raise funds for the establishment of a scholarship which would enable young artists from Wales to pursue their studies further in London or abroad.

My idea was warmly received by many of these personalities, such as Richard Burton, Geraint Evans and others, who were delighted to be of assistance. Unfortunately these celebrities were working all over the world, and it was impossible for any of them to be available on the date that I had booked the Albert Hall. There was general consternation in the Delysé camp until Matti Prichard came up with a stupendous idea: "Why not invite the congregations of all of the Welsh churches and chapels in the London area to gather for a mammoth *Gymanfa Ganu* [a hymn-singing festival] in the Royal Albert Hall on that date?"

The idea appealed to me immediately, and I decided to go ahead with the project. The date at the Albert Hall was confirmed, and the administration of the event was placed in Ronnie's capable hands. Time was short, however, as all of the churches and chapels in the area had to be notified of our choice of hymns, and leaflets containing the words had to be sent to the ministers, along with a letter from me informing them about the recording and asking for their help and co-operation. I explained that, although the project would be handled as a commercial proposition, there would be a substantial royalty payable to a fund that would be distributed to all of the religious institutions that took part. They were told that the event was scheduled to take place on 3 May

1963, and that the recording would begin punctually at 8pm. The letter also asked them to rehearse the hymns on the list, and explained that the event would be conducted as much like a religious service as possible. The able and experienced musician Dr Terry James would conduct the choirs, and Cyril Anthony was engaged as the organist. Matti Prichard, whose advice was invaluable, also recommended that I should invite Emyr Jones, an eminent Welsh scholar, to read through each hymn before the singing began.

I couldn't have coped without the enthusiastic support of my faithful and able staff at the Delysé office, for I was fully occupied with the artistic and technical aspects of this great undertaking, in which I was nobly and competently assisted by Allen Stagg, who was looking forward to the challenge of making a fine recording in the notoriously difficult building. The Albert Hall has an echo which is fiendishly hard to control, but I consoled myself by thinking that, even if only half of the hall's full capacity turned up on the night, that many bodies would dampen the acoustic nicely. Allen had decided to place the equipment in a room under the stage, and it was planned that I would convey my instructions from my position on the stage by telephone.

What memories this would bring back of seeing Uncle Fred sitting in front of the conductor in the midst of an orchestra, in the same hall, directing a recording by Elgar or of Handel's *Messiah*, communicating by Post Office telephone line to the studios! I couldn't have imagined then that I would be doing almost the same thing in years to come.

Meanwhile, back in the office, the letters of invitation were sent out. My able accountant, Mr Kaye, worked out how the royalties would be collected and paid to the various churches, while Mr Lennox prepared himself for (hopefully) a mammoth task in the dispatch department and Mabel Tobin and Sue Caplin, my assistant and secretary, tried to stop me from going mad! Matti Prichard, who felt responsible for the whole project, was constantly rushing into the office with the latest reports from the religious institutions, for without their support the whole undertaking would be a fiasco. However, from the information she was receiving on the Welsh grapevine, she seemed pretty confident that we would have adequate support, at least.

The great day arrived. I went to the hairdresser in the morning and decided which dress I was going to wear for the event, which had to look reasonably glamorous and yet business-like. It was a difficult decision, but the act of choosing helped to save me from having a nervous breakdown! I then went to my parent's flat in Portland Place for lunch and gave them tickets for seats in a box near the stage. They were also in a state of great excitement and anticipation, and when my mother bade me farewell and wished me good luck she shook her head and said, "Whatever will you do next, Isabella?"

It was, of course, a great gamble, as the publicity that had been generated for the event in the press was considerable, and if we had little support and the event turned out to be a failure it would make Delysé a laughing stock. Nothing ventured nothing gained, however, and the Delysé staff converged onto the Albert Hall to help in preparing for the evening. Allen and his team of engineers had been there for hours already, setting up the equipment below the stage and arranging the microphones. This was a difficult and critical decision, for none of the microphones could be moved once the session had begun.

I went home to dress and returned to the Albert Hall at around six o'clock. As I approached, I saw signs of activity, as coaches began to jostle for parking positions, but I didn't dare feel too optimistic, for they might have been going to some other event in the area. I went straight down to the artists' room, where I found Pompy and Roguey, who had just arrived from work. I told them to go out and about to see what was happening while I went down to the basement to consult with Allen.

On my return to the artists' room at about seven o'clock, I found Matti in a state of gibbering excitement. She threw her arms about my neck and told me that people were arriving in their thousands! Coach after coach was depositing its passengers and going off to find a parking space, and the huge hall was filling rapidly with excited Welshmen and -women, not only from the London area but also from the north of England, South Wales and even North Wales. I was quite overcome, not only with relief but also with gratitude to these wonderful people, who had gone to this great effort to support me and to indulge their passion for singing hymns.

I went to find my parents in their box, for I was in such a state of excitement that I couldn't be alone. They were safely seated with Waylett, their chauffeur, who had driven them to the hall, and were also amazed at the sight of the thousands of singers who filled the huge hall from the arena to the top of the gallery. As I left them, in order to start proceedings, my father called out, "*Coraggio, mia fia,*" in a Milanese accent.

I returned below stage to the control room to tell Allen that we were about to begin and greet Terry James and Emyr Jones, and to make sure that Cyril Anthony was seated at the great organ console. From the back of the stage, I could hear the roar of thousands of voices coming from the hall, and I have to admit that my heart was beating very quickly. I told Terry and Emyr that it was time to go onto the platform, when they would be introduced, and that I would tell the assembled masses exactly how we wanted them to help us make the recording.

My heart was throbbing when I faced this vast concourse of people. The Albert Hall has a capacity of 6,000, and that evening it was packed. Allen came onto the stage with me and was introduced so that he could get the feel of the hall now that it was full. (I have to admit that I was glad that it wasn't me who had the responsibility of transferring the sound of this massive assembly onto tape!) Allen went below, and Matti took her place beside me, so that she could introduce me in Welsh, and then proceeded to introduce Terry James, Emyr Jones and Cyril Anthony.

My instructions to the "congregation" were simple, although unfortunately not in Welsh. I explained that Emyr Jones would read the verses before each hymn was recorded, and that, from the moment that the red light went on, we would be recording, at which point they should stand still and keep absolutely silent. When Emyr had finished his reading, Terry James would raise his baton, which would be the signal for Cyril Anthony to begin playing the introduction. Then, when the singers reached the end of the hymn, they had to wait for the red light to be extinguished before they could sit down and relax.

I had told Allen before the session started that I wanted to play back the first hymn so that the congregation could hear how magnificent they sounded, for I needed them to be encouraged and inspired for the rest of the session. Allen wasn't too happy about this, for it was technically difficult, but I insisted, as I knew that it would make all the difference to their performance. He told me that he was going to keep the technical side of things as simple as possible by using three-track equipment, the outer channels of which would be fed by the two microphones suspended high above the stage facing the audience, which would also pick up the organ. The voice of the speaker, Emyr Jones, who would announce each hymn, would feed the third and middle channel, which would be switched off when the singing began. Terry James's instructions to the singers would also be carried on the middle channel, as I presumed would be my words to the multitudes when I explained how I wished them to proceed when the session began. I'm sure that no other recording engineer would have had the common sense to use these simple technical procedures – they would have used many more microphones – but Allen knew what he was doing, and I had complete faith in his technical expertise.

There was no musical editing to be done, for there were to be no repeat takes, but when we returned to the studios and heard the sound that we had achieved in this mammoth recording we were quite overcome with wonder and excitement, and so the master was cut and sent as soon as possible to the Decca factory. The only delay was in the printing of the record cover, because we'd had to wait for the actual event to take place so that we could photograph the audience from the stage, for this black-and-white image would cover the entire surface of the 12" sleeve. It was a most effective shot, and a great incentive to purchase the record, for many of those taking part in the *Gymanfa* found themselves immortalised on the sleeve. The dealers – many of whom were intrigued enough to be present at the Albert Hall – couldn't wait to see the finished product in their shops. The record was a tremendous success, not only in the UK but also all over the world, wherever the Welsh had settled. I received wonderful letters of appreciation, and when I heard that, as a result of the royalties received from the sales, the participating congregations had been able to install new roofs and central heating systems in their chapels, I felt a real sense of triumph.

A Nation Sings (ESB 3167/DS 6067) was such a success that I was entreated to repeat the performance and to hold another *Gymanfa Ganu* in the Albert Hall, which I did two years later. Although this recording might have been technically superior and the performance more polished – the congregations had obviously practised very hard – I felt that this second version lacked the magic of the first. It was again a great success, and even boosted the sales of volume one, but I felt in my heart that one should never repeat a spontaneously inspired recording.

Recording 6,000 voices in the Albert Hall was a feat that lifted the reputation of Delysé to great heights in the recording industry. The very audacity of the project seemed to have a stunning effect on my Welsh catalogue, for it had been based on Uncle Fred's advice to concentrate on the gaps in the lists of the major record companies. If I stuck to this method, and continued to make recordings of quality, I couldn't fail. In 1963, both Delysé and Envoy were thriving, for the children's stories were selling very well and the Irish and Welsh recordings were also enjoying excellent sales on both sides of the Atlantic.

14 Wyn Morris And Mahler

For some time, I'd heard talk of a young Welsh conductor called Wyn Morris, who had recently returned to England from the United States. His friends persisted in telling me that I had to hear him, for they were convinced that his talent would place him amongst the greatest conductors. I was told that, after leaving the Royal Academy of Music, he had studied in Salzburg under Igor Markevich, who considered him to have been his most talented pupil since Guido Cantelli. Following this, he went to the United States, where he won the much-coveted Koussevitzky Prize, awarded by the Boston Symphony Orchestra at Tanglewood. The official citation described him as being "one of the most outstanding talents for conducting in the history of Tanglewood". After studying under Georg Szell, he became conductor of the Cleveland Chamber Orchestra for a period before returning to England.

As you can imagine, these reports made me very curious to hear this young Llanelli-born conductor, who was now married to an American. I had also heard that he was sometimes arrogant and somewhat unpredictable, and perhaps difficult to handle, and for this reason I was rather unwilling to meet him personally, knowing my weakness for becoming involved when confronted by great talent, but I was finally persuaded by one of his friends, Dafydd Gwynn Evans, and by Matti, to attend his debut at the Royal Festival Hall at the end of November 1963, when he was to conduct Mahler's ninth symphony.

On the night of the concert, I was given a seat in a box, in which Dafydd sat with Wyn's wife, Ruth, and her mother and father, who had come over from America for the occasion. There was a feeling of expectancy in the hall, which was filled almost to capacity, for the rumour had spread in musical circles that on that night London might witness the first appearance of a great new talent. We needn't have feared disappointment for he conducted the massive score from memory with the utmost confidence and inspiration. Not only was it a great performance but it was something of a *tour de force*, for at that time Mahler's works hadn't yet become part of the standard orchestral repertoire, and the Royal Philharmonic can't have been too familiar with the symphony, which is of outstanding difficulty. However, they gave their best, and played as though inspired. One could sense how delighted they were by the great ovation which both they and Wyn received at the end of the performance.

After the concert, we adjourned to the Savoy Hotel, where Wyn's father-in-law had arranged a reception. It was a happy and delightful occasion, for everyone was pleased that Wyn had achieved such a great success. He was in seventh heaven, of course, relieved that the performance had gone so well. Indeed, the warmth of the reaction he had received from the audience must have given him immense satisfaction. On this first meeting I found Wyn to have an engaging and forceful personality, and he was also vivacious in manner, which is unusual for a musician. It was difficult to talk while he was surrounded by so many people wanting to congratulate him, and so it was decided that we should soon have a meeting to discuss his ideas and aspirations. We had no cause to fear the opinion of the critics, either, as they were unanimous in their praise, and to an extraordinary degree. The favourable reaction was best expressed by the critic of *The Times*, who wrote, "Never since Bruno Walter do we remember such persuasive and thoroughly idiomatic rendering of this mammoth score."

Mahler's ninth symphony was a work that held a particular significance for me. Uncle Fred had been in Vienna in 1938, three months before the *Anschluss*, when he had recorded this great work with Bruno Walter and the Vienna Philharmonic just before he was forced to flee the country. It was an historic and unforgettable event, which thanks to my uncle was recorded for posterity. I had listened to it many times, and felt fully confident that my assessment of Wyn's performance was justified.

During the course of many meetings, Wyn revealed his ambition to conduct and eventually record all of Mahler's works. I told him that I was anxious to support him in such a series, but that it had to be remembered that Delysé was Isabella Wallich, and that the financial burden would be a heavy one, as recording any of Mahler's works – which necessitated huge orchestral forces – demanded considerable financial involvement. In the meantime, after much discussion with Wyn, I decided that I would record

Mendelssohn's *Elijah*, a work comfortably within the scope of the Delysé catalogue. If I could also persuade Geraint Evans to sing the title role, I would have a winner which could help to raise funds for the Mahler project that we had in mind.

Like all Welsh conductors, Wyn loved conducting the great choral works, and so he took on the *Elijah* project with enthusiasm. I telephoned Basil Horsfield, Geraint's agent, and asked him to find out if he would like to take part in the recording and when he would be available. As I expected, Geraint was enthusiastic, and so I set about planning the sessions with Wyn, deciding on which orchestra he wanted to use and working to tie up their availability with Geraint and the other singers. There was also the question of the recording venue, and after discussing things with Allen Stagg we chose Watford Town Hall, which was the most suitable in every way. All of our plans fitted together beautifully, and the recording was scheduled to take place in March 1966. This was a long way ahead, but Geraint was fully booked for performances all over the world until then, and so we had to accept the fact that we would have to wait for another twelve months.

The delay suited me well, for it enabled me to continue to build the Delysé and Envoy catalogues and thus prepare myself for the considerable expansion which lay ahead. In the meantime, I continued to visit Dublin, where I made a number of interesting and successful recordings, including the charming *In Dublin's Fair City*, for which I used The Guinness Choir, and I also continued my series of recordings with Dermot O'Brien And His Clubmen, as they had been so commercially successful.

My schedule also included a visit to the north-east of England, where I'd heard that there was a fine choir called The Consett Citizens' Choir, which was very popular on regional television. If I could persuade the well-known Geordie baritone, Owen Brannigan, to sing with them in a programme of popular songs, I felt that this, too, could be a success. In any case, it would be fun to work with a group of singers from the other side of the British Isles. Owen proved to be pleasant and easy to work with, and when I brought the choir together in the Conway Hall for the sessions they behaved like a lot of schoolchildren on holiday. Once again, Arthur Wilkinson wrote the arrangements. *Songs Of The Tyne* proved to be a charming recording, and it did very well, considering that I was dipping my toe into the likes and dislikes of a new regional public. Owen

Brannigan's participation proved to be of enormous help in the following marketing campaign.

At this time, an extraordinary stroke of fate occurred which would place me in direct opposition to EMI. While I had been recording in Dublin, I had told Harry Christmas that I was proposing to record *Elijah* with Wyn Morris and Geraint Evans. He received the news with horror, as it placed him in a very difficult position, as I'd sworn him to secrecy. As a director of EMI, he naturally owed allegiance to his company, but he was also a great friend of mine. He then revealed that EMI were well advanced in preparations for their own recording of *Elijah*, complete with an international star cast. Of course, I realised that I had to cancel our arrangements, as it certainly wouldn't do to come out with the same release at the same time as EMI. Harry and I promised to say nothing of what we had told each other.

I returned instantly to London to cope with what seemed to be a disastrous situation. There was no question about the recording not taking place in March, for the orchestra had been booked and no record producer can ever go back on that obligation. Geraint, I knew, would be understanding, but my credibility with this great artist would be diminished.

Wyn, however, remained remarkably calm in face of this apparent disaster, and reminded me of one of Ronnie Young's much-quoted sayings: "When you're handed a lemon, make lemonade out of it!" He begged me to keep calm and see what sort of lemonade we could make with the resources at our disposal. He came up with an idea that would shoot Delysé to the very top of the international record scene. He told me that we should consider the assets that we already had. We had the services of one of the leading orchestras definitely booked; we had the knowledge that Geraint Evans was available to work with us on a definite date; and we also had Wyn himself, who had just made a great impact on the musical world with his performance of Mahler's ninth symphony. The answer was obvious: we had to record Mahler's *Des Knaben Wunderhorn*, which at that time had only been recorded once before, and not very significantly at that. Furthermore, Wyn observed that each of the baritone songs would give Geraint a chance to display his great dramatic talent. Here was a ravishing and exquisite work just waiting to be recorded.

However, we still had to find a mezzo-soprano who would be able to learn the difficult score in time for the sessions. After much discussion, we decided to approach Janet Baker, who was just then at the beginning of a distinguished career. She agreed, and so I was then in a position to issue contracts, order the copying of orchestral parts and set the whole project in operation. It was a momentous decision because, by recording a major work and by using large orchestral forces and distinguished artists, I was entering into direct competition with the major companies.

In the midst of all this preparation and excitement, my personal life wasn't exactly peaceful, for we had decided that our house in Clifton Hill was by now too large for our needs and too expensive to run. The boys were now grown up, and I knew that Pompy was dissatisfied with his present job and feeling frustrated. I could hardly bear to think of it, but I knew that he was seriously considering leaving England to work in America. He had been a wonderful friend and companion to me, and also a devoted elder brother to Roguey, who would soon be entering his third and final year at Oxford and was already leading an independent life. I had long had my sights set on a small apartment building which was almost next door to the EMI studios in Abbey Road at 10 Grove End Road, where there was a vacant flat on the third and top floor of the low building, and so, after consulting the boys and my parents, I took the plunge and made the decision to move.

The flat was a charming place, with a large sitting room and a circular dining room, which I found especially attractive, along with two good-sized bedrooms and a smaller one leading from the excellent kitchen. A few years before it wouldn't have been large enough, but as Roguey was nearly always away now it suited us well.

I was fortunate indeed to have had the help of a devoted and efficient staff, for I needed every ounce of help that they could give me, as I was deeply involved in the artistic, technical and financial preparations for the recording of *Des Knaben Wunderhorn*. At the same time, I was travelling to Ireland and Wales to build on my catalogue of regional recordings, and also visiting Europe to negotiate overseas distribution deals, which were becoming increasingly important.

To add to our burdens, the time had also come to record the second volume of *A Nation Sings* at the Royal Albert Hall. Although this event was still a considerable administrative undertaking, we were confident that the great hall would be filled to capacity on the day of recording. We had been besieged by people asking for tickets, and I had been informed that every Welshman living in or near London would be there to join the vast number arriving in coaches from every part of Wales. This time I suffered no haunting fear of there being an empty house. In fact, nearly every famous Welsh actor, singer and politician who could be free on that night had promised to join in.

The event proved once again to be memorable and moving, although it seemed to lack some of the magic of the first *Gymanfa*, even though the singing was of a finer quality than that of the first occasion (although this was probably because my adrenalin wasn't flowing quite so fast!). Again, Allen performed his difficult technical task in his lair under the stage with consummate skill and calmness. I never worried when he was at the control console, for I knew that, short of an earthquake or some other natural disaster, I could rely on him to deal with almost any unexpected eventuality. On this occasion, to my great relief, everything once again went smoothly.

Because of these and future large-scale undertakings, I had to increase my staff. As well as Ronnie Young, Mr Kaye, Mr Lennox, Mabel Tobin and Matti Prichard, I had also engaged a new young secretarial assistant, Susan Caplin. I remember so well the day that she came for her interview, when Ronnie and I talked to her together. She was a lovely girl, and I was drawn to her immediately. I had some fear that she might be too highly strung for this hectic job, working for a company that seemed to be nearly always in a state of nervous tension, but she was obviously fascinated, in spite of this warning. It was difficult to explain what her duties would be, except that she would be mainly concerned with making herself useful to me in every way possible. I told her that I would like to consider the matter further, and after she left I voiced my fears to Ronnie that she might not be strong enough to cope with the job. He felt that I should give her a try, and in doing so I made one of the happiest decisions of my life, for she turned out to be both efficient and enthusiastic, and because we were such a small organisation her charm and easy manner were invaluable.

When I asked her in later years why she had been so determined to join Delysé, she replied that it was because her parents had told her that she would never hold down a job! They were quite wrong in this, though, because, in spite of the fact that she had no musical knowledge, her natural common sense and shrewd intelligence proved to be an asset through many of the hair-raising experiences that followed.

The recording of *Des Knaben Wunderhorn* was now upon us. This was my first venture into a symphonic work, and it would bring Delysé into direct competition with the major record companies. Both EMI and Decca had been very helpful to me in the distribution of my records, and up until this time they had been happy to handle my catalogues, which were largely concerned with regional repertoire and recordings for children. Now, though, I was entering into their own field of activity, although in choosing Mahler – who at that time was a composer still largely absent from most major catalogues – I hoped to avoid direct confrontation. If my recording was a success, it would prove an asset for them and it would benefit them to issue it – under licence, internationally – on their own labels. In the United Kingdom, of course, *Des Knaben Wunderhorn* would be released on the Delysé label. It was a bold venture but a calculated risk.

Now, though, I had to put these worries behind me and concentrate entirely on producing a great recording, which was scheduled to take place on 28-9 March 1966. The ingredients of success were all there: a musical work as yet practically unknown to the general public; great artists; and the finest available engineering, under Allen Stagg's control. Wyn had returned from New York on 14 March, and I had arranged with both Geraint and Janet to start rehearsals two days later. For these events, I had engaged the services of Nina Walker, the principal coach at Covent Garden, to act as accompanist and to be present at the sessions at Watford Town Hall. Geraint and Janet were happy to fall in with my rehearsal plans, and I must say they worked well with Wyn on these occasions.

In spite of the fact that Geraint had been unable to rehearse with Wyn while they were both in New York, he had obviously worked hard on the music himself, and for this I was grateful, for the type of orchestral lieder-singing that Mahler demanded was new to him, and very difficult, not only musically but also in the correct pronunciation of the German text. For Janet, too, this was a new experience, but with her exceptional musical intelligence and her beautiful voice, which was so well suited to Mahler's music, I knew that I had little to fear.

Without the rehearsals, we could never have completed the recording in the four sessions for which I had budgeted. This was a calculated risk, based on my belief in Wyn's deep sympathy with Mahler's music and the extraordinary way in which he had achieved such a magnificent performance with the Royal Philharmonic Orchestra. I felt complete confidence in his capacity to inspire the London Philharmonic in the same way.

As we rehearsed in my flat, the atmosphere was most cordial, and indeed we all enjoyed the serious music study. Geraint was in splendid form, and seemed to sense that the delightful songs were well suited to both his dramatic talent and his voice. Janet, with her intense capacity for serious study, worked with utter concentration, and she, Wyn and Geraint got along well together, as far as I could judge. Nina Walker was a great help to me, for she was an experienced *répétitrice*, and well known to them all. She also had a keen sense of humour, which, together with Geraint's clowning, kept the atmosphere free from any tensions which might have arisen.

After the company departed at the end of the last rehearsal, Geraint stayed behind for a quick chat. He was in splendid form, and amused me vastly by giving demonstrations of his dramatic handling of certain parts. He was a natural actor, as we well knew from his magnificent portrayals of Falstaff and Iago in the past, and I asked him if he had ever considered appearing on the straight stage, to which he replied that, when he felt that his voice was beginning to age, he might do just that. We then became involved in discussing the terrible character of Shakespeare's Iago, and Geraint proceeded to give me an unforgettable impromptu demonstration of how he would act the part in *Othello*.

The first session was due to begin on Monday 28 March at 2pm. I was terribly excited and nervous, but I knew that I had to hide this from the artists. I arrived at Watford Town Hall some hours before the start of the sessions accompanied by my team, which consisted of Mabel Tobin, Sue Caplin and Ronnie Young. Allen had been there with his boys since early that morning, setting up the equipment in the control room and the microphones over the orchestra. As always, it was a tremendous relief to find him there, apparently calm and in excellent humour. He assured me that all was well in the hall, without any unexpected difficulties, such as noisy repair work or drilling out in the street – at least so far. This was a relief, as I knew only too well how strange things could happen unexpectedly when recording on location.

The members of the LPO straggled in, exchanging jokes with each other and with Allen, and gradually their pleasant, casual behaviour made me feel quite calm and able to receive them in a manner which I hoped indicated that I was quite accustomed to producing large orchestral recordings!

At two o'clock on the dot, I asked Wyn to begin the rehearsal while Allen and I worked together to fine-tune the orchestral balance in the

L-r: David Hughes (tenor), Isabella, Allen Stagg and Matti Prichard, 1962

L-r: Dr Terry James, Allen Stagg and Isabella discussing a musical matter at the Royal Albert Hall

Setting up the equipment at the *Gymfana Ganu* with Allen Stagg and the boys, 1963

Introducing Allen Stagg on stage at the Royal Albert Hall for the *Gymfana Ganu* hymn-singing festival, 1963

The 6,000 people who attended the *Gymfana Ganu* at the Royal Albert Hall in 1963

Delysé's first big hit, the recording of the TWW show *The Land Of Song* with Ivor Emmanuel and the Children's Choir

Allen Stagg and Isabella listening to a playback in the control room at IBC Studios

In Richard Martell's dressing room in Brussels, 1968. L-r: Mausi Wagner, Richard Martell, Isabella and Wyn Morris

Wyn Morris slipping into rehearsals, Christmas 1970

Isabella holding the sleeve to the recording of the Prince of Wales's investiture

At the recording session for *Des Knaben Wunderhorn* at Watford Town Hall, 28/29 May 1966. Middle (l-r): Ronnie Young, Janet Baker, Geraint Evans and Mabel Tobin. Front (l-r): Wyn Morris and Isabella

Isabella and Michael Gray in the
control room during the recording of
Mahler's eighth symphony, 1972

Wyn Morris (standing) and Michael
Gray (seated) in consultation during the
recording of Mahler's eighth symphony
at Walthamstow Town Hall, 1972

Lord Louis Mountbatten adjusts
Isabella's microphone at the press
reception at the Imperial War
Museum, 1970

Wyn Morris conducting Mahler's
second symphony at EMI studio
one, 1979

Wyn Morris during rehearsal sessions at St Jude's Church, Hampstead, in 1979

At the control room in St Jude's Church, Hampstead, 1979. Around desk (l-r): Allen Stagg, Wyn Morris, Isabella and Mausi Wagner

The concert of Mahler's ninth symphony at the Royal Festival Hall, 1979

Wyn Morris and Charles Rosen during the recording of Beethoven's second and fourth piano concerti at EMI Studios, 1977

Isabella (l) in her sitting room in Paris, where these memoirs were written, 1999

Isabella (second l) with (l-r) youngest grandson, Philip Corbett; daughter-in-law, Jeannie; and youngest son, Roguey; accompanied by Fahré

Isabella relaxing in her Paris garden, 1999

control room. Once we'd arrived at an acceptable sound, we asked Wyn to listen and give us his opinion. When we were satisfied, we asked Janet and Geraint to sing into their microphones so that Allen could work on mixing the voices with the orchestra. All of these trial takes were numbered. Mabel marked the continuity sheets as she sat beside me, and noted every remark about each take against the bar numbers. In this way, we knew exactly what had to be done later in case of an emergency cropping up while the sessions were edited at IBC.

The twelve folk songs presented under the title *Des Knaben Wunderhorn* are based on the German folk verse collected by Arnim and Brentano, and Mahler set them to the most beautiful music. It was amazing how Wyn captured the atmosphere of these traditional peasant tales, handed down through the centuries, and how he seemed to breathe this atmosphere of folk legend into the songs, some of which depicted spectral armies and other, more humorous characters. This had to be understood and communicated to the orchestra, who were playing this music for the first time and drawing complete absorption of the text and the music from Janet and Geraint. Wyn succeeded in this admirably. It was a *tour de force* on his part, and the way in which he, Geraint and Janet conveyed the atmosphere of this wonderful composition was quite amazing.

From my position in the control room, the sessions seemed to be progressing absolutely as I had planned and hoped. As Allen had predicted, the acoustics in Watford Town Hall gave us the free, almost-out-of-the-door sound that the music required. The orchestra played as if inspired, and the soloists were obviously happy with the beautiful songs, which suited them so well. As we worked on the tapes during the next few days, we were thrilled by the beauty of the performance and the sound that we had recorded. There was little in the way of editing to be done, and we concentrated almost entirely on the spacing of the songs. Allen Stagg was a martinet when involved in the production of a perfect master. I never ceased to be amazed by the care with which he performed this meticulous work.

I sent the masters to Decca for processing, and as soon as I received white-label samples I forwarded some of these to the principal critics, such as those who wrote for *Gramophone*. Most importantly of all, I walked around the corner to the EMI headquarters in Manchester Square and left a copy for David Bicknell marked "Urgent", and asked for it to be left in his office.

I had no idea what an extraordinary effect this would have. At that very time, the EMI international A&R conference had convened to hear the two classical producers David Bicknell and Walter Legge presenting their projected schedule of recordings for that year. David, who had been my uncle's favourite assistant, walked into his office having decided to take a breather from the conference and found my note and the sample record waiting for him. He later told me that he had burst out laughing, for the conference had been largely concerned with Walter Legge's desire to obtain authorisation to record *Des Knaben Wunderhorn* with Elisabeth Schwarzkopf, Dietrich Fischer-Dieskau and the Cleveland Symphony Orchestra, conducted by Georg Szell. He told me that he walked back into the conference room and threw my white label promo onto the table and said, "You'd better listen to this version of *Des Knaben Wunderhorn* before you decide if you want to proceed with ours." Apparently, dead silence fell on the conference, and Walter was furious. I don't blame him!

What an extraordinary series of events! It had been EMI's decision to record *Elijah* which had forced me to cancel our plans to record that work in the previous year, and now the same thing was happening again, only now the shoe was on the other foot. In all fairness to the A&R board and to Walter Legge, after listening to the Delysé recording they agreed to postpone the version that they were considering, and to my great relief they decided to license and distribute my recording for international release on their prestigious Angel label. It was certainly a moment of great triumph for Wyn Morris, Allen Stagg and me.

There was a final sequence to this rather strange series of events some 18 months later, when Walter Legge approached Allen – who by then had left IBC to become manager of EMI Studios – and begged him to engineer his version of *Des Knaben Wunderhorn*, which he was just about to produce for EMI. In spite of considerable pressure, Allen refused, much to Walter's disappointment, and when asked for a reason Allen answered enigmatically, yet with great diplomacy, "I never compete with myself."

When I heard the finished master of *Des Knaben Wunderhorn* for the first time, I felt a thrill of creative satisfaction. The production seemed to have all of the necessary ingredients for a memorable recording. The chosen artists suited the repertoire perfectly, and all three – Wyn, Janet and Geraint – had given magnificent performances of this strange and unique music, engineered in virtuoso style by Allen Stagg. There was no doubt in my mind that it was an inspired recording, and indeed the critics agreed. The success of my first major recording meant a great deal to me, possibly because it was the realisation of a childhood dream I'd had when I was privileged enough to follow my Uncle Fred from the concert hall to the studios and hear the great orchestras and artists with whom he was working. Many other recordings of great importance followed, but *Des Knaben Wunderhorn* was the jewel in my crown. I remember thinking at the time that it could not be bettered, either artistically or technically, and that, if I never made another, I could retire happily. To our great relief and joy, the critics in the UK, the US and Europe praised the recording to a degree that really astonished us. In fact, I have rarely seen such reviews as those that we received not only for the initial Delysé release but also for the international reissues. The seriousness with which the critics regarded our efforts gave us immense satisfaction and confidence in the future.

Perhaps because of the unforgettable relief I felt in our success, I may be forgiven for quoting a few excerpts from some of the reviews. *Gramophone* published the following:

> How wonderfully well this 1965 Delysé recording of *Des Knaben Wunderhorn* comes up, both technically and musically. It was well thought of in its day, but this latest reissue struck me with the force of revelation. Twenty-eight years on, the sheer commitment of the music-making – fearless, imaginative identification ever the father of true insight – is very apparent; that and the living, still-breathing spontaneity of it all. For once, I wasn't tempted to return to Szell's famous 1968 EMI recording for succour and renewal…Wyn Morris's accompaniments are splendidly vital and distinct, the more so as Allen Stagg's vividly-transferred original recording has a quite exceptional clarity and stereophonic immediacy; orchestra and voices both properly forward within a clear, open acoustic…

Meanwhile, *Records And Recording* printed the following:

> If the recent glut of Mahler performances in our concert halls indicates how completely the British public has succumbed to the spell of this strange figure after decades of neglect and downright

hostility, it still seems remarkable to find an important new Mahler recording emerging from Watford Town Hall through the efforts of one of our smaller companies, using British singers, a British orchestra and a British conductor. And this is an important issue, for, whatever one's feelings towards these gargantuan symphonic edifices, there can be little doubt that the quintessence of Mahler's genius is to be found in his orchestral songs...Throughout, Mahler's orchestral mastery provides unending delights, and Delysé were fortunate to find in Wyn Morris a conductor who clearly revels in the vivid and subtle colours of the scoring and is able to shape each song in thoroughly convincing fashion...All in all, then, this is a splendid issue – one, moreover, which can be recommended even to those who do not particularly relish Mahler's large-scale compositions...

The 13 January 1983 edition of the French publication *Telerama* featured the following review: "Here returned to us are two of the most wonderful Mahlerian recordings ever heard. What has become of Wyn Morris, that conductor born in 1929, celebrated – even if not in this country – for his interpretations of Mahler and Bruckner?...Wyn Morris was one of the few able to express the strange Mahlerian universe: the terrible violence, plunging us into the ecstasy which follows."

Meanwhile, Roguey celebrated his 21st birthday on 8 February. By this time he was in his final year at Oxford, but we decided to organise his party at home. He had hired a coach to drive him and his friends to London, where all of the arrangements for the festivities were laid on, including the hiring of a small group of musicians to play dance music and the preparing of masses of food and drink. He arrived with about 20 of his friends in a very happy state, for he had installed a small bar in the coach. Amongst his friends was a very attractive girl by the name of Jean Collar, a fellow student, who was to become my daughter-in-law in the not-too-distant future. It gave me such pleasure to see so many young people enjoying themselves, but I'm afraid that my neighbours in the building must have suffered greatly, as the party went on all through the night. It was a relief to know that they were being driven safely back to Oxford in the coach, for a considerable amount of champagne had been consumed. So that they wouldn't feel the pangs of hunger at dawn, Ronnie had prepared a Cornish pasty for each guest with his own hands, and every one of them had to be eaten on the way in lieu of breakfast.

I had known for some time that Pompy was considering emigrating to America, and that he was in correspondence with an agent who put British scientists in contact with interested employers in the States. When he told me that he'd been offered a position with the General Electric company in Philadelphia, and that he was seriously considering it, I knew that I couldn't stand in his way but should instead encourage him to make the right decision. He was keen to work in the aircraft industry, but because of the uncertain economic situation in Britain during the years after the war there seemed to be little activity in this field of employment. Neither did the job at GE have much to do with actual aircraft; he would be working on defence systems, sponsored by the US government.

The truth was that Pompy wanted to make a complete change in his life and move on to pastures new, and I could only wish him well and give him every encouragement. My parents were very upset at the thought of him leaving England, but I reminded them that every generation of our family had seemed to do the same thing, and so on 28 January 1968 I accompanied him to Heathrow to see him off to Philadelphia. It was a great wrench for both of us, as we'd been very close and shared many experiences, some happy and some tragic. It wasn't an easy decision for him, as he loved his home, his red Élan sports car and dear old *Maggie*, but he felt that it was the right one. He went off bravely and tackled the problems of a new job in a new country, and also learned how to look after himself. Luckily, we had family in America, which was some consolation to me, as I was sure that they would be a help to him during the first difficult months.

As things turned out, I needn't have been so concerned, for Pompy's decision to go to America indeed proved to be the right one. In May, I was obliged to attend meetings in New York to discuss the American release of *Des Knaben Wunderhorn* and *Das Klagende Lied* with Bob Myers, who managed the Angel label in America. The trip was very successful for both Bob and John Coveney, EMI's artists manager in America, who made much of me and spoiled me delightfully.

While I was there, Pompy came to meet me in New York. He was in good spirits, although I sensed that he was concealing something important from me. On this occasion, however, he told me nothing of his plans, and

I didn't press him, but when he came over to London on a flying visit in September he revealed that he was engaged to marry Shirley, a beautiful girl with whom he knew he would be comfortable, for she was the daughter of Dan Hinger, the principal timpanist of the Philadelphia Symphony Orchestra, and according to Pompy her family was very similar to ours. When I did finally meet her, just before the wedding in October, I was relieved, for she was indeed delightful in every way.

In the early spring of 1967, I was involved in a heavy schedule of work, for not only was I about to embark on my second major symphonic recording but I was also releasing more material for the children's catalogue, which continued to be successful. My list of well-known stories told by famous personalities had been growing apace, each of which had to be produced, engineered and presented to our distributors, EMI and Decca, for marketing purposes. Thankfully, my faithful staff proved to be highly competent, and lifted a lot of this work from my shoulders.

The great success of *Des Knaben Wunderhorn* encouraged me to embark on a second large recording. Once again, I asked Wyn Morris – who had considerable knowledge of Mahler – if he could suggest another work by that still little-known composer. This would give us the initial advantage of breaking the ice, by presenting the public with something new and the critics with the opportunity of writing about a relatively unknown work. Wyn responded immediately by suggesting *Das Klagende Lied*, which Mahler had written when he was only 21 years old and which would follow on well from our recording of *Des Knaben Wunderhorn*.

Once again, this work revealed Mahler's fascination with folklore. The poems that he used in this work he wrote himself, and these formed the basis of the text, which told the tale of two brothers who entered a forest to seek a flower which would reward the finder by the providing him with a queen as a bride. The younger brother found the flower and the elder murdered him while he slept. According to the legend, a minstrel happened onto the scene and fashioned a flute from the rib bone of the unfortunate younger man. When the minstrel played the bone flute, he recounted the sinister tale as a lament. It's a wild story, encompassing the search for a queen, a castle wedding and other mediaeval adventures. Mahler originally planned the work in three parts, but eventually dropped the first part and published the full score in two parts, which Wyn was now suggesting as the follow-up to *Des Knaben Wunderhorn*.

It was quite an undertaking, for the work is scored for full symphony orchestra, choir, soprano, mezzo-soprano and tenor soloists. After studying the score carefully, and after much discussion, I decided that I was justified in giving the recording the green light, and the arduous task of choosing the artists and setting up the sessions began. Wyn, of course, was engaged as conductor, and we then had to find artists experienced in both German opera and lieder repertoire, for Mahler demanded that his singers were practised in both styles. It wasn't going to be easy, for most of the artists able to cope with the difficult music were busy performing all over the world. Fortunately, however, luck favoured us in the form of the tenor Andor Kaposy, who at that time had been singing in Düsseldorf. I flew over to listen to him, and although I can't remember which opera I heard I was obviously sufficiently impressed to engage him on the spot to come to London for the rehearsals and recording sessions on 1 and 2 April 1967.

We had heard much of Anna Reynolds, whose beautiful mezzo voice was beginning to be known throughout the world. Unlike most British singers, her career had begun abroad. She was already famous in Italy, where she had appeared in leading roles in the Rome Opera before being engaged to sing at the Metropolitan in New York and in the great European opera houses, including Covent Garden and Glyndebourne. She would be ideal for the role, if only she were available and interested enough to learn the difficult score. Luckily, Anna, who was a fine musician, was free on the session dates, and was also very generous in the time that she gave for rehearsals.

We then had to find a soprano, and in this too we were fortunate, for Teresa Zylis-Gara was free. At that time she was singing at the Metropolitan, performing roles which indicated that her voice was suitable for our requirements. On the strong recommendation of Basil Horsfield, who was both her agent and a good friend, as well as a man whose judgement I trusted, I decided to engage her as the solo soprano. We were very lucky, for she was a fine artist, and her voice had just the quality that we needed.

After this, all that we had to do was hire an orchestra – this time my old friends from Philharmonia, who were now renamed the New Philharmonia – and to arrange for John McCarthy to organise professional singers for the chorus. Allen Stagg had been informed of every step in our preparations, since we had to be prepared for the extremely complicated aspects of these recording sessions. He was present at all of the rehearsals, especially those that dealt with the chorus, but also those involving the soloists, which were held in my flat. For one rehearsal, however, Wyn and I flew to Düsseldorf very early one morning to rehearse with Kaposy at noon, catching a plane back to London in time for an evening of work with the two ladies.

We were lucky that we were able to have so many rehearsals with the singers, for again Wyn was faced with conducting a very difficult work of which the orchestra had no previous knowledge. He seemed to share some deep affinity with Mahler, and his mastery of the score was quite extraordinary. He was able to intertwine the orchestra, singers, and chorus with complete assurance, which was essential in such a complicated work.

Allen's task, too, was far from easy, as he had to balance the voices in such a way that the listener would be able to imagine the position of the voices in relation to each other and the text. Mahler didn't help us in achieving this separation, for he uses the two female voices as a sort of commentary, interweaving vocal lines with the chorus to achieve a kind of Greek chorus effect in song, while the tenor plays the part of the *spielmann* (minstrel). There is also an outside band, composed of a group of brass players, who have to sound as if playing "from the interior of the castle during the ill-fated wedding feast". Allen achieved this by positioning this group of musicians behind the conductor, as far away as was possible in the hall. In this way, we achieved a naturally distant sound which we couldn't have achieved if we had recorded them separately in the studios and mixed them artificially. Nina Walker acted as second conductor for this, as Wyn had his back to the "distant" band during this part of the sessions. It wasn't easy, but it worked extremely well. I later had to attempt this sort of effect in future Mahler recordings, and I grew to understand the difficulties only too well.

The sessions of *Das Klagende Lied* were remarkably successful. The artists worked together splendidly and happily, and there were no perilous moments whatsoever. I was delighted with the way in which the New Philharmonia – many of the members of which I knew from our adventures across Europe with von Karajan – responded to Wyn. Wyn is at his best when recording. I think that he enjoys the intimacy of working under those conditions with other musicians, and thus creates a relaxed atmosphere. We were delighted when we hurried the takes back to the studios to began the painstaking work of producing a master. When the test pressing came back from the factory, we felt that once again we had achieved an outstanding recording.

There was considerable anticipation in the air before the release of this latest Delysé recording, because, as *Das Klagende Lied* was relatively unknown, it was awaited with interest by both critics and Mahler enthusiasts. We needn't have feared any adverse criticism, however, for the reviews were without exception both appreciative and enthusiastic. Their approval gave me immense pleasure, for I believed the work to be very beautiful and an outstanding achievement for such a young composer. The fact that we had made such a successful recording was reward in itself, and we were soon delighted by the warmth of the reviews. We can surely be forgiven for feeling triumphant when such a highly respected critic as Christopher Breunig wrote in a 1967 edition of *The Audio Record Review*, "The test pressings of *Das Klagende Lied* arrived with no fewer than 28 pages of draft notes by Jack Diether…I have never read anything which excited me so much to hear…The recording was made last April [and] is beautifully sung, and Wyn Morris has secured a striking cohesion and power, welding everything together and getting drama from forces who can hardly be over-familiar with the score. The stereo recording is very well balanced, with soloists, orchestra and choir properly related in space…A strongly recommended record."

This was only one of the many laudatory reviews, and when the Bruckner-Mahler Society awarded Wyn with the Mahler Medal of Honour in recognition of his exceptional recordings and performances of the composer's works, our delight knew no bounds. It was indeed a triumph for a young and small company to achieve such a success with its first two major recordings. The team was very proud.

15 Bayreuth And Brussels

By the end of 1968, both boys had married, and so it was time to take stock of my position and, for the first time, to make decisions which affected only myself. I had already been compelled to move the office from Marylebone Road, for the Methodists from whom we had rented the building since 1961 wanted it back. For a long time I had been interested in a new, small apartment building on the corner of George Street and Marylebone High Street. As well as being in my favourite area of London, it was also very convenient for all of my musical activities, and I would be able to do without a car, as I could walk to nearly all of my meetings. This would be a necessary economy, for the rent on the flat in Heron Place was high.

I went to visit the building and found that there was still one apartment available on the fifth floor, which had an immensely long living room, with windows at either end as well as halfway down the outer wall, for the room was on a corner. There were two excellent bedrooms, each with their own bathroom, and a very small but well-equipped kitchen. As soon as I walked into the living room, I knew that it was just what I wanted, and I decided there and then to sell my flat in St John's Wood and move into Heron Place. The sitting room was so large that my grand piano fitted in comfortably, as did all of my books, music and equipment, so I would be able to work conveniently and comfortably from home. Needless to say, 11 Heron Place became a popular rendezvous for countless members of the musical world, and also a venue for many publicity parties, when we celebrated our new releases. I made the move on 1 February 1968.

The previous year had been one of great activity and success. Not only had we launched two major recordings, which had both achieved considerable success, but I had continued to build on my Welsh catalogue with a second recording by The Cor Godre Aran, the splendid North Wales choir that had been so successful before. I also continued to add to my children's catalogue, releasing more enchanting stories written and recounted by the wonderful Johnny Morris, as well as other material, including poems by Edward Lear, *Alice In Wonderland*, and *Paddington Bear*, all of which were read by David Davis in his inimitable and quiet way, which children seemed to love. Marjorie Westbury, who was so popular on BBC children's programmes, also contributed to the Delysé catalogue with readings from *Squirrel, Hare And Red Fox*. However, it wasn't long before major companies such as EMI also decided to release children's records, although their ventures into unknown territory didn't prove very successful and soon fizzled out.

I also made many trips to Dublin to record interesting and talented ballad singers for the Envoy label, and also continued to release material by the ever-popular Dermot O'Brien. I paid three visits to Belfast for EMI, where I produced recordings of Veronica Dunne with the Belfast Symphony Orchestra, conducted by the talented and pleasant Havelock Nelson.

The year had certainly been successful, and the marriage of both of my sons also brought much family happiness into our lives. As I lived so near my parents (their flat in Park Street was within a stone's throw of Heron Place), I was able to visit them frequently. It was delightful to walk over there on summer evenings, after a long day, to pass a happy time telling them all about my adventures. My father, who had long since retired from business and was in rather poor health, loved to talk about the financial and marketing aspects of my activities, and often gave me very sensible advice. Their Italian housekeeper, Maria Rosso, had been with them for many years, and was very much a part of the family. She was a splendid cook, and was capable of turning her hand to anything. I can hear her voice now, saying, "I do, I do," when asked for help. How we all missed her when she decided to move back to stay with her family in San Remo after the death of my father in 1971. After this, my mother engaged a Yugoslav to replace Maria, but she could never get on with the girl, whose name was also Maria, although she remained with my mother until her death in 1973. When dear Maria Rosso came to visit me in London a few years later, she told me how deeply she regretted having gone back to Italy before my mother's death.

Mausi Wagner had been popping in and out of my life ever since we first met at the Toscanini rehearsal in 1937, and as 1967 drew to a close she begged me to come to Bielefeldt to be present at the opening night of *Lohengrin*. This was the first time that she had produced a Wagner opera, and was an event of enormous importance to her and to her friends, for we knew that it was the realisation of a deeply-felt ambition. She was also fully aware that it was unlikely that her brother Wolfgang would ever give her this opportunity in Bayreuth. The portals there were tightly closed, and in any case Mausi was *persona non grata* there because of her anti-Nazi activities during the war.

I arrived in Bielefeldt on New Year's Eve for the opening night, and Wyn joined me there, for he was also most anxious to see how her ideas as a producer would finally be realised. Her excitement was quite touching, and her fears that I would somehow be unable to get away from London revealed her loneliness. In a letter dated 10 December, she implores me to arrive on time: "Only trouble now is this: we have a *Hausprobe* at 7.30pm on the 29th, and everybody I know will be in it. I would love to meet you. Can you not come on an earlier plane? It gets awfully foggy around Hanover anyway, and a daytime arrival would be much safer. See what you can do!"

This was just one of many such letters informing me of the progress or otherwise of the rehearsals and the lack of funds, etc. Both Wyn and I arrived from our various destinations on time for the performance to find Mausi in a state of controlled excitement and nervous fear. In spite of the difficulties, we thought that her production was beautiful, imbued with warmth and colour, which suits this opera so well. It was a production which revealed a tender side of Wagner, and I felt that Mausi emphasised this most poignantly. The sets and costumes were simple, tailored in pastel shades, which fitted in with Mausi's overall concept. There was a wonderful after-show party that night, at which many of Mausi's friends were present. As the performance had gone very well, spirits were high and relief was felt by everyone involved, especially Dacre, one of Mausi's pupils from her masterclasses, who had designed and built the beautiful sets.

Mausi and I were true friends as young girls, even though we had come from rather similar backgrounds in nationality and cultural interests, and we had lived through many experiences together, both happy and tragic. Because of the war, Mausi had known Dick only briefly, and when she returned to Europe she found me a young widow with two sons. We had picked up the threads of our friendship with the utmost ease, however, and it was during the course of our long talks at that time that I really began to understand the extent of the unhappiness that she had suffered after her father's death.

Until that time, she had enjoyed a wonderful, magical childhood in Bayreuth. Fêted and spoiled during the weeks of the festival by the world-famous visitors, the four children lived in a musical paradise, and Mausi, her father's favourite, was given the affection and security that she craved. However, this ended suddenly with his death in August 1930, while she was at school at Brighouse, Yorkshire, and she wasn't summoned by her mother in time to be present when the tragic event occurred. It seemed that there was little sympathy between Mausi and her mother, Winifred, who appeared to be bewildered by her daughter's independent character. In 1935, she sent her to the dreaded Heiligengrabe School in Germany. As Mausi told me during our long talks when she visited us in London, from that time on she had virtually decided to leave her family and their home, Wahnfried, where she felt increasingly disenchanted with her mother's growing adulation of Hitler and the all-pervading Nazi influence.

As young girls, we had experienced many wonderfully happy days in London, full of laughter and hard work and great music, when Mausi forgot her troubles and became the happy carefree girl she would have been if her father had lived longer and been able to protect her. She knew that she was in danger in Germany, and in the spring of 1939 she went to Lucerne to stay with her aunts at Triebschen, Wagner's old home and refuge. In 1968, Mausi told me that, on 10 February 1940, there was an encounter with her mother in Zurich, in which Winifred tried to force Mausi to return with her to Germany. It was a terrible meeting, and one in which Winifred warned her daughter that, if she continued to disobey the Führer's commands, she was in danger, even in Switzerland. Mausi refused, and after her mother returned to Germany on the following day she never saw her again until after the war.

In later years, Mausi had been invited to Bayreuth by her brother Wieland, who was running the festival together with Wolfgang, after Winifred had been prevented from resuming artistic control. She returned each year, running her masterclasses there from 1959 to 1967. However, this ended with the premature and tragic death of Wieland. She was utterly unhappy then, and felt completely alienated. Without his protection, she felt that she had to leave Bayreuth in the hope of establishing her masterclasses elsewhere.

The Wagner family situation became impossible in 1970 and 1971, when a great upheaval occurred in their lives. It was finally agreed, after a bitter argument and years spent in endless litigation, to transfer the ownership of the *Festspielhaus*, the Villa Wahnfried and all of the manuscripts and archives of Richard Wagner to the German State. Although very large sums of money were involved, Mausi and her sister Verena opposed the scheme. They wished to retain the family interest in the festival, particularly on behalf of some of the young Wagner generation who, now grown up, might eventually wish to take over proceedings. However, Winifred and her younger son, Wolfgang, forced the issue and the deal was made. Mausi took possession of her share of the money, and for the first time in her life – although much against her will – she had cash to spend.

In spite of her immense generosity, and the fact that she was at last able to live without worrying about her financial position, she was unhappy with the situation. From this time on, the fraught relationships that she had with some of the other members of the family became even worse, and she realised that she had to give up any ideas that she might have had of working in Bayreuth.

The '70s proved to be very adventurous and exciting years for Mausi, for in 1972 she was offered the chance to become artistic director of an arts complex, the brainchild of an arts council in the north-east of England. She was delighted, as she saw in this an opportunity to create a platform for her masterclasses. She became so involved that she bought a large property called Southlands, in the village of Eaglescliff, in which to house the faculty, and a small house in which to live in Norton, near Stockton-On-Tees. *The Friedelind Wagner Masterclasses Scholarship Trust* was published in both America and Europe, and the first class took place in 1976. Unfortunately, the whole scheme proved to be a fiasco and a fearful financial burden to her, as the county boundaries were suddenly altered and the financial support from the council never materialised. The concept was eventually abandoned, and the whole project came to nothing. She was very bitter about this, and it was a terrible disappointment to her.

During her last years, she worked to draw the attention of the music public to the compositions of her father, Siegfried Wagner. She believed that his talent had been overshadowed by the genius of his father, and she wanted to use every means at her disposal to remedy what she considered to be the neglect of his considerable creative output, which comprised both operas and purely orchestral works. In 1975, she launched a campaign to promote Siegfried Wagner's works by organising a concert performance of *Der*

Friedensengel in association with the Pro Opera Group at London's Queen Elizabeth Hall, at which Leslie Head conducted the fine cast, which included such eminent artists as Martha Mödl and Hanne-Lore Kuhse. In 1980, she promoted a performance of *Der Kobold* with the same group, at which several members of the Wagner family were present. It was quite an event in the music world of London, and created much interest. Then, in 1983, Daniel Barenboim included Siegfried Wagner's tone poem *Sehnsucht* in his concerts with the Orchestre de Paris at the Salle Pleyel, and in 1985 I released the recordings that I had produced for Mausi in Aalborg on my Delysé label.

Mausi spoke to me often about her father's industry, and when I looked at the long list of his compositions I marvelled when I realised that he also found time to be a well-known conductor, which entailed much travelling and study, as well as run the Bayreuth Festival. No wonder he died when he was still a comparatively young man. I could see much of her father in the meticulous care and concentration that Mausi displayed when she undertook any task, and also in her impatience with inefficiency. Happily, she also inherited her father's warmth, which made her such a delightful friend. Her character was both resolute and courageous, and she never flinched at doing what she believed was right, even if the price she had to pay was high. Her physical resemblance to both her father and to Richard Wagner was so marked that it never failed to fill me with awe. I didn't intrude too much, but I knew that she was a true friend.

A few days after my return from Germany, I flew to Athens to stay with Fiorella and Frixos Theodorides, where Fiorella was to sing Violetta at the Greek Opera. I was looking forward to seeing her on the stage. She had begun her career in Rome at the age of 18, when at short notice she had replaced one of the stars of the Rome Opera in the role of Violetta in *La Traviata*. In fact, she had no notice at all, for the prima donna in question had been taken ill suddenly only hours before the performance, and there was no one within even flying distance of Rome free to replace her. When Fiorella's singing teacher heard of the situation, he volunteered the services of his brilliant young pupil, and said that he was sure that she would be fully capable of taking over the role. So Fiorella, who had never even walked onto the stage of the opera house, took her place in the demanding opera (after a piano rehearsal, I presume) with her coach and a brief indication of stage positions, and triumphed. She became the toast of Rome, and her future career was assured.

When I first met Fiorella and Frixos in London in 1962, they had already been married for some years. She had met Frixos while she had been performing with La Scala Opera Company in South Africa, singing her role in *La Traviata*. Frixos, who was in the shipping business in Johannesburg, heard her performing and fell deeply in love with her. When they told me this story, I wasn't surprised, for Fiorella was very beautiful and Frixos very handsome, but I was sorry that she had eventually given up her career. During our long and great friendship, we discussed recording Ermanno Wolf-Ferrari's *Il Segreto Di Susanna*, which she knew well and I am sure would perform enchantingly. I laid on arrangements for recording the project, but at the last moment the plans fell through. I never quite understood why, for Fiorella had continued to keep her voice in fine condition. Perhaps Frixos – who was one of the most delightful men I have ever known – was, in his Greek way, afraid that she would become once again too involved in a career. Luckily, I hadn't booked the orchestra, so no harm was done, but it was very disappointing, as it is an attractive and little-recorded work, and one which would have suited Fiorella admirably and fitted well into my catalogue.

None of these disappointments interfered with our friendship, however, and Frixos helped me through many of the difficulties that lay before me. When he transferred his activities to Athens and they left London, I missed them greatly, but I did visit their beautiful home several times. On this particular visit, I was accompanied by Felix Aprahamian, who came with me to hear Fiorella's performance as Violetta. He thought her a fine artist, and gave her a favourable review in *Opera* magazine. Frixos and Fiorella were delightful hosts, and we had a wonderful time as they showed us the glories of Athens. As well as being an eminent critic, Felix is also a charming man, and I think that Fiorella and Frixos much enjoyed his company.

It was a fine performance of *La Traviata*, in which Giacomo Aragal sang the role of Alfredo. Not only did the roles of the cast suit their voices admirably, but also both Fiorella and Aragal looked extremely handsome onstage. I was very much relieved, for Felix had accompanied me to Athens on my recommendation, and I was delighted with the successful outcome.

The early days of 1968 were filled with family activities. Not only did I move into my flat in Heron Place but also Roguey and Jeannie left their home in Hampstead to live in Southampton, where Roguey joined the staff of the university there. This decision suited them well, for Jeannie's family lived there, and they had also been building their own boat in one of the sheds in Moody's Boatyard. I would still escape to dear old *Maggie* as often as possible at weekends, in spite of the fact that my crew had deserted me! I often invited friends to join me on board, which was very pleasant, but when I was alone on the boat it was rather melancholy, for she was full of the memory of happy family times.

Meanwhile, Mausi returned to London on 14 February and stayed at a small hotel in Bentinck Street just around the corner from my flat, which was very convenient for both of us. She was full of projects and plans for her two favourite protégés, the great soprano Hanne-Lorre Kuhse, who for years had been forced to remain in East Germany, and the American tenor Richard Martell, for whom Mausi had worked ceaselessly for many years. I hadn't yet met him, but after seeing the photographs of this handsome and prodigious young man, whom she assured me was a major Wagnerian tenor, I couldn't wait to meet him. I willingly agreed to go to Bayreuth in August, where he would be appearing as Siegmund in *Die Walküre*. Before this event, however, Mausi had plans to visit opera houses all over Europe to see how her production was faring. My diary was filled with different addresses and performance dates, which began in Amsterdam, followed again by Bielefeldt. Mausi's next stop was Berlin, after which she was off to the United States before returning to Bayreuth in time for Richard Martell's debut as Siegmund.

In the midst of the agitation that usually occurred when Mausi was in town, I was also preparing for my next sessions, which were scheduled to take place in the Decca studios. This was a rather dreaded event, for it would mean that, for the first time after many years of working with Allen – who by this time had left IBC to be the manager of the EMI studios at Abbey Road – I would have to accustom myself to the presence of a new engineer. Allen's departure was of course a great tribute to his achievements, and indeed richly deserved, but it meant that he wouldn't be able to accept any outside commitments, which was a real blow. I'm afraid that I rather hoped that he would become bored with his new job, which, although certainly very prestigious, was mostly concerned with administrative work and grappling with politics, which is nearly always a considerable part of working in a huge organisation. However, I had no alternative but to grit my teeth and go to Decca, whose technical reputation was very high. Through my long business relationship with the company, I knew that they would certainly treat me well. In any case, I consoled myself by knowing that I would find a lot of engineers trained by Allen awaiting me there. This was indeed the case, and I was looked after with the utmost consideration.

I had planned to make three recordings in their studios in Hampstead. Although I found it difficult to convince myself that the recordings should have been made in a studio rather than in a cathedral, I greatly admired the skill with which Alec Rossner achieved a sound appropriate to the material. It wasn't his fault that my ear had been so long attuned to a natural sound, as opposed to an artificially-created ambience, and in truth his achievement was considerable. Those involved were the highly skilled and disciplined McCarthy Singers, all of whom were professionals, under the direction of John McCarthy, who was an expert on the specialised religious music I was about to record. The singers he had selected were versed in singing the liturgical repertoire that I had chosen, which was unaccompanied, and so impeccable intonation was therefore of the utmost importance. I was tremendously impressed by John's knowledge and conducting skill, and the result of this effort, *Music For Holy Week*, was so successful that I decided that I would certainly follow it up with music for the other great feast of the Christian year with *Advent To Christmas*.

Walter Legge and Elisabeth Schwarzkopf paid a brief visit to London during the spring of 1968, and Walter invited me to dinner at the Savoy Grill, which he knew to be my favourite restaurant. He was no longer active in the world of music, and I couldn't help thinking how our situations had reversed since my association with Philharmonia. In retrospect, I was very thankful that I hadn't accepted his offer to remain with the orchestra as joint manager with Jane Withers, for not so long after that time Walter had very suddenly terminated his relationship with Philharmonia and virtually removed himself from his job at EMI, and even from England. I felt that it was much better – in spite of all the difficulties and the risks that I had run – to be free to make my own decisions, for better or worse.

I much enjoyed our meeting in the dear old restaurant, so full of happy memories of meals there with Uncle Fred, for the Savoy Grill had always been the favourite rendezvous point of many great artists. Walter was one of my oldest friends, and very much part of my childhood, and I was sad to think that he was no longer active in the career to which he had contributed so much, for he was a man of great talent. I asked him on this occasion if he would consider helping me to build on the Delysé catalogue. He appeared to be quite interested, but nothing came of this suggestion, and indeed I thought at the time that perhaps he wasn't in very good health. I remember, though, that suddenly his old sparkle returned when, on hearing a fire-engine in the distance, he said, "My God, it's getting very late. That must be Elizabeth coming to look for me!" This was one of our last meetings, and I'm happy that we both enjoyed it so much, for Walter didn't live for very much longer afterwards.

Letters from Mausi were falling like snowflakes, for the time was drawing near to make good on my promise to join her in Bayreuth to hear Richard Martell make his debut as Siegmund in *Die Walküre* on 17 August. I must say that her letters filled me with some foreboding, for they were full of vivid descriptions of the intrigues against her and the difficulties she would have to face to obtain tickets, as no one in the management was allowed to give her any. Poor Mausi. It was hard to imagine a brother behaving in this way to his sister, but having seen Wolfgang on previous visits to Bayreuth I understood the situation completely. It was obviously going to be a very exciting visit, when there was so much intrigue and skulduggery going on. I was certainly looking forward to hearing the performance and seeing Mausi again, but I was sure that it was going to be a pretty rough ride in that atmosphere, where one could still feel the sinister aura of Nazism. Although Mausi was anxious that Wyn should also hear Richard perform, he was unfortunately too busy to leave London, so on 16 August I flew alone to Nuremberg, where I was met by Mausi.

We had a delicious lunch in that famous old city, and Mausi warned me of the dramas that lay ahead. The friend who was delegated to obtain the tickets had still not done so, but Mausi seemed confident that she would succeed. I gathered that they would be issued in my name, and that Mausi would literally sneak into the *Festspielhaus* just as the lights dimmed. The plan was that Richard, Mausi and I would all meet for supper after the show at an inn in the country just outside the city, and that in the long interval I should go to Richard's dressing room to confirm the arrangements. This prospect made me rather nervous, as I feared that I might be arrested by one of the severe-looking uniformed guards, who seemed to be hovering everywhere.

However, the first beautiful act passed magnificently. Richard sang extremely well, and acted the part of Siegmund most convincingly, although his handsome looks were of considerable help in this. Leonie Rysanek, who sang the role of Sieglinde, also sang very well, and together they created an inspired performance. I could hardly believe it when Mausi told me that this was the first performance she had attended during the season, and that she was only present now because she was ostensibly there as my guest. However, we were very conscious of the guard who was seated nearby, and we feared that at any moment we might be asked to leave. I was so furious when she told me this that I was certain that, if it did happen, I would stand up in the *Festspielhaus* and make a public demonstration. Luckily, this didn't occur, but I felt very angry indeed.

When the first act was over, Mausi showed me how to find the dressing rooms. I plucked up my courage, hoping that I wouldn't bump into the formidable Wolfgang, and assuming what I hoped was a very relaxed manner I found my way to the long, marble-floored corridor onto which the doors to the dressing rooms opened. Opposite every door sat a "dresser" waiting to be summoned to the artists, and on every door was a label giving the name of the occupant. As I tap-tapped down this elegant corridor, looking vainly for the name of Richard Martell, I thought of dear, shabby old Covent Garden, and wished that we were all safely there.

I finally spotted Richard's name, and addressed the attendant. "Is Herr Martell able to be visited?", I asked

"What name, Madam?"

According to instructions given by Mausi, I answered, "Frau Martell."

At this answer, I saw the first sign of normal human behaviour, when the dresser inquired politely (but with a twinkle), "Which Frau Martell?"

When I told Richard about this, we both burst into fits of laughter, for it seemed that Richard – who is very good-looking indeed – was regularly besieged by a bevy of female admirers. This lightened the atmosphere considerably, and we enjoyed a happy and relaxed supper party after the show. Richard was in good form, for he was pleased that his performance had gone so well, even though he said that he wasn't in top physical condition. However, I've never yet met a singer who is entirely satisfied with the state of his or her health, and this doesn't surprise me, for the demands of nearly all of the great operatic roles are so severe that I always marvel at the way in which a singer can survive the physical and mental strain of a performance.

Mausi had been through a dreadful time during this visit to Bayreuth. The courage that she had shown in the face of the insults to which she had been subjected was amazing. She hadn't been allowed to enter the *Festspielhaus* and had been turned out of the best hotel in the town, and yet she had borne these insults with apparent good humour. She even looked in good physical form, for which I was thankful, for I was concerned that her health might have been impaired by all that she had endured. In her last letter to me from Bayreuth, she had written, "My sister's health is so poor right now that she felt that she wouldn't survive the shock if anybody did anything to me [at the *Festspielhaus*], so I promised to wait until she left." This was outrageous behaviour! And all because Mausi dared to open her mouth and voice her horror at what was going on in Bayreuth. She had become public enemy number one. No wonder I was nervous about joining her there. In the event, however, I forgot all about being afraid, and I wanted to fight everyone. It must have been very hard on Richard, for he was Mausi's protégé. However, at that time he was also standing in for Windgassen's Tristan, and tenors who can sing Wagner roles are few and far between, so the management had to behave itself and treat him with some respect.

As I write these words, I can see a photograph that was taken in the gardens of the *Festspielhaus* during the long interval of this performance, when I had returned from visiting my "husband", Richard Martell, in his dressing room. Mausi and I are both dressed elegantly and looking very pleased with ourselves, with triumphant smiles stretching from ear to ear. To be attached to a Wagner – especially this Wagner, about whom there was so much talk – was like walking through the gardens of Buckingham Palace in the entourage of the Queen. My admiration for Mausi's courage was boundless. She fought nearly every member of her family, except her sister, Verena. It all seems unbelievable, yet on reading Gottfried Wagner's biography (*The Wagner Legacy*, also published by Sanctuary Publishing), this harsh behaviour in the Wagner family is all proved to be true. It was an unforgettable experience, and I'm proud that I stood up for her in public.

A few days after my return to London, I received a letter from Mausi, dated 20 August, in which she thanks me "for having conquered everybody". She also wrote that "Richard is receiving funny looks from brother Wolfgang, and so he will probably soon be sacked, even though he is getting nothing but rave compliments from the *Festspielhaus*." This dreadful behaviour in the Wagner family goes on from generation to generation, and the battle over who will control the festival once Wolfgang has finally given up is raging to this day.

By the beginning of September, it was time again for me to make a recording, which I had long been anticipating. Ever since I had produced *Das Klagende Lied*, I had promised myself the treat of working once again with Anna Reynolds, whom I considered to be not only a fine musician but also the possessor of a wonderful mezzo-soprano voice. She knew how much I admired her, and during the Mahler sessions I had asked her if she would be prepared to record some lieder for me. I suggested that she should consider Mahler's *Lieder Und Gesänge Aus Der Jugendzeit* and Robert Schumann's *Liederkreis*, opus 39. She agreed, and these sessions were scheduled to take place at the Decca studios.

I had long admired Anna as an artist, and when I had finally worked with her during the recording of *Das Klagende Lied* my admiration had grown further. She was famed mainly as an operatic singer, having achieved great success in the major opera houses of Italy and making her Metropolitan debut in New York in a performance of *Das Rheingold*. She was also heard in coast-to-coast broadcasts throughout the USA. Curiously enough, however, her fame in England hadn't matched her international reputation until not long previously, when she had appeared at Covent Garden, Glyndebourne and the Edinburgh Festival. I had long wondered at her late recognition in her own country, and after the wonderful way in which she sang in *Das Klagende Lied* I was determined to persuade her to record for me again. There was no problem in achieving this, for Anna loved singing lieder, and she was beginning to enjoy success with this format.

After a few very pleasant meetings, we chose our repertoire for the planned recording with equal enthusiasm. We both looked forward to the sessions, and it was pleasant to think that we had no orchestra, chorus or other soloists to consider, and that we could therefore take our time. To add to our satisfaction, Geoffrey Parsons was also happy to act as Anna's accompanist. As his services were in constant demand by many great singers, including Victoria de Los Angeles, Elisabeth Schwarzkopf, Nicolai Gedda and Rita Streich, I was indeed fortunate in finding him available. Alec Rossner was again the engineer, and the sessions – which were to be my last recordings in the Decca studios – went smoothly. Alec was a fine and capable engineer, and it is no criticism of his work that I missed Allen Stagg in the control room. I had been used to working with Allen, and he had been part of my team, but I was lucky in my sessions with Decca to have had the help of such a competent and sympathetic colleague as Alec.

The last few months of the year were very busy indeed. The fun part of my work was the actual recording and the meetings at which the choice of artists and repertoire was discussed, which were always fascinating. The rough part was the costing and the search for finance, in which I had to persuade my financial adviser that the project was commercially viable. As well as this, there was also the business of actually selling the records. To succeed in this, we had to invest in promotion, and I had to attend many marketing meetings with our distributors and travel far and wide to meet the dealers in order to persuade them that our labels were really of high enough quality for them to make a huge effort to sell them. I had learned early on in my career that it doesn't matter how wonderful the recording may be; success or failure depends on the point of sale to the public. Of course, the reviews from the critics, the amount of time that a recording receives on air and, most important of all, the amount of exposure that the artists concerned enjoy in performance are also essential factors in the financial success of the product.

The organisation and co-ordination of these aspects of my work was very time-consuming and often exhausting, but I knew full well that our survival depended on how successful I was in carrying out this side of the business. I often thought of Sir Edward Lewis, the chairman of Decca, who had been a good friend to me at the very beginning of Delysé and who had offered to take over the distribution and marketing of my records, thus leaving me free to attend to the artistic production of the catalogues. It had been a tempting offer indeed at the time, and on looking back was one that I should probably have accepted. However, it would have meant losing my independence, and I couldn't accept that. Who knows whether I made the right decision? Life might have been easier, but then I would have been part of a huge organisation. Having seen what sometimes happens in that situation, I think that I made the right choice.

By this time, Mausi was back in Bayreuth, keeping a very low profile. At least, that's how she described it, but knowing Mausi I rather doubted this. Richard Martell was due to pass through London on his way back to the States, and she was most anxious that he, Wyn and I should meet and discuss the possibility of recording Wagner's *Rienzi* in some sort of deal with a television company. Richard was most anxious to sing this role, which I'm sure would have suited him admirably, but alas nothing came of the project. As Wyn had never actually heard Richard perform, we agreed to go to Brussels on 4 December that year, when he would be singing the role of Walter in *Die Meistersinger* there.

On 29 November, I flew over to Athens to hear Fiorella sing in a concert programme. It wasn't easy for me to get away at this time, for I was shortly due to be in Brussels, and of course the month coming up to Christmas is always a hectic time, but I couldn't resist her warm invitation. As always, it was a joy to see Frixos and Fiorella and spend a few hours in their beautiful home. I don't remember very much about the concert, however, and I think that this visit was really an excuse for old friends to see each other again. I returned to London just in time to prepare to leave for Brussels for the performance of *Die Meistersinger*. Mausi had bombarded me with letters from Brussels, where she had been with Richard during the build-up of the production work. It seemed that all had not gone well, for the climate of Brussels at that time of the year didn't suit him, and he had developed a nasty case of bronchitis, which forced him to stand down for the first two performances, which was most unfortunate, both for him and the management. The situation is best described in the following letter from Mausi, dated 5 November:

> The theatre was very upset about his cancellation of the opening night, for the other Stolzing is just not within reach of Richard's stature in either voice, looks or stage presence. All in all, it was not a bad performance. Some of the staging was very good, though the local papers expected the "Meister" to be solemn stuffed shirts, and did not like the producer's having loosened them up. Brother Wolfgang turned up for the dress rehearsal, which Richard did in pantomime, but Wolfgang reassured him that he knows his voice and that it didn't matter. Richard warned me of Wolfgang being backstage, and so I entered by the auditorium, but Eva, Wolfgang's daughter, had the shock of her life when she saw me, and turned to a pillar of salt. Needless to say, she didn't greet me, and I went upstairs to avoid a public spectacle of Wagnerian bad manners.

Having experienced Wagnerian hospitality in Bayreuth back in July, I wasn't surprised by Mausi's letter, but once again I was truly shocked by the uncivilised behaviour of the family, even in a foreign country. I was also very sorry to hear that ill health had forced Richard to miss his first two performances, but Mausi told me that he had fully recovered and was looking forward to his performance on 4 December, at which Wyn and I would be present.

When we arrived, Mausi was delighted to see us. She had been having a pretty difficult time keeping up Richard's spirits, which had been low because of his bronchitis. Nothing is more pathetic than a singer who can't fulfil an engagement, and this staging of *Die Meistersinger* was an important one in Richard's career. Mausi was convinced that he was the ideal von Stolzing, both vocally and physically, and many important people were coming to Brussels to see and hear him perform. It was certainly very bad luck that he had to miss two of his performances, but now we were there to support him and Mausi, and indeed it was a fine performance in every way. The cast was very good, with Helga Dernesch an attractive and vocally excellent Eva; Norman Bailey a very experienced Hans Sachs; and Richard, now restored to good health, was in fine voice again, and his handsome presence helped him create the role of the young lover.

After seeing him in this part, Wyn and I felt that Mausi had been quite right in her estimation that Richard could corner the world market in the role of Walter von Stolzing, for there were very few tenors who could sing this role adequately. I usually felt consumed with nerves when the dreaded moment of the 'Preislied' approaches in the final act, but when Richard began this ultimate test at the end of the long and arduous opera I felt confident that he would surmount the ordeal triumphantly, and indeed he did.

16 The Investiture Of The Prince Of Wales

I have always been moved by the romance and colour of historic English traditions, especially those concerned with the monarchy, so I was gratified to learn that I had been granted sole rights to the recording of the investiture of His Royal Highness the Prince of Wales at Caernarvon Castle on 1 July 1969. My friends felt confident that, if I applied to the Earl Marshal for permission to make a record of the ceremony, this would be granted to me in recognition of the part that Delysé had played in making known Wales's contribution to the musical and literary arts.

The Earl Marshal wrote back to me on 7 January consenting to my request, and it was full speed ahead from that moment. Time was short, for I had committed myself to releasing the recording on the market only six days after the ceremony at Caernarvon. I was told that I was mad to have embarked on such a risky venture, but it represented something about which I felt passionately, and I was determined to carry it through to a successful conclusion. The first thing I did was to approach the BBC, who would actually be recording the ceremony and from whom I would take delivery of the tapes. There were many legal and commercial arrangements to be discussed, but the BBC was wonderfully efficient and co-operative throughout, and I was truly thankful for their help.

During the months that I'd waited for my application to be accepted, I'd attended many meetings with Raymond Ware of Decca, who was to be my main contact during the technical operation, which was to be carried out by his company. I also attended a meeting with Arthur Haddy, their highly respected studio manager, which was vital, for the success of my delicately-timed plan depended on his co-operation. It was arranged that I would take possession of the tapes at Caernarvon Castle on 1 July, the night of the ceremony. I would then drive back through the night to the Decca studios in London, so that the waiting engineers would receive them on the morning of 2 July, and the editing could then begin at once. As it was felt that it was unwise for me to undertake the journey back to London alone, it was also arranged that Mr Lennox should join me in Caernarvon and accompany me on the night drive back to the studios.

The next important matter to be tackled was the design and printing of the sleeve, without which the record couldn't be released. During the previous months, I'd had many meetings with the excellent and enthusiastic printer Claude Day, who was primed to start his operation as soon as we could provide him with the artwork.

The question was, who would design the cover? I wanted it to represent the pomp and circumstance of the subject matter, and I knew that whatever I chose as a design had to conform to the wishes of the establishment. I finally decided to approach Lord Snowdon, whom I knew to be a talented artist as well as a man closely associated with the royal family. He was kindness personified, and took infinite pains to name several artists whom he thought would be suitable. John Piper was his first choice, an artist whom I also greatly admired, but unfortunately he was involved in another project and so didn't have the time to submit designs. The same difficulty applied to other artists that Lord Snowdon suggested.

As time was growing short, I decided to follow the advice of Rodney Dennys, Somerset Herald-of-Arms, with whom I'd already had several meetings, and thus invited Gerald Cobb, MVO, FSA, to design the front cover under his personal supervision. As Mr Dennys had already written the superb sleeve notes, his offer of help was indeed generous, and his assistance didn't end there, for the fees which he and Mr Cobb requested for their beautiful design and artwork were derisory. In fact, you might say that they contributed to the creation of the record cover for practically nothing. I was touched by their kindness, and deeply appreciative, and I kept Lord Snowdon informed of our decisions regarding the design, for his advice had been very helpful. The back-cover notes were in Welsh, and I gratefully left the correction of the printing to Caradog Prichard. I knew that I could rely on him and Matti.

I sometimes wondered if I would ever reach the end of this responsible and delicate undertaking. I longed for the moment when I would finally be seated as a guest on one of the charming little red cushions designed by Lord Snowdon to watch what I knew would be a beautiful and moving ceremony. When I reached this stage, it would be up to the BBC to do all the hard work until the time came for me to take delivery of the tapes.

High on the list of priorities was the letter that I had to write to all of the eminent personalities scheduled to part in the ceremony. I had to formally inform them that I had been granted exclusive rights to issue the recording of the investiture. As the recording was to be issued on one 12" LP, lasting approximately 60 minutes, only a short excerpt of each individual contribution could be included. I was therefore asking their permission to proceed with this, and to donate their part of the performance to the Welsh Council of Social Services. I would like to include here my personal thanks to all those who took part in this memorable event by reproducing the credit list that was printed on the record cover:

The front cover designed by Gerald Cobb, MVO, FSA, Somerset Herald-of-Arms.

The photograph of HRH the Prince of Wales by Godfrey Argent and supplied by Camera Press.

The BBC recording edited by Raymond Ware, by kind permission of the Decca Record Company Ltd.

The following artists took part in the ceremony. They have kindly agreed to donate their services should any part of their performance be included in this recording:

SOLOISTS
John Rhys Evans
Margaret Price
Marjorie Thomas
Rowland Jones
Delme Bryn Jones
Geraint Evans
Helen Watts
Gwyneth Jones

CONDUCTORS
Roy Bohana
Arwel Hughes
Wyn Morris

Ann Howells

Trevor Anthony
Stuart Burrows
Kenneth Bowen
Elizabeth Vaughen
Patricia Ern
Rhyland Davis
Maureen Guy
The Investiture Choir
Cor Godre Aran
The BBC Welsh Orchestra
Kneller Hall Trumpeters
State Trumpeters of the Household Cavalry

COMMENTATORS
Richard Baker
Emlyn Williams
Cliff Michelmore
Raymond Baxter
Alun Williams

Directed by Isabella Wallich

During the weeks leading up to the ceremony on 1 July, I must have rarely been in the office, for I was frequently in Cardiff discussing matters relating to the ceremony and also visiting the record dealers, hoping to gain their co-operation in the selling of the records. I couldn't neglect to do this throughout the major cities, where, in order to gain the support of organisations such as WH Smith, I had to assure them that the record would be on sale on 5 July. However, these activities took time and were very tiring, and so I was thankful to leave the normal office routine in the capable hands of Mabel Tobin and Sue Ronson. I had complete confidence in both Mr Kaye and Mr Lennox, and was sure that the accounting and dispatch of goods would be in perfect order. I really don't know how I could have managed without the efficient help of these faithful friends.

As in all matters relating in any way with the royal family, the announcement that I'd been granted rights to record the investiture brought the press out like bees around a honey pot. I was constantly giving interviews, both in London and in Cardiff, and I must say that the press was very generous in the amount of coverage they gave me, which, although very time consuming, did me no harm at all, and certainly helped with the promotion of the Delysé catalogue.

At last, on 28 June, the day approached. I left for Caernarvon by car, breaking up the journey at Cardiff, where the National Eisteddfod was held that year and where I must have had a Delysé stand on the field, with Matti in charge. I spent two days there, and then drove north-west to Caernarvon, where I arrived late in the afternoon of 30 June, the eve of the ceremony. The town was teeming with thousands of visitors. After depositing my luggage at the Golden Lion, which I could see at a glance was the social centre of all activity, I set out to find the BBC headquarters, where the engineers were setting up vast arrays of equipment for both radio and television transmissions. To my relief, they were expecting me, and kindly reassured me that everything was going to plan. I knew that they were highly experienced in covering these great events, but I wanted to be sure that they hadn't forgotten about me in the excitement. How thankful I was that I wasn't in control of those momentous sessions.

I returned to the Golden Lion to find many of my friends gathered there, and I spent a delightful evening gossiping and exchanging news. The faithful Mr Lennox was due to arrive the following morning and help me collect the tapes after the ceremony and drive back with me to London through the night.

Unusually for Wales, where it nearly always rains, especially on important occasions, 1 July was a beautiful day. The sun shone on the vast gathering of people, and the weather stayed fine throughout the ceremony, which wasn't due to begin until 2.30pm. I was summoned to take my place almost two hours before this, yet I didn't mind the long wait for the surroundings in the magnificent old castle were beautiful and the excitement so intense that there was always something to watch. I had many friends there, too, who came to spend a few minutes to chat and exchange news while I was seated on my little red cushion, designed by Lord Snowdon and given to guest. For a few hours, my shoulders were free from responsibility, and I prayed that all would go well.

In the event, the ceremony was not only visually beautiful but also intensely moving. The atmosphere created by the Queen and the Prince was one of devotion, as they moved in an almost mystical way through the intricacies of the ancient traditions. The Queen looked wonderful in a short yellow silk coat and little cap of the same colour, shaped in a mediaeval design, a charming outfit that I believe had been designed by Lord Snowdon. The touchingly young and handsome prince, meanwhile, conducted himself throughout the difficult ritual with elegance and assurance, which I thought remarkable, since this was the first occasion in which he had ever featured as the central figure. My admiration swelled even further when, after Sir Ben Bowen Thomas had read the homage and the royal address from the people of Wales in Welsh, the Prince replied in the same language. This was a considerable achievement, for Welsh is a difficult language, as I knew from long experience.

The most moving part of the investiture, however, was the presentation by the Queen of her son to the people of Wales. First they proceeded to Queen Eleanor's Gate, and then to the King's Gate and the lower ward of the castle, where the Prince bowed to the people as they voiced their acclamation. The presentations were supported by the magnificent fanfare composed by Sir Arthur Bliss, Master of the Queen's Music, and played by the trumpeters of the Royal Military School of Music. Bliss had written ceremonial music of the highest order for the processional atmosphere required in the presentations, and he had also written the antiphonal music played during the departure of the Queen and the Prince, which was very impressive and just right to accompany the farewell epilogue spoken by Emlyn Williams, which created a fitting end to this wonderful and unforgettable ceremony.

When it was all over, I made my way through the crowds to the Golden Lion to seek refreshment, for which I felt considerable need, and found Mr Lennox awaiting me as planned, standing in the entrance of the hotel. We greeted each other with considerable relief, for a most responsible and tiring task lay before us.

That night, a great dinner was laid on at the Golden Lion for all of those artists and distinguished persons who had contributed to the ceremony. I had received a most beautifully printed invitation for this event, but unfortunately I was unable to attend as I was waiting to be summoned by the BBC engineers to take delivery of the tapes, so Mr Lennox and I sat rather sadly in a small room, eating a hasty meal while the sounds of junketing came from the dining room of the hotel. Our summons came at around 8.30pm, and we drove immediately to the headquarters of the BBC, where the tapes of the entire ceremony were waiting for us, amounting to about 40 in all, comprising both television and audio versions. These were packed into my faithful Armstrong, and at about 10pm Mr Lennox and I set off through the night on our journey to the waiting engineers at the Decca studios in London.

We were received with great cheers and congratulations and cups of lovely hot coffee and fresh rolls, which we both needed badly. The huge reels of tapes were handed over to Raymond Ware, who had been a faithful friend throughout the negotiations with Decca leading up to this day, and he took over the editing responsibilities. After a brief rest at home, I returned to the studios to help them in the mammoth job of completing the miles of editing that had to be done before the master could be delivered to the factory. Raymond and his team successfully accomplished this task with amazing and unprecedented speed, and the masters were received at the factory on 4 July, while pressing was completed on the following day and the discs were inserted in the sleeves.

A monumental task had been completed. Decca had placed their whole factory at the disposal of Delysé, and my gratitude knew no bounds. The release was announced at a press conference at the Savoy Hotel on 7 July. The story received enormous coverage, and the media treated us handsomely on this occasion. Matti Prichard, who had worked very hard to publicise the undertaking, was delighted with the success with which her efforts were crowned. I've never heard of anyone who could compare with her in the field of public relations. The Prince of Wales graciously accepted a presentation of the record, and I received a charming letter of thanks and appreciation in return.

When the excitement was over, I asked myself whether it had been worth the great investment of effort. The answer is, of course, yes, for it satisfied a heartfelt desire within me to express the respect and admiration that I felt for the monarchy, and the beauty of the ancient pageantry was as appealing to me as a fine musical composition. It's wonderful when one's efforts are appreciated, and I was delighted when one of the musical critics summed up his review by describing the recording as "the greatest royal record ever made".

17 Pye And Lord Mountbatten

During the excitement of the hectic weeks leading up to the recording of the investiture, I'd been approached by several members of Pye Records, who wanted to judge my reaction to a business proposition. Finally, at a meeting with the managing director, Louis Benjamin, I decided to accept their invitation to work for them as a producer, on the condition that they waited until after the investiture release to conclude the deal.

This was a difficult decision to make, as I'd been closely associated with Decca ever since my early days in the industry, and some years previously I'd actually refused a similar offer from their chairman, Sir Edward Lewis, who wanted to unite our catalogues. This also applied to my relationship with EMI, who had successfully handled my distribution both in the UK and abroad. I accepted Pye's offer because their classical catalogue needed my services as a producer, which gave me the opportunity to undertake the work I really enjoyed without being burdened by excessive administration. I would also have the benefit of financial support, as the production charges would be shared and office costs and expenses would be much reduced. I had made up my mind about this just before the investiture ceremony, and a contract was signed between Delysé and Pye to be effective from 1 October 1969 until 27 September 1971.

On 27 September 1969, I moved the Delysé offices to Pye Records' premises in ATV House, just around the corner from my flat in Heron Place, where I was allocated two large offices to accommodate me and my personal assistants, Mabel Tobin and Sue Ronson. Mr Kaye, my accountant, and Chris Lennox had previously decided to retire, as neither of them wished to become part of a large company again. I was very sad to lose their skilled and devoted services, but I understood their feelings. Shortly after the move, I was also deprived of Sue Ronson, who left to have her first baby.

I knew most of the executives with whom I would be working at Pye, and they were friendly and co-operative. At first it was rather strange, as I had to accustom myself to being part of a large organisation, where I could no longer act on my own decisions; everything had to be discussed at meetings. However, it was consoling to feel that, for at least two years, I wouldn't be the sole provider of financial resources, and that there would be others with whom I could share problems and decisions. I remember strolling back to my flat on balmy, early autumn evenings, feeling relieved at not being entirely on my own, even if the respite lasted for only a short time.

Under the terms of my contract, I had agreed to render exclusive services to Pye as a producer, although I would still record material for my own labels. Luckily, the recordings that I had made for EMI in Belfast had been completed in September, and therefore I wouldn't be contravening our agreement. After joining Pye, however, it didn't take me long to realise that they were inexperienced in the field of classical recording.

The company's executives were experienced businessmen who had held high positions in major record companies, and were certainly enthusiastic, hard working, kind and eager to help. Alas, however, as is so often the case, they lacked a record man at the helm. Although Louis Benjamin was highly intelligent and capable, he was a theatre man, probably brought in by Sir Lew Grade, chairman of ATV. Monty Pressky, Tom Grantham and Geoff Bridge, meanwhile – whom I had already met frequently at federation conferences – were experienced negotiators and legal diplomats, and were very useful executives, but nevertheless lacked the specialised knowledge and expertise needed to manage the company's artists and recording affairs.

I had attended no more than one meeting before I realised why Pye had so eagerly approached me to act as an exclusive classical producer. It was revealed that I was urgently needed to rescue them from a situation into which Louis Benjamin had taken them some time previously, and there was no one in the company who had the expertise or knowledge to deal with it. Apparently, some time previously, when the opportunity had presented itself, Benjamin had acquired the rights to the enormously popular television series *The Life And Times Of Lord Louis Mountbatten*, which was to be reissued in an edited version on record, and which Benjamin believed would contribute highly to Pye's prestige. In this series, Lord Mountbatten described his life story, using his own material as well as that drawn from the national archives, and the series had been brilliantly produced by John Terraine.

I must confess that, on first hearing of their dilemma, I was seriously annoyed, because if I'd known of this during our preliminary talks I might well have turned down their offer. However, on thinking it over, my love of history and my interest in all matters royal persuaded me to agree to produce a recorded version of the series based on the original screened version. I knew what difficulties and problems lay ahead, but to be honest I had always been fascinated by Lord Mountbatten's personality, and I suspected that the challenge would be intriguing.

My conditions, however, were strict, as the task was sure to be heavy and time consuming. The company had to agree to hire Graham Samuel, a brilliant political and historical journalist, to help me edit the tapes. Also, they could not interfere during the time in which I devoted myself to sessions for Delysé, and the recordings of which I would be in charge, for Pye. I then demanded a repertoire meeting to be held at once, at which the recordings planned for Pye would be discussed and the timetable confirmed so that the agreed schedule would enable me to give sufficient time and energy to these heavy demands. I also insisted that I had first refusal on the services of editing engineer Alan Florence, one of Pye's top technicians, whom I had known and worked with during the early days of IBC. I knew Alan to be a gifted editor, and he would be vitally important in the delicate business of cutting the masters, as in this case the task would require special skill and sensitivity.

The Pye board agreed to my terms, and the editing of the tapes began in November 1969 and were completed in May 1970. It was a mammoth undertaking, as the editing sessions had to be scheduled in a way to suit both Graham's and my own commitments, but the task was eventually completed, and proved to be absolutely fascinating. I'd been right to choose Graham to help me, for we shared a great admiration for Lord Mountbatten's achievements during the war. It was intriguing to hear the last viceroy of India tell the story of the part that he had played in the handover of that country to its newly-created government, following the most complicated negotiations with Ghandi, Nehru and Jinnah, which eventually led to the final separation of India from both Britain and Pakistan.

When the editing was completed, Graham and I thought that, in order to make the audio version more intelligible, it would be necessary to make a few additions, mainly linking passages, to be recorded by Lord Mountbatten himself, and so we prepared a list of these suggested amendments. I then wrote to Lord Brabourne, Lord Mountbatten's son-in-law, indicating that, with his consent, I would drive down to Broadlands with equipment and two engineers, if Lord Mountbatten would be prepared to spare us a couple of hours or so at his convenience. Meanwhile, I sent Lord Brabourne the amendments which we wished to record, as well as an acetate containing the completed edited version of the TV tapes to date, so that he and Lord Mountbatten could listen and hopefully approve of what we had done so far. Within a few days, I received an answer from Lord Brabourne: "Lord Mountbatten, my wife and I listened to these acetates with great care during the weekend at Broadlands, and I would like to begin this letter by sending you our very warmest congratulations on the really excellent results of your labours. We all fully realised how extremely difficult it was to cut down so much material to three long-playing records, and on the whole we think that you have done an amazingly good job."

Lord Brabourne then made two very important suggestions, the first relating to the material covering the post-surrender period of the Japanese war, particularly the Potsdam Conference, when Indo-China was split, which had been referred to as being the main cause of the Vietnam war. His second major worry was the way in which the whole series would end, in which Lord Mountbatten himself alluded to his determination "never to allow ambition to interfere with the work in hand", which was followed by a list of honours and decorations, described by the narrator. Although Lord Brabourne approved of the piece, he suggested that, instead of this, we should end the series with the speech about ambition, spoken by Lord Mountbatten, played out by the *Preobrajensky March*. This would surely provide the whole programme with a grand ending. As I had been unsatisfied with the way in which the television series had ended, spoken by the narrator, I was happy to accept this suggestion. In fact, Lord Brabourne was tireless in giving me his advice when needed. As a successful and highly gifted film director, his contribution was invaluable.

Early in the morning of 15 May, I drove to Broadlands in Hampshire with my two young engineers and their equipment. They had taken great pains to perfect their appearance, and like me were obviously very excited by the occasion. We had no problem in finding our way, since Romsey, the little market town in which Broadlands is situated, was only a stone's throw from Moody's Boatyard, where my boat *Maggie* lay. I contemplated how strange it was that, throughout the years in which the boys and I had rushed happily down to Southampton for wonderful sailing weekends, I had never imagined for one moment that I might be driving almost to the same spot with two engineers to record Lord Mountbatten in his home.

When we arrived at the beautiful house, we were received by John Barratt, Lord Mountbatten's private secretary, and by his kindly man-servant, whom I later learned from Lord Mountbatten himself had served with him throughout his years in the navy. After a quick glance at the soft green lawns stretching down to the river, the engineers and I were shown into a small library, where we were told that Lord Mountbatten would soon be with us. While we waited, we began to set up the equipment.

It's strange how certain incidents remain vividly in one's memory. I can still hear Lord Mountbatten's footsteps coming down the staircase and his slow approach across the stone floor of the hallway, and I think that, by this time, we all felt rather nervous. As he entered the room, his presence was extraordinarily impressive. As he greeted me, the words "this man is a born prince" flashed through my mind, and I could see by the attitude of my young team that they were similarly affected.

Lord Mountbatten gave us a warm greeting, and after I had presented my engineers he asked me exactly what I wanted him to do. He then examined the script and the equipment, and was prepared to start work immediately. I explained that I'd brought an acetate of the speech that he'd made in the original film, in which he had made his affirmation of faith in personal ambition, which we had agreed would make the perfect end to the entire series, just before the play-out of the *Preobrajensky March*. I asked him to listen to the acetate, as it would help him to judge the pace of his original recording and enable him to match his voice as closely as possible to the audio version, and asked him to sit in the comfortable chair in front of the microphone. He had the scripts in his hand, and confirmed that he was quite satisfied with the linking passages and the amended ending, although told me that he'd made one or two minor alterations that he hoped I would approve. I then had to remind him that he should repeat the recording of each episode, in case there was any editing to be done. He agreed to this readily, and after the first take I ran a playback, hoping that he would approve of the sound of his recorded voice. There were no problems, as he was obviously used to working with technicians.

When we had completed the session, I asked him if he wanted to listen to the tapes, but he declined, declaring that he had complete confidence in my work. He then asked me if I was satisfied with his performance, and when I answered, "Entirely," he looked touchingly pleased.

The session was then declared to be at an end. While the boys were dealing with the tapes and packing up the equipment, Lord Mountbatten led me into his beautiful drawing room to show me the photographs of his daughters and his grandchildren. He also pointed out pictures of the royal family, to which he was so closely related. It was a great honour to be shown this glimpse of his personal life, and I was touched by his kindness. He also asked me if I would care to visit the huge kitchen quarters in his basement, which had been converted into a museum to house his trophies. As I knew that he had a large weekend party arriving shortly after lunch, I hesitated to accept this offer, but his servant volunteered to act as my guide, and proudly described many episodes in Lord Mountbatten's career, for which the man had been awarded magnificent decorations and swords of honour.

When we returned upstairs, the servant led me into a delightful little kitchen and a cosy dining room, which had been already prepared ready for the dinner party that evening and which Lord Mountbatten had arranged to have moved from the basement so that his old servant could enjoy an easier life. I was amazed to learn that he was the only live-in servant in this large house, and that the daily chores were performed by local help. I reflected that only a naval man could organise his life so efficiently.

Lord Mountbatten bade us a genial farewell, explaining that unfortunately he couldn't ask us to stay for lunch, as his party would be arriving shortly. I told him that he need have no cause to concern himself, as we'd spotted a delightful inn on the way to Romsey. We drove off very happily after a successful morning's work. The boys were pleased that Lord Mountbatten had been efficient and considerate, and we agreed that he had succeeded in transforming what might have been a delicate operation into a pleasant and memorable occasion. My young team obviously regarded it as an historic experience, and they were thrilled to have been involved. As we departed, I promised Lord Mountbatten that I would arrange for him to have as many copies of the album as he wished, for I knew that he intended to give one to each member of his family.

As we left Romsey, we stopped for some much-needed refreshment at the pub that we had noticed earlier. I was driving, and so the boys were able to indulge themselves with enthusiasm and relax after a successful job well done.

The long task of editing the television tapes finally came to an end after the visit to Broadlands. With the help of my colleagues at Pye, I was now able to concentrate on the presentation of the album, which had been decided at the board meeting on 5 May the previous year and had since been agreed by Lord Brabourne. The recording was to be a triple-album boxed set. On the cover would be a superb photograph of Lord Mountbatten in the uniform of Admiral of the Fleet, taken for us by Godfrey Argent, surmounted with the title *The Life And Times Of Lord Louis Mountbatten*, followed by the words *Based On The Television Series By John Terraine*. Inside the box would be a booklet, which would be printed on very fine-quality art paper containing black-and-white photographs and biographical notes, as well as the programme of each record, while Lord Mountbatten had given us permission to reproduce his magnificent coat of arms on the front cover of the booklet. I was assigned the task of collating all material relating to the cover of the box, the booklet and the recordings. In addition, it was also my responsibility to organise the launch reception, which was to be held at the Imperial War Museum on 21 October at 6pm, courtesy of its director, Dr Noble Frankland.

For the next few weeks, my concentration was almost entirely focused on preparing the reception, which had almost taken on the air of a naval operation. The experience I had gained in recording the investiture was of immense value to me, for it propelled me into a world of traditional behaviour and customs in which every decision had to be referred to St James's Palace. *The Life And Times Of Lord Louis Mountbatten*, however, was different. I had worked very closely with this almost legendary figure, principally through the medium of Lord Brabourne, and it was very obvious that the affection between Lord Mountbatten, his two daughters and his grandchildren created a feeling of geniality and warmth that pervaded the entire operation. To have met Lord Mountbatten in his own home was of great assistance to me in organising the launch party, at which I wanted to create an atmosphere subtly influenced by naval tradition and yet one which would allow him to create his own aura of characteristic charm and graciousness.

Lord Mountbatten wanted to know exactly what Lord Brabourne, Dr Frankland and I had planned for the reception. (This was now the naval officer on the scene!) For instance, did we want him to make a short speech? Had we planned for the record to be played in the small theatre next to the reception room, where any guest who wanted to could retire and listen? Yes, we had. The invitation had been approved, as had the guest list, and on my recommendation the catering firm Searcey Tansley had been engaged to provide refreshments for 150 guests.

We then sent the timetable that we had drawn up to Lord Mountbatten for his approval or otherwise. The plan was that Dr Noble Frankland and I would be at the front door of the museum to greet him and conduct him upstairs to the reception, where he would meet Mr and Mrs Benjamin and the other directors of Pye. After short introductory speeches from Louis Benjamin and himself, he would then no doubt wish to mingle with the guests. It all sounded very formal and rather dreary, but thanks to Lord Mountbatten's genial personality and the informality engendered by the cheerful presence of his daughter and two grandsons it turned into something of a family party. During the reception, the boys disappeared into the museum's display rooms, which no doubt were much more interesting to them.

I was soon made aware of Lord Mountbatten's penchant for teasing. During the months of working on the album's production, he had been a shrewd enough judge of human nature to have spotted that I was a worrier, and he decided to play a little trick on me. Shortly after his arrival at the reception, while I was briefly concerned with some minor problem, he sent an urgent message requesting that I join him. When I found him, he was standing with John Terraine, the producer of the television series, in front of the board displaying the album, which we had prepared for the dealers and the press. When I saw them gazing at the board, my heart sank, for I instantly imagined that they had discovered some awful blunder in the presentation. However, when they saw my stricken face they greeted me with friendly congratulations, a glass of champagne and much laughter.

I considered that this behaviour deserved a *revanche*, and so I responded with Queen Victoria's famous remark, "We are not amused." I scored a palpable hit with this, and pleased Lord Mountbatten greatly. While I was there, I asked if I might present Graham Samuel, whom I knew was longing to meet Lord Mountbatten, who was his hero. As I had expected, Lord Mountbatten warmly thanked Graham for his help in the difficult task of editing the television tapes, for I had previously explained how much I owed to his skill and judgement. Graham was delighted, and I could see how amused and touched Lord Mountbatten was by Graham's romantic Welsh enthusiasm. There was no doubt that this meeting was of great significance to Graham, and I was so happy to have been able to bring it about.

Lord Mountbatten left at 7.15pm, for he was due to dine with the Royal Yacht Squadron at 7.30, and he bade us farewell, expressing warm thanks to Mr and Mrs Benjamin for a very happy and successful party. When the excitement was all over and the post mortem carried out, it was decided that the effort and expenses invested had been worth it in terms of the immense promotion that we had attracted. Louis Benjamin admitted that the production of the album had been undertaken mainly for reasons of prestige, and certainly the outcome had exceeded his hopes. The editors of nearly every major newspaper had been there, and representatives from the BBC and independent television companies had all attended. Many top-ranking navy and army officers had also made a point of being present, as well as prominent politicians and the high commissioners of Pakistan, India, Malaysia, Ceylon and Canada. Very important, too, was the presence of Tony Pollard, editor of *Gramophone* magazine, probably one of the most important publications of its kind in the world, although of course Tony was a social asset to any gathering.

We were also very relieved by the number of buyers from the major record stores who attended, whose presence was so important. I had given many such press receptions for Delysé throughout my years as a record producer, so by this time I had become a pretty good judge of their success or otherwise. In this case, because of the presence of Lord Mountbatten, I was delighted with the result, as were the directors of Pye.

When I first heard the news, some years later, of the murder of this wonderful man and the death of one of his much-loved grandsons on a sailing holiday with his family on the west coast of Ireland, I was utterly shocked. His tragic death brought back to me his grace of manner, his kindliness and his humour, and above all the privilege I had felt at having been involved in recording such a significant period of our country's history, interpreted and spoken by the chief protagonist, Lord Mountbatten himself.

18 Maggie, Sir Arthur Bliss And Mahler

Although it might seem that my life was filled by all of these activities, I still found plenty of time to devote to the boys when they made frequent visits to London – Pompy and Shirley from Philadelphia and Roguey and Jeannie from Southampton – and these were very happy occasions. My flat was a great attraction, as Heron Place was in the very centre of the West End, so there was always plenty to see from the fifth-floor windows. My office, meanwhile, was converted into a spare room. (In a few years' time, when my two American grandsons arrived on the scene, it became a nursery!)

I would still go down to Southampton as often as possible to see *Maggie*. By this time, Roguey and Jeannie were building *Cottontail* in Moody's yard, so this was also an opportunity to see them fairly frequently. As I was now without a crew, I wasn't able to sail the boat, but we did manage one unforgettable sortie to the Isle of Wight, which involved three of my friends and became a somewhat perilous adventure. I had told Roguey that I would love to invite friends to spend a last weekend on board, as *Maggie* was about to be sold, and he kindly volunteered to skipper us to Bembridge on the eastern tip of the island. So on 13 August 1970, Jerry Northrop Moore (an American, and one of my greatest friends, but no sailor), Graham Samuel and his friend Mary Thomas set off in high spirits for Southampton to spend a few days on board.

Before relating our adventures on the high seas, I must explain how I made Jerry's acquaintance. For some time before our meeting, I had received letters from America in which he wrote of his great interest in the life and career of Uncle Fred, and indicated his desire to write his biography and expressed his hope that I might be willing to help him. Our first meeting didn't take place until the late spring of 1968, and after this I decided to introduce him to my mother, who had been so close to both my Uncle Fred and his brother, Will, in the early days in London. I was sure that she would like Jerry, and indeed they got along splendidly. This added to my conviction that he should be the one to write the book about my uncle's life, and this conviction grew steadily stronger as I got to know him better.

With our skipper, Roguey, at the helm, Jerry, Graham, Mary and I set sail on a beautiful summer's day, mightily happy. On the Wednesday, we sailed down the Hamble River into the Solent and past the entrance to the great naval base at Portsmouth. It was an uneventful and pleasant cruise to Bembridge, where Roguey saw us comfortably moored up in the harbour. Unfortunately, he couldn't stay with us, as he had to return to work, but we settled down to a good dinner and much musical gossip. Afterwards, filled with fine sea air and a few bottles of wine, we passed an excellent night.

Over the next few days, we explored the immediate countryside and even tried to visit Osborne House, which still belongs to the Queen and was so loved by Queen Victoria and Prince Albert, but we failed to gain an entrance. We enjoyed those happy days very much. Indeed, we were so relaxed that we didn't notice the worsening weather – at least, my guests didn't, but with my long experience of conditions on the Solent I began to think with some concern about our return voyage. I said nothing to the others, however, as I didn't wish to spoil their enjoyment.

During the Saturday night, the storm grew worse, and there was soon no disguising our unhappy position, for I knew that Roguey had to get us to Southampton on Sunday evening, as we all had to be back at work on Monday morning. There was nothing for it but to grit our teeth and risk the crossing in gale-force winds. As arranged, Roguey turned up at Bembridge, having sailed on *Cottontail* across the Solent to the island on the Saturday with Jeannie and a friend. They were to sail back to Moody's yard on the Sunday. This made us very anxious, for not only did Roguey and I have to worry about our passengers on *Maggie* but we also had to be concerned about Jeannie and her crew on *Cottontail*.

In the event, we set off bravely, for we had no choice, and soon realised that we were in for a bad time. The Solent can be very nasty, but our guests were brave and behaved admirably, keeping quiet and not bothering Roguey, who was hanging onto the wheel and steering the boat with great skill, which was not easy, as *Maggie* wasn't at her best in such conditions, being long and narrow in the beam. We all huddled together in the deckhouse, being careful not to disturb to the skipper. Just as we were coming up to the entrance to Portsmouth Harbour, Jerry looked over his shoulder and said, "Sorry to disturb you, Roguey, but there's an enormous vessel coming up fast behind us, and it looks like they intend to turn right into the harbour." Nobody said a word while Roguey coped with the situation, and I must say that I was filled with admiration for the way in which he handled *Maggie* in the rough seas, and felt such remorse at having put my friends in such a perilous situation. There was no sight of *Cottontail* on the way, and we just prayed that Jeannie had had the sense to leave the island sooner and had thus avoided the full strength of the gale.

We were so relieved when we finally left the turbulent waters of the Solent and sailed up the Hamble to find Jeannie and *Cottontail* safely waiting for us on their mooring, and I performed my usual miraculous feat of producing an enormous meal for the crews of both boats on board *Maggie* within minutes of tying up. After enduring other experiences similar to this one, I often asked myself whether I really enjoyed sailing as much as I thought I did! Many years later, Jerry told me that his long weekend spent on the Isle of Wight on board *Maggie* was one of the most unforgettable incidents of his life, so perhaps I needn't have felt quite so guilty.

It was fortunate indeed that Jerry survived our perilous yet exciting cruise on the Solent, for he was thus able to write his fine book based on Uncle Fred's career in the creation and development of the record industry. *Sound Revolutions* was originally published by Hamish Hamilton in 1974, and was reissued in 1999 by Sanctuary Publishing.

After the reception at the Imperial War Museum on 21 October 1970 to celebrate the release of the Lord Mountbatten recording, my first year with Pye came to an end. Naturally, my thoughts looked to the future, as my agreement had only one more year to run. I didn't regret throwing in my lot with Pye for one moment, for I had thus far enjoyed many new experiences, including that of careering around the British Isles with my team of young engineers. This had reminded me of the early days with Delysé, when Allen Stagg and his young cohorts engineered the recording of Welsh and Irish choirs, which formed such an important part of my early catalogue. Above all, the difficult and fascinating task of producing the Mountbatten record required endless patience and skill, and Graham Samuel and Alan Florence, who assisted me brilliantly, were rich in these qualities. Although it was the most important project, the Mountbatten recording was far from being the only one with which I was involved during that first year.

In as early as December 1969, not long after my move to the Pye offices in ATV House, I was approached by Geoff Bridge and Monty Pressky, who asked if I would help them out of a difficult situation. They wanted me to take over as producer of a number of Golden Guinea sessions during the same period that I was editing the Mountbatten tapes. Monty and Geoff were good negotiators, and they knew that there would be times when the editing studio was unavailable, so I couldn't really use this as an excuse to refuse their request without appearing ungracious. They explained that these recordings would involve a considerable amount of travelling at times, and that everything possible would be arranged for my comfort, including air travel and luxury hotels. As I was always happy to perform what I felt was my real job, actually producing, I agreed to help in any way that I could.

However, I had a counter-proposal up my sleeve, and this was a good opportunity to use it. I knew that Pye had for a long time contracted the recording of the most famous brass bands and choirs in the north of England, and that they were behind in their schedule, so I put it to them that, if they were prepared to finance two major recordings for their Virtuoso label, which was close to my heart, I would agree to carry out the Golden Guinea sessions. As my repertoire suggestions were so obviously beneficial to the building of their Virtuoso catalogue, they were forced to agree. It was now my turn to crow, and I must admit that Louis Benjamin took this in good heart.

As soon as the bargain was struck, at the end of 1969, I began to produce my first recordings for Golden Guinea, starting with The Black Dyke, England's most famous brass band. My young team of engineers drove up to Bradford with the equipment, and I flew up on the following day, arriving when they were set up and ready for me to begin the sessions. The band was excellent and highly competent, and the two conductors, Geoffrey Brand and Roy Newsome, were both first-class and pleasant musicians who couldn't do enough to be helpful. All went smoothly, and I was soon able to fly back to London.

My next recording was of popular hymns with The Huddersfield Choral Society, and this was followed by a recording of The Colne Valley Male Voice Choir, who performed a programme of well-known Yorkshire airs. These recordings were so successful that later in that year Pye decided to make further recordings of these famous choirs and a number of other musical societies, including The Metropolitan Police Choir in London, The

Felling Male Voice Choir in Newcastle, and a recording of Handel's *Messiah*, about which I remember little, except that it was recorded in Bradford with the fine choir of that city and with Forbes Robinson as one of the soloists.

It was a hard year, in which I covered quite a broad field of work, and when it was time for me to be recompensed Pye handed out the funds for me to begin production of Sir Arthur Bliss's *Pastorale* and *A Knot Of Riddles*, as well as Mahler's first symphony, with Wyn Morris conducting the New Philharmonia Orchestra. This was my reward for the mammoth task of recording the diverse types of music that I had undertaken on their behalf during 1969.

I often look back on this period and wonder how I ever found the energy to accomplish this heavy recording programme, which seemed to grow in size like a snowball. Throughout that arduous year, the planning, organisation and recording of the two important works for the Virtuoso label, which dangled before me like a carrot before a donkey, kept me in a state of happy expectancy.

Some months previously, long before I had joined forces with Pye, Wyn had spoken to me of these two delightful works. *Pastorale* was scored for chamber orchestra, mezzo-soprano and solo flute, and Wyn suggested that it would make an ideal coupling with *A Knot Of Riddles*, which had been written for baritone and solo members of the orchestra. Although not expensive, as orchestral projects go, these two works would boost the catalogue considerably, and to the best of our knowledge neither had previously been recorded. During a recent tour of the United States, Wyn had introduced *Pastorale* to American audiences, with great success. As an added gesture, Pye dedicated the recordings to Sir Arthur Bliss, as a celebration of his 80th birthday, which pleased the composer immensely. When I had completed the estimate and presented the programme of repertoire to the board of directors, it was enthusiastically received as an unusual and attractive addition to the Virtuoso catalogue.

Other than getting to know these two delightful works by Bliss, the pleasure of meeting him would almost have been reward enough. He was still handsome and attractive at 80, radiating good humour and obviously enjoying life. Not only was he one of England's most distinguished composers but also, in his position as Master of the Queen's Music, he enjoyed a full and satisfying social life. It was rare that a musician of such eminence showed so few signs of arrogance and conceit. He and Wyn got along together splendidly, and the sessions at Barking Town Hall were a happy occasion. For *Pastorale*, which Bliss had written after a visit to Italy, we engaged the London Chamber Orchestra and the mezzo Sybil Michelow, who sang the charming pagan voices, while Norman Knight played solo flute. Meanwhile, in *A Knot Of Riddles*, the distinguished baritone John Shirley-Quirk gave a delightful performance, and Sir Arthur was in a state of enchantment and yet still very efficient when his help was required.

Working with Sir Arthur reminded me of when, thanks to Uncle Fred, I had been privileged to spend time with Sir Edward Elgar as a young girl, particularly those memorable days in Paris when Uncle Fred and the Menuhins flew there for the première of Elgar's violin concerto. Obviously, I couldn't resist comparing the two composers. They were born in completely different *milieux*, for Elgar was a countryman and Bliss was essentially a product of London, public school and Cambridge. Neither could be other than English gentlemen, although I imagine that Bliss was capable of being pretty wild. He was also a little younger, and had fought in the First World War. There was, indeed, no comparison between them as creative artists, but as fate had been kind enough to me to throw me into their lives – even if, as with Bliss, for only a brief period – I felt profound interest in considering them as men and artists.

Sir Arthur and I became good friends. He was most generous in his hospitality, and invited Wyn and me to his home in St John's Wood on a number of occasions, where we were entertained by his American wife. The couple were also kind enough to take me with them to one of the garden parties at Buckingham Palace. He seemed to take great pleasure in life, and even enjoyed accompanying Monty Pressky and me to trade shows when his record was released and exhibited on the company's stands. He was thoroughly amused by these events, and made witty speeches at them, much to the delight of the dealers and the public.

The next nut was going to be more difficult to crack, however, for the financial investment was much greater. However, after the outstanding success of my earlier recordings of Mahler's *Des Knaben Wunderhorn* and *Das Klagende Lied*, Pye knew that the opportunity was one which they couldn't refuse, especially as in Wyn Morris they had a conductor who was acknowledged as being one of the finest conductors of Mahler in the world, and so they decided unhesitatingly. Although the financial estimate for this production far exceeded anything that they had previously envisaged, they agreed to allow me to proceed with the sessions.

Wyn and I were overjoyed, to put it mildly, for I hadn't been in a financial position to undertake this task myself. Even so, I was sad not to be producing the recording for my own Delysé label, for I was sure that it would be an authoritative version of this beautiful work. However, at least it would be recorded for posterity.

19 *Symphonies And Symphonica*

The beginning of 1971 saw the gradual dissolution of my association with Pye and the inauguration of the Symphonica project. It had been a period of intense activity for me, for not only had I steered the Mountbatten project to a happy conclusion for Pye but I had also produced a considerable number of recordings for their catalogues, necessitating much travel and hard work. When my contract with them finally ended, I found myself free once more to consider my position in relation to my own catalogues, and in 1972 Wyn and I began to hold serious discussions concerning Symphonica.

After the highly acclaimed recordings of *Des Knaben Wunderhorn* and *Das Klagende Lied*, which had achieved such spectacular success, it might be considered that we had established ourselves as Mahler exponents with an international reputation, as these recordings were selling all over the world. We planned to record Mahler's eighth symphony in November 1972, and therefore my main preoccupation leading up to this date was with setting up a financial and management company to direct the operation: Symphonica.

I've often been asked why I was so enthusiastic about the Symphonica project. I've always believed that my answers to this question were both practical and culturally viable. By engaging a group of the finest and most experienced musicians available in London – including eminent soloists, members of celebrated string quartets, chamber orchestras and other principal players of established symphony orchestras – to come together to record great musical works, followed immediately by public performance, the artistic intimacy of the relationship between conductor and musicians would remain fresh. This concept aspired to the heights of performance, aided by economic common sense, for by combining the functions of recording and public performance we found that we could save on the amount of rehearsal time and financial investment necessary. I have never changed my mind about this. and still believe that it is a practical means of sharing the costs of recording, performance and promotion.

During this critical and troubled period, the family suffered a great loss with the death of my father in February 1971. This wasn't a complete surprise, however, as he had been getting progressively weaker, and we had been conscious of the apparent aimlessness of his existence after his retirement from his chairmanship of the British division of Coty. Not only had his work satisfied his interest in conducting a model business but also his love of beauty was satisfied in working on the tasteful presentation of the high-quality products. He was certainly interested in his family – he adored his grandchildren, and he was the kindest of fathers – but nothing seemed to take the place of his beloved business. My personal loss was great, for not only did I miss his warmth and affection but also his calm and experienced advice, especially in this time of considerable stress. My mother, whose very foundation must have just disappeared, showed her usual stoical courage in the face of loss. After nearly 60 years of marriage, life must have presented her with a great emptiness, but somehow she managed to continue to live peacefully and show loving interest in the rest of her family.

People often asked us why Wyn and I chose Mahler's mightiest work, the eighth symphony, with which to make Symphonica's debut. We explained that the very courageousness of the project would attract considerable notice and publicity, and would bring about the necessary support, both financial and otherwise. So, without further ado, the decision was made to forge ahead, and with the help of John Raffael, an enthusiastic young businessman, and Colin Hadley, a PR specialist whom I had met during my time with Pye, the machine started to roll.

A highly successful deal was set up with a publication called *Arts Mail*, which was distributed and sold through all venues concerned with the arts, and their subscribers were for a limited period able to order our recording of Mahler's eighth symphony directly at cost. This arrangement proved to be highly successful, and by this scheme we recovered a considerable amount of our initial production costs. Unfortunately, however, this wonderful little publication didn't survive for very long, probably because it wasn't sufficiently supported by the arts public, or, more likely, because the distribution and sales organisations of the major record companies saw it as a threat to their own activities. For whatever reason, we were unable to benefit from it for our future releases, and missed it sorely after its withdrawal.

Those who took considerable interest in the Symphonica project appeared to be artists' managers, and thanks to my years in the industry I had grown to know many of them and was now in a position in which to assess their merits. One of these managers was Basil Horsfield, a most intelligent and knowledgeable agent who not only dispensed wise advice but was also a most helpful associate. He introduced me to many fine artists and interesting people, including Dolly Burns, one of the few musical hostesses remaining in London, who had a beautiful house in Chesterfield Hill, just off Curzon Street. She loved to entertain visiting celebrities there, and offered the most generous hospitality. The food was always delicious and the company amusing. I remember on a number of occasions sitting next to Larry Adler, a witty raconteur, who would never stop talking.

Through Basil, I also became friendly with the great American soprano Beverly Sills, one of his most important artists, who was frequently in London. She was a delightful, kind and unassuming woman who was usually accompanied by her husband, and when they came to London they often brought their little daughter with them as well. I remember visiting her dressing room in Covent Garden with Basil just before her performance of Donizetti's *Lucia Di Lammermoor* and seeing her little girl playing with toys on the floor while her mother put on her make-up and dressed for the demanding role she was about to sing. When I later heard her perform, I was quite overcome with admiration as I listened to her phenomenal virtuosity in the great *coloratura* arias of the third act. I found it hard to associate this fantastic performance with the gentle and almost matter-of-fact woman I had visited in the dressing room. Beverly and I later became good friends, and after she attended one or two of my sessions she wanted to engage me as her personal producer, although her husband thought this unwise, as it would have undoubtedly offended her own record company. In any case, at that time I had too many things happening in my own career to commit myself to other responsibilities.

In the family, too, there was a lot going on. On 25 March, I went down to Southampton University to be present when Roguey received his doctorate. I was so proud of him, for he had achieved success entirely unaided by anyone. It was a moving and happy occasion, and I only wished that his father had been there with me. Also on that very day,

Jeannie's sister, Barbara, married Richard Seabrook, and we went to the reception after the event at the university to join the Collar family there. Jeannie had decided that she should be present at the wedding, and so missed the awards ceremony at the university.

In spite of the fraught atmosphere in which I was living, there were times when life was very amusing and lively. I was surrounded by many good friends, and I remember that, if I wasn't at a business function, there was a gathering in Heron Place almost every lunchtime when John Porter was there with his accountant and partner, John Peters. Mausi and Wyn often stayed with me, too, and the atmosphere was always lively and stimulating. To add to the general liveliness, we were also attended by Rene Haines, who looked after the flat for me, and often her husband, Nob, was there too, to add to the good cheer. How I loved those two dear people, who gave me the most devoted service for several years.

The date for the recording of Mahler's eighth symphony was fast approaching, and so Wyn returned from Llanelli, where he had been studying the colossal score and resting in the care of his mother. During the days before the sessions, we had rehearsed with The Mahler-Bruckner Choir (formed by Wyn himself), The New Philharmonia Chorus and The Ambrosian Singers, as well as with The Highgate School Choir, The Orpington Junior Singers and The Finchley Children's Group, who were all taking part in the recording. We had hired conveniently-placed halls all over London so that they could reach the rehearsals on time, and the experienced and talented musicians Anthony Saunders and Nina Walker had been engaged to play the difficult arrangements of the orchestral score so that the choirs could have some knowledge of the music before their ears were confronted by the orchestra.

The eight soloists all came to rehearsals held at my flat, and Nina and Anthony accompanied them. We were so rushed, and were concentrating so hard on these activities, that we hardly had time to feel fear, and it wasn't until I walked into Walthamstow Town Hall on the morning of the first session, on 20 November 1972, that I realised the immensity of what we were undertaking. I remember whispering to myself, "What would Uncle Fred say to me now?"

The vast hall was crammed to capacity with crowds of orchestral musicians, choral singers and children, all looking utterly lost and bewildered. When I arrived, Wyn was already there, standing on the podium and studying his score, looking very small indeed in the midst of this vast concourse, which he somehow had to dominate. I greeted him, trying to appear very calm and self-confident, and then walked into the control room, where I found Michael Gray, EMI's chief recording engineer, looking pale and nervous, along with the other engineers, as usual fiddling with the equipment. I asked him if all was well, and he replied, "No problems with the equipment at the moment," so at least for the time being I didn't have to worry about that. To tease him, I reminded him I had recorded a capacity crowd of 6,000 people in the Royal Albert Hall some years previously, but this recollection didn't seem to cheer up either of us.

The huge orchestra of 90 musicians were seated on the floor of the hall, with the choirs arrayed on the built-up platform behind them. The children, meanwhile, were arranged in a fan shape in the front of the platform built behind the orchestra and directly in front of Wyn, while the adult choirs reached almost to heaven behind them and on either side. It was a mightily impressive sight. There were only the eight soloists to bring into the picture, which was no simple task, as they had to contend with these enormous forces. In the event, we had built a small, narrow platform for them on the floor to Wyn's right, and they would sing into a separate microphone while Nina stood in front of them to act as a second conductor in case Wyn wasn't always clearly visible. It was a tremendous challenge for Mike Gray to obtain the maximum sound and separation so that we could mix the channels to the best possible effect in the studios, but he surmounted these difficulties wonderfully well.

Wyn began to rehearse the orchestra and soloists for the first take while I made my way through the crowd to the control room, where I asked Wyn to start the session, as I wanted to work on balance. We had agreed to begin with the very last section of the whole work as, according to working practice learned from Allen Stagg, I always started to get the right balance with the most heavily-scored section of the work, at a time when everyone concerned was performing, so that I could be sure that not only would all of the performers be heard but also that they would be properly balanced. Wyn and I agreed to begin at the very end of the last movement, at "Alles vergänglist nur ein gleichniss," which was the beginning of the great build-up to the conclusion, with all soloists, choirs and full orchestra, complete with bells, harmonium, piano, celeste – the lot, in fact.

The hour of reckoning was upon us, so I told Michael that we were ready to begin the session. Mabel Tobin, my assistant, was at my side with the continuity open in front of her. I spoke to Wyn through the telephone and told him that we were ready to record take one, which Mike would announce on the tape, and that everything performed, even false starts, should be numbered, even if the material was only a few notes in length. After the first few takes, Wyn, the principals in the orchestra and the soloists (Joyce Barker, Norma Burrowes, Alfreda Hodgson, Raymond Myers, Elizabeth Simon, Joyce Blackham, Gwynne Howell and Alberto Remedios) came in to listen. We were intensely moved and encouraged by the beauty of the magnificent sound, and the realisation that our dream was really coming true.

The session went unbelievably well, and we completed our recording schedule for the first day. However, when Wyn and I listened to the takes involving the solo artists, we realised that Remedios was unhappy. I should have listened to him during the rehearsals in my flat, when he expressed his fear of the difficulties in the work, which he felt was completely alien to him. We realised then that we had to find a replacement. But where? Helden tenors were few and far between, and I knew that there was no one in London at that moment who was capable of singing this music.

I telephoned Basil Horsfield and told him of our dilemma. To my amazement, he said that he thought that he could help us. The great English tenor John Mitchinson had just the voice we needed, and had unexpectedly returned to London only the night before from an engagement abroad. Basil offered to telephone him at once and explain our predicament. I knew that John was suited to the work, and only hoped that he was familiar with it. In any case, he was an intelligent artist, and if he was willing to rehearse with us that evening I was sure that he would be able to master the difficulties, both vocal and musical, and as he was one of the nicest men in the profession just having him with us would be a blessing. Fortunately, he was free, and agreed to help. When I told Remedios of our decision, he appeared relieved at being able to withdraw from the engagement.

We had by now completed two of our scheduled sessions. They had cost us blood and tears, but now that we had solved the problem of the tenor we felt that a great worry had been lifted from our shoulders. John Mitchinson was versed in the German school of singing essential for performance of Mahler, and I blamed myself for having inflicted suffering on Remedios as well as on Wyn and myself. But we had been miraculously rescued by God, Basil and John Mitchinson, and after this – considering the enormous difficulties of the work – the sessions went remarkably smoothly.

We waited until early January 1973 before starting work in the studios, but in the meantime there was still the concert before us at the Royal Albert Hall on 11 December, and we had to concentrate on this. It was another mighty undertaking, for once again we had to hold rehearsals for choir and soloists, and there was also the complicated organising of the concert itself. I engaged Charlotte Nichols to handle the promotion and publicity and to attract the 6,000 people needed to fill the hall. This required considerable effort, but she was efficient, and she did a good job. Of course, we had already gained some publicity when the Symphonica project was first announced.

In the event, the house was filled with an enthusiastic audience. It was indeed a wildly exciting and triumphant occasion. Wyn was in splendid form, confident after the experience he had gained from the recording sessions, as indeed was the orchestra, and judging by the enthusiasm of the audience and the excellence of the reviews the event was a definite success. Wyn was at the height of his powers as a conductor, and I was filled with admiration for his performance. Once again, I was amazed by his understanding of Mahler, as indeed were the critics, who gave the performance outstandingly good reviews. "A massive scheme, massively realised," was just one quote from a critic in *The Guardian*.

On 15 September 1973, the family sustained another great loss with the death of my mother, Louise. Her end came quite suddenly. I'd had no idea that her heart condition was so serious, as she rarely spoke of her health to either me or Mondy. On that afternoon, she had telephoned to say that she wasn't well, and that the doctor had taken a cardiograph. I went around to her flat in Park Street immediately, where I found her in bed. She seemed quite cheerful, but nevertheless I decided to spend the night with her. In the morning she appeared to be fairly normal, and ate a little breakfast. When she said that she wanted to get up to go to the bathroom, I suggested that she should stay quietly in bed and that I would bring her everything she needed, but she insisted on getting up. I waited outside the door until she came out and then walked closely behind her. Suddenly she gave a little sigh and a jerk and fell back into my arms. I caught her, but she was already dead.

It was a terrible shock, and at first I was stunned by the abrupt transition from life to death. My first thought was that she had died as she would have wished, giving as little trouble to others as possible. I called Mondy and Catherine, who were then living in Paris, and they flew over at once. It had been so sudden that we simply couldn't believe that it had happened, and that she was no longer with us. Looking back, I don't think that she ever got over my father's death, two years previously. I had tried to draw her out and urged her to enjoy some of the activities that she had been unable to do because of my father's long illness, but she didn't seem capable of doing this. At the time, I had been looking at flats that would be large enough to share with her and house all of my activities as well, but alas this was not to be.

Mother was a gifted musician, but she seemed to prefer to live for others – her husband and her children. The birth of her grandchildren had given her an immense interest, and my boys had adored their "Bam-Bam". She had never seemed to tire of being with them, helping to nurse them through their childhood illnesses and taking part in their endless "chats", during which wonderful adventures were imagined and shared. I had to try not to give in to this great sadness, as I was carrying such a burden of responsibility at the time. However, it wasn't easy to put the loss of her behind me, for I had loved her very much.

The success of the Mahler eighth concert and recording filled us with elation. The reviews were outstandingly good, and indeed far exceeded our expectations. Meanwhile, our distribution both in the United Kingdom and internationally was well organised, and thanks to our arrangement with the publication *Arts Mail* the record's immediate sales figures were a tremendous help in recouping the initial costs of its production. The concert – which was principally undertaken for its promotional value – had also paid its way, even better than expected. Now we had to prepare ourselves for our next venture, which was the recording of Mahler's fifth symphony and his *Lieder Eines Fahrenden Gezellen*, which was added to complete the necessary time for an LP release. I had already instructed Sidney Saxe to begin engaging the orchestral players, as this had to be arranged as soon as possible in order to ensure that we obtained the musicians that we really wanted. I had also booked studio one at EMI for the recording, which was scheduled to take place on 1-3 November.

In spite of the success of the Mahler eighth recording and concert, it was proving difficult to raise the funds to finance this next venture. The results of the previous project had amazed the industry, but we couldn't expect financial help from the major record companies. The banks certainly showed interest, and we received offers of assistance from friends, but these fell through, and in the end I decided that the only way forward was to borrow from a bank and to guarantee the loan with my own funds. Finally, John Raffael introduced me to the manager of one of the major banks, with whom he was on friendly terms, in a branch at Guildford. I well remember driving down with John to that delightful, busy little Surrey town, which I knew so well from my early married days, praying that we would be able to arrange the deal. I was successful, and although this placed me in a dangerous financial position I was thus able to fulfil my commitment to Sidney Saxe, by handing over to him the funds necessary to pay the orchestra in advance, and to settle in full my account with EMI for the use of their studios. There were also other obligations that I could now meet, and once again I could sleep at night.

My next problem was finding a suitable hall in which to perform the concert, which, as we announced in our advance publicity, would take place immediately after the sessions. This concert would be taking place in November, the very worst time of the year to find a vacancy, and the situation seemed hopeless until I was inspired to try something quite original which had the advantages of both novelty and panache.

I knew that the Theatre Royal in Drury Lane was empty at that time, and so I went along to see the manager to try and persuade him to allow us to use his beautiful theatre as a concert hall. He was delighted with the idea, and so I put the suggestion to our board of directors, who accepted it with enthusiasm. I explained to the manager that we would have to extend the proscenium of the stage forward into the stalls, for otherwise the sound would be unacceptable. He understood this at once, and was most helpful to us throughout the whole operation. It turned out to have been a brilliant idea, for the beautiful historic house lent itself to our purpose most magnificently. We achieved some helpful publicity, and the advance bookings were excellent. Before the concert, however, there was still the actual recording to do, and we aimed to produce as fine a result at these sessions as we had at those for the Mahler eighth.

Unlike the recording of the eighth symphony, for which monumental forces had been engaged, the sessions of Mahler's fifth symphony were far less harassing, and in fact took place in a most relaxed atmosphere. For one thing, Mike Gray felt much more at ease, as he was working in his own studio, and we only had to deal with the orchestra, as there were no choirs or soloists. Also, the sheer beauty of the music thrilled us. From the very opening of the first movement, with the magnificent affirmation of the horns and trumpets, to the divine inspiration of the *adagietto*, we basked in its beauty. Indeed, after we had made one take of this movement, recorded from beginning to end without a single stop, Wyn was so overjoyed by the performance that he didn't want to repeat it. The orchestra, too, begged me not to insist on a second take. Nevertheless, for security reasons I told them that I had to insist on a repeat performance.

There was a general feeling of elation when we completed the recording of the work. It seemed to both Wyn and myself that we had achieved something to which we had long aspired, and we approached the *Lieder Eines Fahrenden Gezellen* in a happy mood. The baritone that I had engaged, the German Roland Hermann, was in fine voice, and the session proceeded most successfully.

All four sessions were pleasant from beginning to end, for which we were thankful, and after their completion we had to summon all of our energy to tackle the concert the very next evening at Drury Lane. The venue presented an unknown situation, and we were therefore pleased that everything had gone so well at the sessions, and that the artists were therefore in an optimistic mood. We arrived at the theatre early the next morning to find the carpenters busy constructing the extended stage, and much of the first part of the rehearsal took place to the accompaniment of hammering. Meanwhile, I tried to check the acoustics in all parts of the theatre. This was a matter of some concern, as the Theatre Royal wasn't a concert hall, and it was difficult to judge the sound in the empty theatre. We just had to pray that it would sound good when it was filled with people.

While Wyn rehearsed with the orchestra, Roland Hermann and I went backstage and sat down in one of the dressing rooms to await his call. We were sitting in front of one of the dressing tables, talking quietly, when I noticed a tall man in a black cloak standing in the doorway that we had left open, just looking at us. At first I said nothing, and then Roland turned and saw him too. After a few moments, the man walked out of the room and into the empty corridor. I jumped up and went immediately to the door and looked out, but there was absolutely no one to be seen in the long passage. Roland and I said nothing to each other about what had occurred, and resumed our conversation quietly. After the rehearsal, I told the manager about this strange occurrence, and he said, quite casually, "Oh, yes. That's our ghost. He must have been disturbed by the sound of the orchestra."

That evening, the concert was well attended by an enthusiastic audience. I think that they enjoyed the novelty of sitting in the elegant surroundings of the Drury Lane theatre, and many of them spoke to me during the interval and suggested that we should use the theatre again for some of our future concerts. Wyn and I weren't entirely sure about the quality of the sound, but the theatre had served its purpose in contributing to the success of the concert and rescuing us from a difficult situation.

As I think back on the wonderful gathering of musicians that made up the orchestra, I can only describe it as a star ensemble, and I would like to pay tribute to them here by naming a few of them. Sidney Saxe, the leader, was a fine violinist and was responsible for "fixing" the orchestra. I can't think of anyone else who could have brought together musicians of such quality, and he succeeded in doing this because they held him in such high respect. I can't name all of the section leaders, but among them were Max Salpeter, second leader; Kenneth Essex, viola; Francis Gabarro, cello; Jack Collyer, double bass; William Bennett, flute; Richard Morgan, oboe; Thomas Kelly, clarinet; Martin Gatt, bassoon; Alan Civil, horn, with his wife, Shirley, playing second; John Wilbraham, trumpet; Derek James, trombone; Alan Cumberland, timpani; Tristram Fry, percussion; and Marie Goosens, harp. When I look over this list, I can't imagine how any conductor wouldn't give everything of which he was capable as a musician to lead them and to obtain performances of the highest musical standard. Indeed, Wyn did just this, and achieved results which were quite outstanding. Our reward came when the critics' reviews exceeded all of our hopes, resounding with almost unanimous praise. Our joy in such an achievement rewarded us for the months of hard work and worries that had plagued us during the creation of Symphonica.

So it was with the happy anticipation of spending Christmas with Pompy and his family in Philadelphia that I flew to the States on 21 December. It was wonderful to be with my family, and the happiness I felt at being able to relax and play with my two little gransons, Eric and Danny, and to gossip with my son and daughter-in-law was indescribable.

After Christmas, I flew to New York to attend meetings with Peter Munves from RCA Victor, at which I negotiated a licensing deal for the recordings of Mahler's eighth and fifth symphonies, and also for the second, which was still to be recorded. He was a great enthusiast, and I liked him very much, and hoped that our business relationship would be a success.

My visit to New York was very pleasant, as I was warmly welcomed and generously entertained by John Coveney of EMI, who was very much involved in the New York musical scene and highly popular with both artists and the management of the musical institutions there. He had also known and greatly admired my uncle. John entertained me generously, taking me to interesting and sometimes exclusive restaurants, and altogether spoiling me delightfully. He also invited me to attend a performance of Mozart's *Così Fan Tutte* at the Metropolitan, which I appreciated most of all. I was tremendously impressed by the standard of the performance and by the quality of the production and *mise en scène*, as well as the atmosphere of financial security which was noticeable to one who was accustomed to the impoverished air of most European opera houses. After the show, John hosted a delightful and amusing supper party, where one of the guests was Nicolai Gedda.

After this very successful visit to New York, I returned to London to begin preparations for the recording of Mahler's second symphony, *The Resurrection*, scheduled next on our list. This was once again a production of considerable size – not, thank goodness, as large as Mahler's eighth, but nevertheless it was scored for choir, soprano and mezzo soloists and an orchestra of the usual immense Mahlerian proportions. There was a difficulty in that, at a certain point in the score, Mahler directed that an "outside" group of instruments had to be integrated into the ensemble but should sound as if coming from a distance. In order to carry this out, I had to increase the orchestra by engaging more musicians for one session after the completion of the rest of the work. We recorded the outside group of musicians at a session in St Gabriel's Church, Kilburn, which has a fine, open sound, as well as a good organ. This then had to be incorporated into the edited master at the studios, a technically difficult task. Nevertheless, Mike Gray did a fine job, and I was pleased that he was praised by a number of critics for his skill in carrying out this operation.

Of course, all of this increased the cost of the production, which was in any case very considerable, as *The Resurrection* is a long work, and this added greatly to my financial worries. In fact, it was impossible for me to overcome this particular obstacle. Then, thankfully, a fairy godfather appeared on the scene in the person of Frixos Theodorides, Fiorella's husband. Both were dear friends of mine, and they came to my rescue and paid for the extra session without any argument, which enabled me to complete the recording. There was no way that I could thank Frixos enough for his help. I invited him to come to the studios to watch us carrying out the delicate operation of integrating the outside band with the main tape, on which all of the technical work had previously been completed. He was fascinated by the whole operation, and I think that he wished that he had agreed to my suggestion that we should make an operatic recording with Fiorella. It was sad that this never happened, for she was a fine artist with a beautiful voice, and there is now no existing recording of it.

20 The Cunard Concerts

The studio work on Mahler's second symphony wasn't completed until almost the middle of January. If I'd had hopes of having some respite from the hard work and nervous strain, I was soon disappointed. The financial problems hadn't disappeared. With so many recordings in the pipeline, and with the Mahler fifth and second recordings not having yet recovered their basic production costs, I was confronted by the seemingly insurmountable task of seeking the finances needed to launch the Cunard concerts. As these were shortly to be announced in the press, this was a serious matter.

Throughout this period I had the good fortune to be blessed by the presence of Jo Harris, who had been one of the girls in Uncle Fred's office. She had just recently reached retirement age at EMI, and she was miserable, for she was one of those devoted and valuable people who give their whole life to their work. When I heard about this, I had the brilliant idea of asking her if she would like to come and work as my secretary. This proved to be an inspiration, as she was delighted to be able to continue in the life to which she was accustomed and I profited by gaining a secretary with years of experience in working with artists and the recording industry. She also kept me on a steady path when events later became quite chaotic.

The concept of the Cunard project was entirely my idea, and therefore the burden fell on my shoulders. It was something quite new in the classical concert world, and it involved three quite separate activities: the concerts, which would take place in the huge hall under the entire length of the Cunard International Hotel; the arrangement and organisation of the dinners, which would take place before the start of each concert, and which was quite an undertaking in itself; and the recording of the whole programme at EMI Studios just before or immediately after the concert. From the idea's very inception, Walter Woyda of Pye was immensely interested in the idea, and considered it to be a novel way of marketing classical recordings. He offered to use the resources of the Pye organisation to distribute the Cunard concert recordings, and I was very grateful to accept this offer, as indeed was the board of IWR (Independent World Releases, the company created to finance these recordings), for it would remove some of the financial responsibility from our shoulders.

The first Cunard concert was due to take place on 24 September, and this was approaching rapidly. I attended a number of meetings with the manager of the hotel to discuss the arrangements, for this was quite a new venture for him, too. It was certainly no easy matter to organise huge numbers of dinners, all of which had to appear exactly on time and disappear swiftly and unobtrusively to allow the orchestra to take its place on the platform erected in the huge room. The concerts had to begin punctually, and I must pay tribute to the hotel staff for the clockwork precision with which the whole operation was eventually handled. During this period, Frixos Theodorides visited while on one of his frequent visits to London, and I was relieved and delighted to see him, for he took considerable interest in my activities and gave me helpful advice in all matters concerning business and finance. I shall never forget how kind he was in accompanying me to visit my lawyers, John Stitt and Ralph Instone, on whom I depended so much for advice.

In the midst of this turmoil, Roguey and Jeannie's first child, Christopher, was born in Southampton on 7 August. This was indeed joyous news, and four days later I drove down to see my new grandson for the first time in the company of Dan and Jean Hinger, Shirley's parents, who had just arrived from America and whose kindly presence made me even more happy. On the way we visited Katie, my dear mother-in-law, about whom they had heard so much from Pompy. She greeted them warmly and gave us one of her delicious teas.

Before this, however, we called in for lunch at a very pleasant little hotel in Hurley. I mention this because, just after we had started on our first course, a group of people came into the restaurant, one of whom was a rather comfortable but very handsome woman, accompanied by two young boys. To our amazement, we recognised her as Sophia Loren. Had we seen her in a restaurant in London we would have thought nothing of it, but seeing her in this rather out-of-the-way country pub was quite astounding. We gathered from the staff that she was appearing in a film which was being shot locally, and that she was staying in the hotel with her family. We finished our lunch in amazement and then drove to the hospital where Jeannie had given birth to her baby. There he was, another human being, and a very special one to me – my dear grandson, Christopher Corbett.

Fiorella Theodorides had meanwhile arrived in London to join Frixos at the Dorchester Hotel, where they stayed very frequently, and I enjoyed many happy dinners with them when the day's work was done. There was always so much to talk about. I would usually sit between them at the table, and was thus entertained by lively conversation from both sides. She loved to speak of her musical activities, past and present, and he of business and finance, and I would eventually leave them somewhat exhausted but always stimulated. How I enjoyed those wonderful evenings, and how I miss those dear friends!

Our first Cunard concert, "the French evening", was almost upon us, and once again the fixing of the orchestra was in the capable hands of Sidney Saxe. Our first soloist was the violinist Jan Pascal Tortelier, the son of a great French cellist, who proved to be both talented and easy to deal with. Indeed, he seemed intrigued to be playing in an after-dinner concert at a hotel. We had decided to keep the programmes for the Cunard concerts light, feeling that, after eating a substantial meal, the audience wouldn't want to listen to anything too demanding. Wyn opened the concert with Lekeu's *Adagio For Strings*, then Bizet's first *Suite l'Arlesienne*, followed by Saint-Saëns's *Introduction And Rondo Capriccioso*, with Jan Pascal as soloist. The second part of the concert began with Debussy's *Prelude À l'Après-midi d'Un Faune*, followed by Chausson's *Poème* and ending with Offenbach's overture to *Orpheus In The Underworld*.

For the sake of all concerned, especially the orchestra, the evening was arranged with meticulous attention to timing. The audience would sit at round tables, each of which was marked to correspond with the number on their tickets. The menu was set and included in the price of the concert; only the drinks were extra. Once the dinner was over, there would be an interval, during which the tables were speedily and skilfully cleared by an army of waiters, who would leave only the drinks. At the end of this interval, the orchestra would come onto the platform and the audience would resume their seats at their tables. I believe that the efficiency of the staff contributed greatly to the success of the occasion, for it created an atmosphere of ease and relaxation.

Much to my amazement, this first Cunard concert was completely successful and went without a single hitch. The audience was enthusiastic, and many came up to me at the end to beg that the second concert would be advertised in time so that they could arrange to be there. Wyn and the orchestra members were pleased with the success, and satisfied with the arrangements. Jan Pascal, too, appeared to be very happy with the performance and his reception, and to say that I was thankful would be an understatement. I could hardly believe that my carefully-planned arrangements had worked so well. We recorded the programme in six sessions between 20 and 23 September, after which there remained only the studio work, which was scheduled to be undertaken at the beginning of October. Walter Woyda and members of Pye were all present at this concert, which they thoroughly enjoyed, and were enthusiastic to take over the marketing and distribution of the recordings. In fact, everyone seemed delighted with the success of the first Cunard evening.

The second and third concerts of the series followed in quick succession, the second being booked for 22 October, with Shura Cherkassky as the piano soloist in an evening devoted to German composers, including the Schumann piano concerto. The recording sessions at EMI preceded the concert by a couple of days, and these presented no problems, as Wyn and Shura worked splendidly together. The first item in the programme was Weber's *Der Freischütz*, one of Wyn's favourite pieces, and he conducted it exceptionally well. This splendid piece created a warm atmosphere of anticipation for Shura's fine performance of the Schumann concerto. As can be imagined, after working together in the studios for two days, this piece proceeded as if on oiled wheels, and was warmly received by the audience.

The second half of the programme consisted of the orchestral version of Brahms's *Liebeslieder* waltzes, for which we had engaged the faithful and talented McCarthy Singers. These wonderful waltz melodies really sealed the success of the evening, and the audience enjoyed them so much that I wondered at one point in the proceedings if they were all about to get up and dance! The programme ended with a lively performance of the overture and scherzo from Mendelssohn's *A Midsummer Night's Dream*, after which the audience departed in a very happy mood.

The third and final Cunard concert was due to take place on 26 November. This concert was planned to be an Austrian evening, and Rita Streich was our eminent soloist. She arrived in London in time for the rehearsal with Wyn at EMI Studios, for which I engaged Nina Walker to play the accompaniments. It was planned that Rita should close the first part of the programme with Susanna's aria from Mozart's *La Nozze Di Figaro*, 'Amanti Costanti', after Wyn had conducted the overture to the opera, followed by the same composer's symphony in G minor, K550.

The second part of the programme was in a much lighter mood, and included pieces by Josef and Johann Strauss. During the preceding sessions at the studios, all had gone well with the Mozart aria, and we had made successful takes. As I had feared, however, when it came to recording the lighter music by Léhar and Johann Strauss the atmosphere hadn't been so happy. At one point, matters had become quite tense and I'd had to intervene to prevent a breakdown in the session. Wyn and Rita simply didn't see eye to eye over these pieces. However, peace was restored between conductor and soloist, much to my relief, as for a few moments I had really feared that there would be no Rita Streich at the concert! However, we had completed the sessions successfully, for which I was also mightily relieved.

I suppose that I had been rather lulled into a sense of ease by the way in which the first two concerts had taken place, and I would have to brace myself to face any possible storm which might blow up on this last occasion. I knew that I had to do everything to make Rita comfortable and relaxed, for I understood that she was performing under unusual circumstances and that she was probably feeling rather nervous. With this in mind, I was waiting to meet her when she arrived at the hotel on the night of the concert, and I led her to a very pleasant room which I had commandeered for her use, where she could change peacefully into her concert dress. She had also asked me if a hairdresser could be present before she went on, and I had arranged for my own to be waiting to help her. These little attentions made her happy and relaxed, and I left her to take my place in the audience with my mind at rest.

I needn't have feared, for she and Wyn performed the Mozart superbly, and she was therefore reassured when she went onto the stage in the second half to sing the difficult aria 'Mein Herr Marquis', from *Die Fledermaus*, and Franz Léhar's 'Lied Du Eva'. In fact, she was delicious, and brought the house down, much to my relief. Wyn also conducted a fine performance of the beautiful G minor symphony, and so he, too, was happy. The concert was undoubtedly a considerable success, and the reaction of the audience was extremely enthusiastic and appreciative.

After the end of the last concert of the Cunard series, the members of our board, IWR, met to review the situation. There was no doubt in our minds that our achievement was considerable. We had established a precedent for bold innovation, and we had also received excellent notices in the press, which enhanced Symphonica's reputation. Once again, both in concert and on record, we had presented performances of the highest quality.

Reviews for our recording of Mahler's second symphony were also highly favourable. The critic in *Records And Recordings* was appreciative of the whole performance, but went out of his way to praise the "quality of the engineering of the various off-stage fanfares and pronouncements". This immensely pleased Michael Gray, who had worked hard to produce these difficult effects. The reviewers heaped high praise on Wyn for his magnificent conducting of the difficult score, and indeed we enjoyed receiving a quality of praise which is rarely given.

We were greatly encouraged by this success, and hoped very much that the enthusiasm that the critics displayed for the quality and the precision of our work would influence the companies Bang & Olufsen and Wilkinson Match, with whom we were negotiating a promotional deal for Symphonica. Forging a relationship with one of them was my chief concern during this year, and I spared no pains in the attempt. There was no difficulty in dealing with Edwin Chilton of Wilkinson Match, whom we met frequently at my flat. He listened to all of our recordings with considerable appreciation, and he really put his heart into making a deal with us, even going as far as accompanying me to meetings with my solicitor, John Stitt, at which Frixos was also often present, in an attempt to come to an arrangement which would be acceptable to Wilkinson's board of directors.

We also seriously considered striking up a relationship with Bang & Olufsen, which the British company approved in principle. The company could see the advantages they would be gaining by forging promotional links with a high-quality record label. Bang & Olufsen had subsidiary companies in nearly every European capital, and in my effort to finalise a deal I made many trips to Copenhagen, Amsterdam, Paris and Brussels. It was costly and exhausting, but I felt that, if I could go to them with the approval of their various European managers, HQ would be much more likely to agree to the project. In the end, although I won support from the main European branches, my meeting in Copenhagen to finalise the details was inconclusive, and I feared that any decision from them would take far too long for me too contemplate.

Meanwhile, Roguey and Jeannie had invited me to spend Christmas with them in their new home in the Normandy village of Serquigny. As a result of the research that Roguey had carried out for ATO Chimie, a subsidiary of the great French oil company Elf Aquitaine, he had been offered a position in France, which both he and Jeannie had agreed that he should accept, and so they had packed up their possessions, including baby Christopher, and departed from Southampton to live in France in the delightful house provided for them by the company, situated in the grounds of the local château. I crossed over to France on the ferry from Southampton, arriving early in the morning at Le Havre. (As the ship entered the harbour, I was reminded of the many times that we had sailed there in dear old *Maggie*, and I felt quite nostalgic.) The ferry arrived early, and I had time to indulge in a little breakfast while waiting for Roguey, Jeannie and Christopher to turn up. I treated myself to a cognac, a coffee and a delicious croissant to keep me warm. After that, I felt that I had truly arrived in France!

It was a delightful little holiday, and I returned to London feeling sufficiently rested to proceed with our plans to find the financial support to resume our recording programme. As is so often the way, however, nature decided to halt these activities, and my physical and nervous resources rebelled. I was rushed to Middlesex Hospital as an emergency case, where I remained for nearly a month, even surviving a ferocious attack of influenza which swept the wards. This illness was a serious shock, but it taught me a lesson that I have never since forgotten. My strong constitution brought me through the crisis, but I realised that one cannot go on indefinitely abusing one's body. I was eventually rescued by dear Jo Harris, who came to fetch me from the hospital. Because of the 'flu epidemic, no visitors had been allowed to enter the ward, and I had felt like some poor refugee escaping from an internment camp.

Faithful Jo had kept the everyday affairs of the office running smoothly, and acted as a source of information for those concerned about my sudden disappearance from the scene. As soon as Mausi heard that I had come home, she returned at once, bringing with her many gifts, including an electric blanket and the complete collection of Somerset Maugham's short stories, which I still possess. Whenever I decide to read one of these, I remember how much Mausi and her thoughtful gifts helped me to recover.

On 16 March, I was formally discharged from Middlesex Hospital and was solemnly warned to behave more sensibly in the future. I staggered back to life from the dreadful experience, and I determined that I would adopt a much keener sense of perspective by allowing approaches to be made to me rather than chasing after every straw in the wind. I had done my utmost to bring about a business relationship with either Bang & Olufsen or Wilkinson Match; I decided that the ball was now in their court, and that they had to come to a decision on their own.

It came as a great shock to Wyn and me to learn that we had been the victims of shady dealings – to put it mildly – by those whom we had trusted. In spite of the assistance that Frixos and my solicitor, John Stitt, offered to regain our share of the rights to the Cunard recordings, we were obliged to accept their disappearance as a *fait accompli*. Wyn was very bitter, but I managed to calm him down by reminding him that we were still in possession of our great Mahler recordings, and that we should lick our wounds and go forward bravely with those valuable catalogue items.

When Fiorella and Frixos came to London in June, I was determined to try to do something to help Fiorella to appear in opera again. I felt so sad that such a fine and gifted singer should not be heard, and so I asked Geraint Evans if he could arrange for an audition for her at Covent Garden, and he complied. Frixos and Fiorella had been so staunch and supportive that, by arranging this, I felt that I might in some way return their kindness. She would be accompanied on the piano by Nina Walker.

On the appointed day, Geraint, Fiorella, Frixos and I met at the stage door of the opera house and were asked to go to the main foyer. We waited and waited but no one appeared, until finally we were informed that, as there was an unexpected rehearsal taking place on the stage, Fiorella would be asked to sing in the foyer. It wasn't unusual for auditions to be held there, but I was particularly upset that a singer of Fiorella's reputation should be treated in such cavalier fashion. Frixos was livid. His Greek blood boiled, and poor Geraint was deeply embarrassed. The least upset was Fiorella, who remained quite calm and said that she didn't mind where she sang. I can't remember what happened in the end, but I felt that it was typical of the sort of ineffectual behaviour one had come to expect at Covent Garden. I was deeply disappointed not to have been able to help this fine artist to stage a comeback and to repay Frixos in some small way. Curiously enough, nearly all of my attempts to do so failed, even in the early days of our friendship, except once, many years earlier, when she had sung as a guest artist with David Hughes on one of his popular television shows.

21 *Recording The Stars*

Looking back over my professional career, it's fascinating to realise how important a part the people and culture of Wales played. This began during the Philharmonia tour in 1952, where I met David Ffrangçon-Thomas and Osian Ellis, after which, fired by their patriotic enthusiasm, I was inspired to record music from their native land, with which I launched my newly-born Delysé label.

Nearly 30 years later, in a strange twist of fate, another Welshman, Geraint Evans, with whom I had previously made two of my most successful recordings, played a crucial role in events. When I told him of my exhaustive search for funds to complete the Symphonica recording schedule, he introduced me to a group of young financiers who had just formed a management company and were seeking interesting projects in which to invest. (Despite the faultlessness of Geraint's intentions, however, this act ultimately plunged us into a situation from which we could not recover.) Christopher Howland was one of the directors of Norton Warberg and was also a personal friend of Geraint's, advising him on his financial affairs. He was also a charming and friendly man to whom I took an instant liking. Geraint then introduced me to the managing director of Norton Warberg, Stephen Gee, whom I found to be most receptive and enthusiastic about the possibility of lending Symphonica the necessary funds to complete the recording schedule. This deal took over a year to negotiate, and was at last finalised in August 1977. The company's demands concerning the amount of catalogue material that we had to provide were considerable, and the terms of the loan were severe.

During this period of uncertainty, I knew that we had to strengthen our position by making a number of important recordings. Two artists of international renown had expressed an interest in working with us, and I decided that we should take the plunge and not miss out on the opportunity of adding their names to our list of artists. This was of the utmost importance, as far as Norton Warberg was concerned. For some time, Wyn had been discussing with Nina Walker (who was Montserrat Caballé's accompanist as well as coach at Covent Garden) the possibility of recording *La Demoiselle Élue*, a little-known work by Debussy, in which Caballé was very interested. Nina had proposed the idea to EMI, but they didn't consider the work to be sufficiently commercial, although it was a beautiful piece, scored for soprano, mezzo, female choir, and orchestra, and we felt that, with Caballé's renown, and as we were a smaller company and thus able to concentrate all of our energies on marketing the recording, we could succeed where a large company might not. We were known for releasing a somewhat unusual repertoire, and had created a sympathetic nucleus of record buyers to give us the support we needed. Caballé accepted our offer to record the Debussy, along with Chausson's beautiful *Poème De l'Amour Et De La Mer*, to complete a recording of fine and unusual French music.

In the event, these proved to be extremely difficult sessions from the very beginning. First of all there was a problem with the arrival of the orchestral parts, which had to come from Paris, and this caused some delay in proceedings, which upset Wyn, for he liked to have plenty of time to mark the scores with meticulous care. Next we had difficulty in finding a suitable venue in which to record, and finally we had to settle on All Saints' Church in Tooting, which was dreadfully inconvenient for all concerned. The worst aspect was that I didn't know the sound of the place, as I hadn't used it before. To add to my problems, EMI were also unable to undertake the engineering as Allen Stagg was still in Germany with DGG at that time, so I was obliged to depend on the assistance of someone I didn't know. Luckily, I was able to engage Bob Auger, a very experienced and able independent engineer, for which I was immensely relieved.

As we were obliged to fit these sessions in with Caballé's commitments at Covent Garden, they were imbued with a nightmare quality from the very beginning, for I never knew from one moment to the next whether Caballé would be able to extricate herself from unexpected rehearsals, and I also feared that her voice would be tired. However, because of her superb vocal technique, this caused no problems.

The first session was held on the evening of 28 June between eight and ten o'clock. We began with the Debussy, and this went well, as Wyn had previously rehearsed the very difficult music with the choir. Although the work was fairly unfamiliar to her, Caballé – experienced artist that she was – surmounted the problems that arose, and Wyn was a model of patience and tact, and so we were reasonably satisfied with the results. There were two sessions on the following day, one unfortunately in the morning. I always tried to avoid this, for I know that the voice is not at its best before it's had a chance to be warmed by exercise. Happily, this didn't seem to worry Caballé, and both this session and the one that had been called for that afternoon passed fairly comfortably.

We had scheduled six sessions, for we had to record both the Debussy and the Chausson. Unfortunately, our luck didn't hold, for when the time came to hold the sixth session Caballé couldn't absent herself from the Garden. I was forced to alter all other arrangements and inform the orchestra that they should proceed to Tooting for a session that would begin at eleven that night and would finish at one in the morning. This was a disaster, for we had to pay for a night session and double overtime for the orchestra as well, which completely shattered our financial budget. Not only did we have to weather this blow but it also was a terrible night, with rain coming down in sheets, and I feared that Caballé might decide not to come. She did turn up, but her voice was tired, and as she was also unfamiliar with the Chausson the whole session proved to be a nightmare for all of us. Wyn, however, was wonderfully patient, and handled the situation with great courage and skill. Much to my amazement, we managed to complete the schedule by the end of the truly awful three hours. I had an exhausting time keeping Caballé going, but I must say that, considering the conditions, she behaved remarkably well.

These were neither the happiest nor most successful sessions I ever undertook, but they taught me an important lesson: never arrange recording sessions to accommodate an artist involved in an opera season. I don't place any blame on anyone. We all did our best under extreme difficulties, but it was a painful experience, and one which cost us much more than it should, as in addition to the heavy orchestral overtime charges we were also obliged to undertake a considerable amount of expensive and difficult technical work in the studios.

In the meantime, life went on in a hectic fashion. The search for finance continued, as I didn't wish to have to rely exclusively on Norton Warberg's final decision – I had become too experienced in disappointment to be caught out by this. We were determined to continue with the enlargement of our catalogue, in spite of all the difficulties, for we knew that our only hope of finding a backer was to have an attractive product to sell.

For many years, I'd had it in mind to record something with Charles Rosen, whom I considered to be the finest pianist since Schnabel and Fischer in the performance of Beethoven. Charles came to London to play a concert at the Queen Elizabeth Hall on 28 February, and once again I was impressed by his fine musicianship, so I invited him to record Beethoven's *Emperor* piano concerto with Wyn. He accepted the invitation enthusiastically, and the recording was arranged to take place at EMI's studios in August. No more rushed sessions for me! I looked forward to working with Charles immensely, for I knew that, with his fine musical mind, the sessions would be a unique experience, God sparing any accident.

We had also planned to enlarge the catalogue by recording Beethoven's *Eroica* symphony, sessions for which were scheduled to take place in July. We were playing a dangerous game, gambling everything on Norton Warberg deciding to finalise the deal. We knew that the only way to achieve this was to include popular classical works in the catalogue, but it was a risk. I was at my wit's end trying to find ways of raising the cash to pay the orchestra up front for the *Eroica* and the *Emperor* sessions.

My life at the time was a nightmare, for Norton Warberg was dragging its heels, and if something wasn't settled soon we would be obliged to cancel the sessions, which wouldn't do our reputation in the recording world any good at all. I spent a lot of time travelling to Paris, Brussels, Amsterdam, and Cologne, working to arrange distribution deals. Luckily, our US distribution had already been finalised with Ray Burford and Paul Myers of CBS during their visit to London, so at least I was spared an exhausting journey to New York.

On 6 May, Roguey and Jeannie's second boy, Philip, was safely born in France, an event which brought great joy and a sense of reality back into my life, which was certainly crazy at that time. The happiness caused by his birth was a much-needed consolation, for earlier in the year dear Jo Harris had died suddenly, and I missed her steady, faithful presence in the office. With the birth of my dear grandson, I realised that there were still normal events to enjoy in life.

A short time later, I experienced what was almost a miracle, a wonderful demonstration of friendship. One morning, while I was working alone in my office, wondering how on Earth I was going to raise the funds to finance the two Beethoven sessions, the telephone rang. It was Mausi. She had stopped at a petrol station on her way to Berlin to tell me that she had decided to contribute financially to the scheduled recordings. I was so overcome that I could hardly speak. She had told me some years ago, when the Bayreuth Festival and its assets had been turned over to the Richard Wagner Foundation, that her mother, Winifred, and her four children had acquired certain sums of money. As this had occurred in 1973, I had thought nothing of it until now. Of course, with this injection of cash I knew that the scales would be balanced in our favour, and that now the deal with Norton Warberg would certainly go through.

It was like a wonderful dream come true. The relief from worry was indescribable, and I hardly knew how to cope with the release from anxiety. I asked her why she had come to this totally unexpected decision, and she said that she admired what Wyn and I were doing, and that she wanted to be part of the project. She explained that it would interest her little to buy bars of gold or invest everything in the stock market, and that she preferred to do something worthwhile with some of her share of the money that her grandfather had bequeathed to the family. I shall never forget that astonishing gesture of generosity, nor cease to be grateful. I realised that Mausi would want to be part of the team and a director of Symphonica Music Limited, and that she would want to attend board meetings, and so everything would be set up in a business-like manner. When I told Wyn that I was going to see Stephen Gee at Norton Warberg's offices to inform him of this unexpected and exciting offer, he nearly went mad with relief. We knew that we could now go ahead and undertake the recordings that we had planned with calm minds.

It so happened that a Dutchman called Willem Smith, who was one of Wyn's most faithful and ardent admirers, was staying in London during these eventful days. For some reason that I find difficult to explain now, it was he who accompanied me to the meeting with Stephen Gee at the Norton Warberg offices when I went there to announce Mausi's offer. Perhaps this happened because I had been alone at the time and wanted someone to act as witness. In the event, I was very pleased to have Willem's company. Stephen was happy, too, for he had really wanted our project to be in a position to be acceptable to his board. I think that he was rather bored by the more mundane applicants for funds, and he told me that, as far as he was concerned, we would soon be able to proceed with our plans, although of course he would have to obtain the agreement of his colleagues. He promised to let me know of their decision before he left the office at the weekend, and true to his word he telephoned me from a call box on his drive to the country and told me that all was well.

Legal agreement following the mutual acceptance of terms was finally reached on 11 August, and the first meeting of Symphonica Music Limited was held on 9 September. Directors Stephen Gee, Mausi Wagner and myself were there, and Wyn Morris was present as the conductor of our orchestra, Symphonica of London. The accountant John Peters, John Porter's partner in his firm, Benelake Investments, was also there as our financial advisor.

In the meantime, we had taken the risk of proceeding with our scheduled programme, and on 3 and 4 July Wyn recorded Beethoven's symphony number three in E flat, the *Eroica*, in EMI Studio One. There were no problems, as far as I was concerned, for I was working with an engineer whom I liked in surroundings that I knew well. It was on Wyn that the heavy responsibility of conducting a great work lay, a work which had already been recorded many times by the world's foremost conductors. It was really the first time that we had openly challenged the major companies, for in our Mahler recordings not only had we championed music almost unknown at the time but also Wyn was acknowledged as being an authority in the conducting of Mahler's works. It's difficult for me to give an assessment of this recording, but as far as I can remember it was a fine performance indeed. How could it not be, as Wyn was working with his own orchestra, in which he had complete confidence, and performing a work that they knew backwards? Wyn and I had gone through such times of stress that perhaps some of the magic was missing, or so it seemed to me, but in the event it was very well received and reviewed, and certainly a contribution to our catalogue of which we could be proud.

Before the agreement with Norton Warberg was actually signed, we still had to record Charles Rosen's performance of Beethoven's *Emperor* piano concerto at EMI Studios, and I was looking forward to this immensely. I had wanted to work with Charles for years, and at last, thanks to Mausi's unexpected generosity, it was finally going to happen. Before the sessions, Charles came to one or two rehearsals with Wyn and me at Heron Place, arriving with his miniature score in his pocket! These were wonderfully enjoyable occasions. He and Wyn worked together in musical harmony, and I dared to allow myself to look forward to the sessions, which I felt couldn't fail to be as fine as I had hoped. I knew that the great work was a part of Charles, and that the recording would be a wonderful experience. The recording had a special significance for me, as it was the first time that I had worked with a great pianist as a producer, and also it was taking place in the very studio in which Uncle Fred had made his memorable recordings of Schnabel and Fischer when, as a very young student, I had been privileged to turn the pages.

There was no question of turning the pages for Rosen, for he hardly looked at his score; he knew exactly what he wanted to achieve. I was on my toes as producer, though, for I knew that Charles would be a severe judge of what I captured on tape. If it didn't meet his requirements, I'd know about it! When the sessions ended, I was relieved by his satisfaction, but I knew that the editing lay ahead, and that he would be very discriminating in how this exacting work was accomplished. He insisted on being present with Wyn and myself at the editing sessions, and I was thankful to have his help in this meticulous task. After working with this great musician, I realised that he was above all a teacher, as indeed had been Schnabel, and that he didn't mind how much time and patience was required to achieve the desired result. It would be impossible to resent his insistence on perfection, and indeed I learned an enormous amount from him.

I invited Stephen Gee to the studios when the editing of the *Eroica* and the *Emperor* was completed, and he was extremely impressed by the results. This was very helpful to me, for shortly after this I took over as managing director of Symphonica Music. In this I was taking on a heavy burden, for I was now responsible for the administration of large sums of other people's money, as well as my own. At the same time, I also had to manage the distribution and marketing of our recordings as well as act as the artists' and recording manager. I was fortunate in being advised by John Peters, who was a fine accountant and who acted as liaison between the banks and myself. Most importantly, he was also a faithful friend, whom I trusted completely. He attended all board meetings, and was tremendously helpful. Mausi, too, was always present at these, as indeed was Wyn. It was comforting to have their support, for at times discussions became quite tough – for example, when I had to explain why the cost of recordings overran the projected budget, which they nearly always did.

However, in the midst of this hard work and administrative responsibility there was a ray of hope to which I looked forward immensely. Charles Rosen had agreed to record Beethoven's *Diabelli Variations*, which had long been one of my favourite works, and to my delight he agreed to do this during his next visit to London. Once again, these sessions took place at EMI Studios, this time with Mike Sheady as engineer. These sessions were a joy from beginning to end, and the recording is one of which I am most proud. There was no orchestra to worry about, no rushing through sessions to complete them in three hours, just this wonderful musician, the piano of his choice, and myself, recording for posterity. When it was all over and the editing completed, I felt as though I'd been on holiday. I can't imagine working with an easier musician. Give him his piano, place him quietly in a studio, and the magic occurs. There were no problems and no mishaps, and I shall always remember the atmosphere of happiness that pervaded as Rosen played Beethoven's enchanting variations.

Our last recording in 1977 was an early and relatively unknown work by Richard Wagner, Mausi's grandfather, called *Das Liebesmahl Der Apostel* (*The Feast Of Pentecost*), scored for large orchestra and male voice choir, and we chose it largely to express our gratitude to her. Once again, we engaged John McCarthy's splendid Ambrosian Singers, and of course the orchestra was Symphonica of London. We gathered at the EMI studios on 19 and 20 November for this exciting musical adventure. This time, my engineer was Michael Gray, my intrepid friend from the Mahler eighth session. The directors of Norton Warberg were invited to attend, and I was amused and delighted by their obvious enjoyment of the experience. It pleased me immensely when I overheard Stephen Gee remark to Christopher Howland, "Isn't it satisfying to be able to help in such a worthwhile undertaking?"

Wagner had written *Das Liebesmahl* for a choral festival in Dresden, and it's an exceedingly difficult piece. Two thirds of the work are *a capella* (unaccompanied), and the singers are joined by the orchestra only in the most thrilling moments of intense excitement, with a great whisper of tremolo strings resembling a wild wind, to be joined finally by the chorus of disciples. The great problem, of course, is for the chorus to remain in tune for almost 20 minutes of unaccompanied singing, so that, when the orchestra is finally added, there is no horrible shock of dissonance. This difficulty can be overcome in a recording situation, but in concert it's more of a problem, and for this reason the work is rarely performed.

To complete the LP, we recorded Bruckner's *Helgoland*, a fine and rousing work also scored for large orchestra and male voice choir. It's an interesting piece, but not as hair-raising as the Wagner. Wyn had also invited some guests to attend the last session, and Mike Gray, with his dry wit, said, "I see the supporters are here for the game." Indeed, there was something reminiscent of a football match in studio one, with the male voice choir and the audience seated in two rows. Luckily, they didn't make as much noise as football supporters! Although the music was very difficult to perform, there was a light-hearted atmosphere throughout the evening, probably because of their presence.

Between these sessions and the time I had to spend on studio work, not to mention the work I had to put in to maintain the smooth running of the company, I was flying to Paris for meetings with Pathé Marconi and to Cologne and Amsterdam to set up distribution and other pressing arrangements with Electrola. It was indeed a hectic existence. Certainly I had a well-set-up company to support me, but banks aren't exactly comfortable bedfellows, and I was conscious all the time that they were looking over my shoulder to make sure that I didn't exceed my budget. We also felt constant pressure about our expected sales, and it wasn't easy to make the banks understand that, before they can buy them, the public first has to be told about new releases via reviews in the press, which often appear only some months after the recordings are on the market. Sales of classical recordings are also relatively small initially, but if one produces a fine record then the demand grows and lasts for many years. One must have patience and, above all, a catalogue large enough to support the situation. In order to help matters, we offered to include all of our previous highly regarded Mahler recordings with the present company's releases, on the condition that Norton Warberg would agree to finance the cost of the necessary processing work.

Thankfully, for Christmas I was able to pack my bags and escape to Serquigny to stay with Roguey and Jeannie and my little grandsons. This was a wonderfully relaxing time, and I forgot my troubles in the happiness of getting to know Philip, now six months old, and observing Christopher's determined and demanding progress as a three year old.

On 1 January, I went straight down to Cannes for MIDEM, the great gramophone record jamboree. Here, in a meeting with the chairman of RCA Japan lasting just over half an hour, which I had previously set up by telephone, I pulled off an excellent licensing deal to cover their territory. I was pleased with my success, as indeed was our board of directors, for now we had distribution in almost the entire record-buying world.

The following year was one of increasing turbulence. It began optimistically enough with plans to record Mahler's great ninth symphony, to which Wyn and I had been looking forward immensely. I think that, in a curious way, we both felt that in returning to Mahler we were re-entering a sphere of music-making in which we had complete confidence, almost as though we were coming home. Also, Allen Stagg was back in England and free to undertake the engineering. I hoped that the coming together of the old team, which had produced such successful results in past years, might rekindle some of the old magic. It was decided that the huge orchestra needed for this mighty work was too large to be recorded satisfactorily in EMI Studio One, and so we approached Watford Town Hall, our favourite venue, where we had worked so successfully in the past. Unfortunately, this wasn't available, and our second choice, Walthamstow Town Hall, was also fully booked, and so the search began for a suitable alternative.

Allen provided a solution, telling us that he had heard favourable reports of St Jude's huge church in Hampstead Garden Suburb. This was not only a venue with sympathetic acoustics but it was also quiet and free from traffic and underground noise. Planes, of course, couldn't be avoided, but the heaviest traffic of flights fortunately occurred in the middle of the day and during the break for lunch. We performed some tests in the church and found the sound to be both spacious and warm, with an acceptable level of echo, and so we decided that, under the circumstances, we should go ahead and use St Jude's as our centre of recording activities.

The church appeared to have many other advantages, for it was within easy reach of Heron Place and there was unlimited space for parking the orchestra's and engineers' vans and cars. The church people were also very helpful, since they were anxious to encourage recording activities on their premises, which could sizeably increase their income. We had decided to return to our usual Symphonica routine of following the recording sessions with a concert as soon as possible, and to this end we had booked the Royal Festival Hall for 22 May.

Mahler's ninth symphony is a work of tremendous musical importance. I think that it's the finest of his purely orchestral works, and it's scored for a large number of musicians. Wyn was at his greatest during the sessions, and with Allen Stagg at the technical helm I felt that we would reach again the heights that we had achieved with *Des Knaben Wunderhorn* and the composer's fifth symphony. However, God has a strange way of dealing with over-confidence, and in this instance what appeared to be an almost assuredly successful recording was put to great risk by the strangest, most unforeseen occurrence.

In the roof high up above us was a nest of baby birds. We were made aware of the presence of this little family when suddenly, excited by the beautiful sounds rising upwards, they decided to join in. Imagine our horror when these tiny but pervasive sounds became clearly apparent above the swell of the 80 musicians. I wouldn't have believed it possible that these little creatures could so dominate the situation. There was nothing that we could do until ladders had been fetched and the nest removed to a safe place in the garden of the church, which couldn't be done until lunchtime. The orchestra was amused and enchanted by the occurrence, and swore that they would refuse to continue recording if the nest was harmed! This was very funny for those who weren't paying the heavy costs, of course, but for us it could spell tragedy. We couldn't continue recording while the birds were still up there. It was eventually decided that Wyn should continue to rehearse for the remainder of the session, accompanied by the birds, after which we would hopefully make up for the lost time in the remaining recording sessions – with the permission of our feathered friends, of course!

It was planned that, after the lunch break, during which the nest would be brought down to the garden, the three hours would be used entirely for recording the results of the morning's rehearsal. It was a desperate plan, and it required all of Wyn's willpower and discipline to keep the musicians in a receptive mood. To our immense relief, he succeeded and elicited a fine performance. Mausi and I, who were in the control room, had been praying that the time would be saved, as indeed it was through Wyn's domination of the situation. It remains a mystery whether or not anxiety inspired Wyn to achieve the results that he obtained from the orchestra, but nevertheless the performance was one of his finest. As we shook our heads ruefully over this near disaster, we swore that never again would we conduct sessions in an untried venue. The church authority was very upset by the incident, but they should have thought of checking the roof for unexpected invaders before we began. I was sure that they had also learned a lesson which they never forgot.

The concert which followed, on 22 May, was an event which aroused considerable interest in the serious newspapers and music journals, which in turn brought a large and enthusiastic audience to the Festival Hall. Our concept of bringing together the finest orchestral and chamber music players in London for the purpose of recording, followed immediately by a public performance, once again caused quite a stir in the musical world, and Wyn stood up to the test magnificently. We had planned a generous programme, beginning with Wagner's exciting overture to *Rienzi* and Felix Weingartner's majestic orchestral arrangement of Beethoven's *Grosse Fuge*, while the second half of the concert was devoted to Mahler's ninth symphony, which, as the critic of the *Financial Times* wrote, was "a work usually devoted as an entire programme". Wyn conducted magnificently, and rose to heights of inspiration and authority in the Mahler. The reviews were excellent, and the critics wrote with meticulous care about how seriously they regarded Symphonica as a musical project. We were delighted by the success of the concert, as indeed was Norton Warberg, but it didn't seem to loosen the purse-strings.

We were now committed to our next recording with Charles Rosen, of Beethoven's second and fourth piano concerti, followed by another concert at the Festival Hall, and once again the tedious and painful task of trying to extract the necessary funds from our backers fell upon me. I hadn't yet received a response from Stephen Gee to my earlier suggestion, that we should contribute our earlier, highly successful recordings to the present catalogue to alleviate the financial situation if Norton Warberg would cover the processing costs.

Our reputation in the musical world was good, and I was absolutely right to insist that we should seize the opportunity of recording Charles Rosen on his next visit to London. Our distributors were also delighted with the fine reviews that we had received for our recording of Mahler's ninth, which they were now busy promoting throughout the world, and insisted that we increased our catalogue as quickly as possible. They were undoubtedly right, but we found it difficult to put pressure on Norton Warberg, who expressed great admiration and appreciation for our achievements but showed a strange reluctance to produce the finances we required. In fact, I was beginning to be seriously concerned about their finances, and wondered if they were as solid as we had believed.

As far as Beethoven's second and fourth piano concerti were concerned, we had no choice; we were committed to Charles Rosen and to the orchestra. There could be no withdrawal, either from the recording sessions or the concert. I told Stephen Gee that there could be no change of plan, and that we had hired EMI Studios for the recordings, which were scheduled to take place in the autumn of 1978. When the recording of Beethoven's fourth concerto was released in 1979, the reviews were outstandingly enthusiastic, prompting headlines such as "Review Selection Of Recordings Of Special Merit" and "Best Of The Month". In *Gramophone* magazine, Richard Osborne wrote, "Rosen's performance is in a class of its own," and "Wyn Morris's contribution is perfectly at one with Rosen. This recording is a must." There was high praise from the American critics, too, such as, "This is easily the most satisfying record of the fourth piano concerto that I can remember." To our intense pleasure, most of the critics repeated their praise of the previously released recording of the *Diabelli Variations*.

Then came the crisis. The Festival Hall concert was upon us, and Stephen Gee told me that there would be no funds from Norton Warberg towards the cost. It was a bitter blow, and I must confess that I felt utterly shattered when I heard their decision. There was only one thing I could do: I paid for the concert myself. There was no alternative, since our reputation would have been destroyed forever if we had failed to meet our commitments. I can remember little of the event, since I was in such a state of despondency, but there is a vivid picture in my mind of Charles bounding onto the platform as though to accept a joyous challenge and giving a masterful performance of Beethoven's enchanting second piano concerto with Wyn conducting. The thought occurred to me then that, if only Charles could be persuaded more often to appear in public, which he obviously enjoyed, instead of spending so much time lecturing and writing about music, then the life of my recording company would be both easier and more lucrative.

As I feared, our association with Norton Warberg had come to an end. Their investment in various enterprises had apparently proved to be unsuccessful, and they were declared bankrupt. I can't imagine how we survived this dreadful period, as our tapes were seized by the Treasury as part of Norton Warberg's assets. I don't speak ill of Stephen Gee and Christopher Howland, for they truly meant well and had felt real enthusiasm and pleasure in helping us. Their company, however, must have spread their finances too thin, as they met with disaster, and we were caught up in this.

I find it deeply painful to write about this period of my life, for we had achieved so much and we believed that we were so close to reaching a firm financial foothold. We survived, somehow, although I had to leave my flat in Heron Place, to which I was very much attached, and for nearly a year I was almost homeless. However, human beings are wonderfully resilient, and somehow I struggled out of the morass of despondency. Thankfully, I had many good friends, and they stood by me. In time, Mausi found me accommodation with a great friend of hers, Lorna Braithwaite, the widow of the conductor Warwick Braithwaite, who owned a pleasant house in Hampstead which had plenty of spare rooms. She seemed delighted to have me there, and I was glad that I could remain in London and look after my business affairs. At weekends, I would escape from my troubles and drive down to Southampton, where Roguey and Jeannie had made their cosy little home available to me. My furniture was moved there at the end of 1979, and I found it a haven of peace and quiet. I blessed the fact that, when they went to live in France, they decided to keep their house at 88 Copperfield Road. I eventually moved there completely, much to dear Lorna Braithwaite's disappointment, for I think that she really enjoyed having me in her home so that she could indulge her characteristic Welsh interest in other people's lives. Her interest and friendship was a blessing at this difficult period in my life.

22 The End Of A Great Adventure

The financial collapse of Norton Warberg in 1979, and the seizure of our Symphonica catalogue as part of their assets by the Treasury, was a blow from which at the time Wyn and I felt that we could not recover. It was dreadful for all concerned, and I felt particular regret that Mausi had also been involved. Staunch, true friend that she was, however, she never uttered a word of complaint, and accepted her loss philosophically, as indeed we all did, as there was no alternative.

I made the move to Southampton at the end of 1979. Roguey and Jeannie lived near Southampton University, on the very fringe of the Meon Valley, which is one of the most beautiful areas of the Hampshire countryside. Jeannie's mother, Mary Collar, whose house was also nearby, knew this part of the world well, after having lived there nearly all her life, and we went on many delightful expeditions together, during which I drove and she acted as a most efficient and knowledgeable guide. She was the perfect companion at that difficult time, for as we meandered along the beautiful country roads she listened to some of my recent misadventures in the musical world and gave me the quiet sympathy which I needed at that time. I remember with real pleasure our delightful visits to Winchester, Salisbury and Old Sarum, to see the ancient fortified remains of the original city, from which we looked down upon the magnificent countryside spread before us and imagined the centuries of people who had shared the same experience. On our return from these trips, we would usually stop for lunch in one of the quaint old inns that we found on the way. It surprises me how well I filled my life during those first years after leaving London. I was helped in this by members of the family across the Channel and from the other side of the Atlantic, who visited frequently, and I managed to stay in both France and America quite often.

I was beginning to spend more time in London at this point, and soon discovered a place in the musical world again. At the end of 1982, at

Mausi's invitation, I made my first recording since the dissolution of Symphonica, after she asked me to produce a programme of piano works by Franz Liszt played by one of her protégés, Lennart Rabes, while Allen Stagg undertook the engineering duties. I was only too happy to do anything I could to please Mausi, and I knew Lennart to be a fine musician, and so this prospect gave me great pleasure. We had the usual problem of finding a recording venue, but even this difficulty brought back nostalgic memories. Eventually, Allen and I settled on the Henry Wood Hall, which I didn't know but which Allen had used before. The resulting sessions were successful, which satisfied Mausi and was a great pleasure for Lennart and his mother, who was present throughout the recordings.

On 22 January 1983, I flew over to Paris to stay with Mausi, who had invited me to be present at the rehearsals of Siegfried Wagner's tome poem *Sehnsucht*, which Daniel Barenboim would be including in his programme with the Orchestre de Paris at their concerts in the Salle Pleyel on 26 and 27 January. I arrived in Paris at about 10.30am and found my way to the flat that Mausi had rented in Montmartre. It was in a large building composed entirely of artists' studios, and I remember that there was a very disagreeable concierge in charge! I finally discovered Mausi's eyrie at the top of the building and waited there for her to return. I suspected that she would be in a state of some agitation, and I decided to proceed with caution.

In the evening we were the guests of Princess Ruspoli and her husband in their beautiful house on the Quai d'Anjou, overlooking the Seine. They were a charming young couple, and they held quite a party. They produced a splendid feast in Mausi's honour, of which she ate very little, as usual, although I made up for her lack of appetite!

The next two days were busy, as Mausi had rehearsals at the Salle Pleyel, and the first performance was to take place on the evening of 26 January. The work was entirely unknown to both the orchestra and the public, but Barenboim made a fine job of conducting and did full justice to the beautiful piece, which was received with warm appreciation by the audience. I couldn't help recalling the time when I had been present at the Salle Pleyel as a young girl of 16, when Paris had heard Elgar's great violin concerto for the first time. My instinct told me that it would be a long while before the French public assimilated this work into their accepted repertoire, as indeed had been the case with the Elgar.

A little later, in 1984, I made a few broadcasts for the BBC for the first time. Presented under the title *My Thanks To Uncle Fred*, they were given much advance publicity by the corporation, and were very successful. I enjoyed making them immensely, particularly because my producer was Alan Haydock, one of the BBC's top presenters, and it was a pleasure to work with him. At this time, I also met another great friend of mine in the BBC, Derek Lewis, the head of the record library, who had been a faithful friend since the early days of Delysé. We would rendezvous at the Hellenic, a little Greek restaurant directly opposite my old flat in Heron Place, which had always been a favourite of mine. During these visits to London, I would seize the opportunity to spend happy hours with Coggie and Stella Margetson in their beautiful home in Hamilton Terrace. We had been friends since our school days, and there was very little that we didn't know about each other's lives. Coggie was not only my friend but also an intimate of my family, with whom she had spent a considerable amount of time in Leighton Buzzard during the war years.

Late in November 1985, Mausi surprised me with another project. She telephoned from her home in Lucerne, and in her usual breezy and casual fashion informed me that she had engaged the Aalborg Symphony Orchestra and their permanent conductor, Peter Erös, to record three of her father's works: the third symphony, the tone poem *Sehnsucht* and 'Un Wenn Die Welt Voll Teufel Wär'. She asked me if I would be willing to produce the recordings, with Allen Stagg acting as engineer. I must say that both Allen and I were rather nonplussed. I asked her why she wanted to go to all the trouble of paying our expenses to fly us to Denmark and putting us up in a hotel for several days in order to record a practically unknown orchestra when there were so many fine and well-known English orchestras that she could engage. The answer was, of course, that she was doing Peter Erös a favour, for he had been a fellow student at her school in New York during the time that she had lived there after the war. I imagine that she felt that the recording would consolidate his position within the Aalborg Orchestra.

Allen was given the name of a first-class engineer living in Copenhagen who had good digital recording equipment and who would be willing to act as his assistant during the sessions. All was finally arranged, and on 15 December I met Allen at Heathrow and we flew to Copenhagen, where we caught a small plane for another hour's flight west to Aalborg. Mausi and Peter Erös were waiting at the airport to greet us, and I don't remember ever having been received with such relief in my life. It appeared that

Mausi was in trouble with the Danish Musicians' Union, for in her imperious Wagnerian fashion, which it's true that she could sometimes assume, she had contravened some of their rules. I was rushed to a meeting at the Musicians' Union headquarters, where I sat at a large table surrounded by dour, unfriendly faces, and was bombarded with all manner of questions. As I didn't yet know what Mausi had said to them, and as I knew nothing of Danish union rules, I was in something of a quandary. After some incomprehensible discussion, I decided that the only way out of the situation was to go on the offensive. I thumped the table hard, reared up and told them that, if they didn't wish the orchestra to earn fees for the recording of three large orchestral works, Miss Wagner had told me that she was prepared to cancel the arrangements and call off the sessions. Fortunately, these were appropriate tactics, and my adversaries collapsed. Later, Mausi offered everyone a drink, and we parted on friendly terms. She was so relieved, for she was quite ignorant of this part of the recording business, whereas I, alas, was only too used to it.

We stayed in a very pleasant hotel called the Hveida Haus, and Mausi couldn't have been a more generous host. The weather was cold, and after our long day Allen and I were both hungry and tired. Surprisingly, the restaurant was at the top of the building, and we enjoyed an excellent Danish meal there before retiring early to rest before the next day's activities. On the following morning, we walked to the hall through the snow, where we met our assistant engineer, and for the first time in my life I saw the digital recording equipment that would be used, remembering the huge consoles that had been trundled around during location sessions in the old days with Delysé, I said to Allen, "I just don't believe that this tiny control console is all we need." It was a revelation indeed. Luckily, Allen and the Danish engineer liked each other and worked well, and even the speakers – which were usually objects of much concern to Allen when he listened to the playbacks – appeared to satisfy his critical ear.

The recordings took place in a municipal hall, and the acoustics there were not very good, but this was something that was beyond our means to improve, and so we had to make the best of it. Mausi asked me, "Do you not think it would be a good idea to say a few words of greeting to the orchestra?" I hoped that they understood English, as I knew nothing of Danish, and went bravely forth to address them. As I looked into their faces, I thought how unresponsive they appeared, and how difficult it must be for Peter Erös to cope with this situation (which, incidentally, he did with fine musicianship and skill). After saying a few words about how these sessions meant a great deal to Miss Wagner, as she would be hearing these works composed by her father for the first time and played by a fine orchestra, I wished us all well and hoped that we would make a successful recording. I then went back into the control room and told Allen and Peter Erös that we were ready to begin with the symphony in C. After listening for a while, I turned to look at Mausi and saw that she was deeply moved. I felt happy that, in spite of the difficulties, Allen and I were there to help her in her long-cherished ambition to record her father's works. The sessions lasted for four days, and then Allen and I flew back to Heathrow where Allen's wife, Sheila, met us. They drove off to return to their home, near Ross-on-Wye, and I waited for my connecting flight to Paris, where I was to spend Christmas with the family.

At the end of my holiday, on 2 January, I met Allen at Fine Splice Studios to edit the Siegfried Wagner tapes. This task successfully completed, I asked Mausi if she would like me to issue the recordings on the Delysé label. I had recently formed a small limited company with Gilbert Burnett in order to have a means at my disposal of reissuing some of the early Delysé children's catalogue or any other material which I felt could be of interest. We issued the Siegfried Wagner recordings in the UK on this, and Mausi released them in Germany. The critics were interested to hear these works, and the fact that the composer was the great Wagner's son added considerably to the importance of the media coverage that the recordings received.

During the years following the collapse of Norton Warburg, Wyn had been investigating the situation regarding the Symphonica tapes, and on one day towards the end of 1986 he asked me to meet him for lunch at a restaurant near the Treasury offices in Westminster. He said that he had finally discovered the name of the Treasury solicitor who dealt with the property of bankrupt companies, and he had made an appointment for us to visit her. This was exciting news, and when Wyn and I met Miss Sargant we found that she was a most pleasant young woman, and I remember being surprised that anyone so charming should be employed in such a horrible job.

The outcome of our meeting was that we came to a preliminary agreement whereby a trust would be set up consisting of the Treasury, Wyn

Morris, Friedelind Wagner and myself, which I agreed to administer. This, however, was only the beginning of the negotiations with the Treasury, as the agreement then had to be incorporated into a legal document in order to satisfy the investigations of any future licensors. To this end, there were a number of meetings between Miss Sargant and Wyn, usually following a consultation between Wyn, myself and any record company which was currently showing interest in acquiring the Symphonica catalogue on a licensing basis.

The deal with the Treasury eventually completed, on 16 October 1989 I was in a position to ask Allen to collect the Symphonica tapes from EMI Studios, where they had been in safe keeping. It was a great moment when we had the masters in our possession once again after ten years – in fact, we could hardly believe that it was true.

As I had feared, however, it took me some time to find our first licensor. The Symphonica catalogue was now quite old, and there had been a number of Mahler works recorded during the intervening years. Nevertheless, the prestige of our earlier recordings had not been forgotten, and in January 1990 I received an offer of a favourable licensing and distribution deal from a young company called MSD, who were then branching out in their interests from publishing children's books to releasing records. Their terms were acceptable, and the advance on royalties was reasonably generous, and so after some discussion with Mausi and Wyn, and after informing the Treasury, we decided to accept the offer and relax in the knowledge that our recordings would soon be once again available to the public. As they were not to be released on our own label, I was no longer involved with the marketing of the product; it would be left to others to cope with the difficulties of arranging distribution both at home and abroad. I wished them well, for all of our sakes.

After this, I found myself with time to spend with my family in America, and so I flew to Huntsville, Alabama, to stay with Pompy, Shirley and my grandsons. This visit gave me the opportunity to get to know the boys, for distance and circumstances had separated us for far too long. Eric was now a handsome young man of 20, and Danny, not behind him in looks, was less than two years younger. We enjoyed each other's company immensely and I was delighted to see the strength of the interests and talents that had been passed down to them. As far as I could tell, both had inherited something of Pompy's outstanding gifts as a scientist, which he had employed by researching the development of defence programming, and they had inherited musical talents from both Shirley's family and mine. Indeed, they had been taught by their eminent grandfather, Dan Hinger, and both boys were fine timpanists. Later, in the years which followed my visit, Eric became first timpanist of the Huntsville Symphony Orchestra, combining this with his career of being a highly considered scientist.

My visit to Huntsville was interesting because not only was it very social, with many luncheons and parties arranged by the wives of the scientists, but also because the town had an active musical life. There was a symphony orchestra, complete with a permanent conductor, and two youth orchestras. There was also a public radio station attached to the University of Alabama, and this played an important part in the cultural life of the area. During my visit there, I was honoured by being invited to make several broadcasts.

Earlier in my story, during the dreadful period around the siege of Dunkirk, I wrote of the uncertainty surrounding the reported death of Henry Walcot, Dick's brother-in-law and father of Elizabeth. Although she was now living in Canada, we had remained great friends over the years, and I knew that she had never been able to accept the mystery that surrounded her father's death. When I heard that she was coming to stay with me in Southampton, I suggested that she and I should go on a pilgrimage to Belgium in an attempt to find some trace of Henry's grave. To this end, I wrote to the War Graves Commission and asked if they had any information concerning the burial of Captain John Henry Walcot of the First Battalion, King's Shropshire Light Infantry, reported missing at Dunkirk. They immediately replied that he was buried in the churchyard of the village of Houtem in Belgium. When I told Elizabeth, she announced that she would be coming over at once.

We drove to Newhaven early one morning, and decided to leave the car there and hire transport on reaching Dunkirk. We were fortunate enough to engage a kindly, efficient woman driver who was accustomed to finding her way in and out of the unmanned frontier posts between France and Belgium. After a long drive through the sad, battle-worn countryside, we finally came upon the village of Houtem, in which stood a huge church. It was here, in its beautifully-kept cemetery, that we found the graves of three British officers, one of which was Henry's. I left Elizabeth alone there for a while and I knew that finding where her father was buried would help her finally to accept his death.

Over the next few years, the fate of the Symphonica catalogue can only be described as confused. MSD very soon sold its interest in the record business to the well-known book publisher Collins, who announced their decision to enter this field of activity with some *éclat* at a press conference held at the Barbican, to which Wyn and I were invited. They had barely dipped their toes into this new venture when, a year later, I was informed that they had sold their interest in the record company to Pickwick. I wasn't really surprised, though, as theirs had never seemed a very serious venture. I had known Walter Woyda of Pickwick for many years, during which he had managed the distribution and marketing company most efficiently. Now that Pickwick had decided to acquire a catalogue to release on its own label, I felt that at last there was a chance for our recordings to be marketed expertly.

In May 1991, before I could discuss the new developments with the members of the Trust, I received a dreadful blow with the news of Mausi's death in a nursing home in Herdecke, Westphalia. I knew that she hadn't been feeling well for some time, but I had no idea of the seriousness of her illness. It was a terrible shock to me, for she had always been a veritable tower of strength, courageously supporting me in my efforts to salvage as much as possible from the shipwreck of Symphonica. Now, though, I had to continue in this struggle alone and deal with all business relating to Symphonica that affected Mausi through Heinz Boettner, a Hamburg accountant.

Once again, in 1991, I signed a new contract on behalf of the Trust, this time with Pickwick, and I sent Walter Woyda a list of the recordings that were available for release, which included Mahler's second, fifth, eighth and ninth symphonies, as well as *Des Knaben Wunderhorn* and *Das Klagende Lied*. The Symphonica list also included Beethoven's second, fourth and fifth piano concerti and his *Diabelli Variations*, all played by Charles Rosen, as well as Debussy's *La Demoiselle Élue* and Chausson's *Poème De l'Amour Et De La Mer*, with Montserrat Caballé as soloist. Knowing that Walter Woyda was an experienced record man, we felt encouraged and hopeful as we received the advance on royalties for each item selected for release. However, the French have an apt saying, "*Plus ça change, plus c'est la même chose*," and this was certainly true in this instance, for in early 1994 we heard that Pickwick had sold out to Carlton Home Entertainments (the record division of Carlton Television), and it was rumoured that Walter Woyda was retiring.

Carlton brought Hans van Woerkens, a well-known and -respected personality in the European recording world, to England to act as chief executive of their record division. The Pickwick name was dropped, and the company name of Carlton Classics now appeared on the labels. Once again, I had to get used to a whole new team and discover the activities allocated to various individuals. Shortly after his appointment, I decided that I had to visit van Woerkens and get to know him, and so I arranged an appointment with him at Carlton's offices in Elstree and asked my grandson, Christopher Corbett – who, much to my delight, had been a student at Southampton University since 1992 – to drive me there to meet the great man himself.

The appointment was for 2.30pm on 7 December 1994, and before the meeting Chris and I decided to give ourselves time to enjoy a good lunch at the famous pub in Elstree, the haunt of many film stars. This was the most enjoyable part of the expedition, as for a while I was able to forget about the critical part of the business which lay ahead and enjoy Christopher's light-hearted company. I walked into the meeting with the unknown van Woerkens and his colleague Charles Padley in an optimistic and cheerful mood, and indeed it all went well, for I found that we had much in common in our background and experience, and that we spoke the same language. I felt that we would work well together. On my return, I was able to report to Wyn reasonably optimistically that we may at last have stumbled on an individual who appreciated what we had achieved and who would help to make our business relationship a success.

After this constructive meeting, things seemed to proceed fairly smoothly. In June 1995, we finally exchanged contracts for the release of the recording of Mahler's second symphony and Beethoven's second and fourth piano concerti, and also his *Eroica* symphony. This encouraged us enormously, as we hoped that it was evidence of the seriousness of van Woerkens's intention to co-operate in the reissue and promotion of the Symphonica catalogue, and of course the substantial advances on royalties for these four recordings was also an injection of much-needed cash. Encouraged by van Woerkens's seemingly sympathetic interest, Wyn was able to arrange a number of meetings with him, in which they discussed new repertoire. I remember how hard I worked on the complicated costing of interesting sessions, which I presented to van Woerkens in the hope that he would be sufficiently impressed to enter into some financial arrangement with us for their production.

There was no response from him. On three occasions in 1996 I was obliged to write to him on matters of policy relating to the release of recordings already licensed to Carlton, and on each occasion I was asked to speak to Charles Padley. I therefore assumed that van Woerkens had already taken leave of Carlton! I received no explanation nor information, which I resented but which didn't surprise me greatly. So there we were, with our catalogue in the power of the huge Carlton Television corporation, and with no one as far as I could see with any experience of the record industry in charge. I had to reconcile myself to accepting the fact that Wyn and I had done everything within our power to co-operate with Carlton and to advise them in the promotion of our catalogue. There was nothing further that I could do, and so I decided to try to relax and enjoy the company of my grandsons, whose presence was a source of great happiness to me.

Christopher had completed his three years at Southampton University and obtained a degree in Philosophy. He then embarked on his great ambition of acquiring his own boat and eventually sailing to the Greek Islands. First, however, he had to find the means to finance such an undertaking. To this end, he moved to Yorkshire to work for a year, and returned to Southampton with cash and an adorable puppy, which was named Fahré, for reasons unknown except to his master! He was half labrador and half Rhodesian ridgeback, and a very handsome fellow indeed. Christopher then obtained a job in a boatyard in Southampton, where he worked for long hours every day fitting out racing yachts, which was physically tough and, at times, not particularly healthy. It was certainly not an easy time, and I remember that he and Fahré sometimes visited me in the evenings, extremely hungry and very tired, both of them covered in white powder from the fibreglass that Christopher rubbed down all day.

After he had acquired sufficient capital to purchase a boat, his next step was to find a way of earning enough money to both live and maintain his craft, and so to this end he enrolled as a student at a teaching college in Bournemouth, and after three months he had obtained an international certificate in the teaching of English as a foreign language, which would enable him to earn a living in the countries that he visited on his travels. I must say that I admired his sense of purpose and his courage.

In September 1995, it was the turn of Philip, my youngest grandson, to enrol as a student at Southampton University, where he would read for a European master's degree in Ship Science, which would involve three years of study, after which, if he had achieved good enough marks, he would study for a further year at the École Centrale at Nantes. During these three years, he was a frequent and welcome visitor, and was often accompanied by a couple of scruffily-attired fellow students called Tom and John, whose exuberant company entertained me greatly.

I was fortunate to be surrounded by the young members of the family, whose enthusiasm for life was a stimulant in itself. My decision to leave London in 1979 after the collapse of Norton Warberg, and to accept Jeannie and Rogue's generous offer to live in their charming little house, had indeed been fortunate, for I was given the priceless opportunity to enjoy both a close relationship with my two grandsons and very frequent visits from Jeannie and Rogue from Paris. This would certainly not have been the case had I remained in London. So in spite of the concern I felt in losing the control of our recordings and our lack of professional contacts, I felt that I had gained something different but of equal importance, and I was content.

London had lost much of its attraction for me since the death of my dear friend Coggie Margetson on 1 July 1995 and of her sister, Stella, in 1993. A few days before her death, I had visited Coggie in St John and Elizabeth Hospital, St John's Wood. I could see that she was very ill, but I didn't realise that her end was so near, and I was thankful afterwards to have been able to spend a few hours with her during the last days of her life. Little more than a year later, the family suffered a great loss in the death of Jeannie's mother, Mary Collar. I can't write of the sorrow felt by her children, of course, but I felt a deep sense of gratitude for the kindness and help that she had given me when I first came to live in Southampton. I shall never forget the many conversations we had concerning our shared love of music and the pleasure we had in the expeditions we took together, which helped me to adjust to my new way of life.

By this time, I had been forced to take life rather more easily, but I was shattered once again in September 1994 by the truly awful and totally unexpected news of Matti Prichard's sudden death. This news was conveyed to me by telephone from someone I hardly knew, who gave me no preparation or warning, and I simply couldn't believe that I would never again enjoy the company of that vivid, warm human being, who had been such a friend and help to me during our great Delysé adventure. The death of these dear friends left me quite bereft, and it took me a long time to become reconciled to the loss.

Fortunately, my young grandsons were a constant source of interest and encouragement to me, with their youthful enthusiasm in all things nautical. Although I followed my family's maritime adventures with great interest, and sometimes with considerable concern, I also managed to keep an eye on the progress (or otherwise) of the Symphonica catalogue in the hands of our distributors. I had no complaints regarding the regularity of the royalty statements, but the sales figures were steadily diminishing, and now that van Woerkens had vanished from the scene there seemed to be no one with whom I could discuss the disappointing situation. Actually, I had recently become less concerned with business matters, although had I been able to foretell the future I would have known that something fantastic lay in store for me.

However, before I was in any way aware of what was to come, I had to submit to the discomfort of an operation to remove a cataract from my right eye. Jeannie came over for the actual operation on 7 May, and although in these days the surgeons are very skilled and the operation routine, and one suffers very little, I was nevertheless thankful to have her there with me.

Many colleagues came to visit me during this time. Johnny Morris not only phoned frequently for a good professional gossip but he also went to the trouble of driving all the way from his home in Hungerford to take me out to lunch on a number of occasions. He had also undergone eye surgery, and so I was worried about the driving, but he made little of it, and his wonderful sense of humour was a tonic in itself. I was also deeply touched when Coggie's nephew, Johnny Margetson, and his wife, Anne, drove down from London to visit me for lunch, bringing with them Coggie's two brilliant caricatures of Toscanini and Harriet Cohen, which I had always admired for their humour and perception and which Coggie had left to me in her will. Even after her death, her generosity seemed endless.

1997 began with celebrations in honour of EMI's centenary, to which I was invited. The first party was held at the Lancaster Hotel on 8 January, and after this a mobile exhibition toured the British Isles, carrying as exhibits many examples of early "talking machines" and souvenirs of the industry's early days, which illustrated Uncle Fred's career and his contribution to record production. Unfortunately, the general state of my health and the uncertain condition of my eyes made it impossible for me to attend all of these functions, although I was determined to go to London for the great jamboree that was held there on 19 February at the EMI studios in Abbey Road, where Uncle Fred had spent much of his later working life and where I, as a young girl, had enjoyed thrilling hours listening to great musicians at work. It later became the venue where I myself produced many of my own recordings, of course, and I was anxious to see what technical changes had been made in recent years.

I was given a wonderfully warm welcome, and heard many glowing tributes to Uncle Fred. I was happy that I had braved the fearful February gale to get there, although the wind blew in from the Channel so fiercely that it was almost impossible for the driver to control the car on the motorway. However, I found myself reliving many nostalgic memories, and I was happy to have been given the opportunity to share them with old friends.

On 22 March, almost a month after the great EMI party, Roguey came over from Paris to visit, and he put a question to me which, if I answered in the affirmative, would alter my life once again and in the most delightful way. Quite out of the blue, he asked me whether I would like to move to Paris to live near to him, Jeannie and the boys. I didn't hesitate for a second: "Would I? Yes!" From that moment, it was all hands on the "go" sign, but first the dear little house in Southampton had to be sold. When I told my friends and colleagues of my decision to leave England at this late period in my life, some were astonished, some dismayed, and others – including my brother – found it hard to disguise their anxiety that I might be making a big mistake. However, I remained utterly convinced that my decision was the right one.

I knew that next I had to tell my old friend and neighbour Albert Nelmes – who had shown me endless kindness ever since the day I had moved from London – that I was leaving. Albert had served in the Merchant Navy throughout the war, and later became a purser on an oil tanker. He represented to me all that was fine about Britain, and his endearing sense of humour proved a safeguard against most trials and tribulations. I knew that my intended departure would be a blow for Albert, who had known us as a family for many years, since Roguey had first joined the university and long before his departure for France. I hardly dared to break the news, but we promised to communicate frequently by telephone, a promise which we have both been happy to keep.

On 2 April, the estate agent came to see me, and it was arranged that the house should be immediately placed on the market. I hastened to make the place as charming as possible, and during the first visiting day, which was on 12 June, three people begged me to give them first refusal. This was not in my power, of course, but was in the hands of the agents and Roguey and Jeannie. However, the house was sold within a week, subject to contract, and to our relief the sale proceeded without a hitch.

Roguey was enormously thankful, for in the meantime he and Jeannie had found the perfect home for me within five minutes' walk from their house in Paris, and they dared not risk losing it by delaying the purchase. As they had already paid a substantial deposit, one can only imagine Roguey's relief when Jeannie phoned him from Paris while he was away on a business trip to tell him that 88 Copperfield Road had virtually been sold on the first day of viewing. I was delighted for my son and his wife that the complicated transactions were being arranged so smoothly, and I assured them that, as far as I was concerned, there were no doubts in my mind about the wisdom of the course that we were pursuing. Now that Christopher had left Southampton and Philip was spending his fourth year of university at the École Centrale de Nantes, there were really few personal reasons for me to remain there. My personal affection for France was also a great incentive, as I had been familiar with the country since my early childhood, through my father's business position. I also had many happy memories of the time that I had spent in Paris as a piano student at the conservatoire. This made me feel a deep intimacy with France, and added considerably to the enthusiasm I felt in accepting the invitation to live there. The language was, of course, no barrier, since thanks to my mother's insistence Mondy and I had both learned to speak French at an early age.

My last weeks in England were pretty hectic. A move is nearly always a nightmare, and when it involves leaving one's country it's a thousand times worse. I shall leave the details to the imagination, but when one considers that my home was also my office it is perhaps possible to estimate the mountains of files, musical scores, tapes and master recordings that I had to sort through. I doubt that I would have been able to handle the situation on my own, but luckily I had the competent and ever-optimistic assistance of Susan Haytor, who had acted as my secretary during the last years in Southampton, and her cheerful efficiency kept my courage from flagging.

To add to the excitement, Pompy and Shirley announced that they were coming over from the States to see if they could be of some assistance. They also wanted to tempt me away from the scene of domestic dissolution and to take me on a brief tour of our old haunts, including the houses in which the boys and I had lived. I must admit that, when they arrived, I was at first rather appalled by the idea of a pilgrimage, for I was afraid that I might find it too exhausting and disturbing.

In the event, though, we managed to cover a large section of south-east England in one day, although it was so tiring that I hardly had time to feel its emotional impact. We left Southampton early one morning and followed the South Downs to Nutbourne, on the outskirts of Pulborough, where we paused to look (from the outside only) at Ludgates, the ancient house which we had always called "Nuts". It looked just the same as it always had, and Pompy and I agreed that the 14th century was really too old a period in which to live comfortably.

Our next stop was in Pulborough itself, where the charming old house Kings Holden was situated above the main road, overlooking the Wild Brooks. Although it dated back quite considerably, it was far more suited to modern living. We paused outside, and a pleasant young couple emerged to investigate. When we explained that we had lived there many years ago, they invited us to come inside. Only Shirley did so, as neither Pompy nor I had the courage to intrude too closely on the past.

We should have avoided visiting Old Pound Cottage at Alfold, for it nearly broke our hearts to find it completely swamped by a housing estate, and the beautiful garden, which Dick had tended so lovingly, almost entirely broken up into separate lots. Although the cottage appeared to be untouched, the surroundings were almost unrecognisable, and Pompy and I swore that we would never repeat this experience.

Mondy and Catherine had invited us to have lunch with them at Chipperfield, in Hertfordshire, and on our way we made a detour to take in Witley. As we approached Gorse Hill, my heart grew heavier, for all of that part of Surrey had become a great dormitory area of London. I realised suddenly that we were approaching the drive on the right, which led up a steep hill to the house. "Well, that hasn't changed at any rate," I said. "They haven't moved the house." However, when we reached the top of the lane, high black iron gates of an incredibly vulgar design stretched across the entrance to the drive, surmounted by gold knobs in the shapes of pineapples! I was so affected by the memory of our past home that I could hardly look as we approached, but Shirley insisted on crawling through a hole in a hedge with her camera to take some photographs. I warned her that if she was seen the police might be called, but her intrepid American spirit seemed quite untouched by this threat. Pompy and I remained in the car in the hope that we wouldn't be discovered, and we agreed that visiting Gorse Hill was another experience that we would never again undertake.

When we arrived at Chipperfield, we were given a warm welcome and an excellent lunch. Pompy was very fond of his uncle, and always tried to see him during his visits to England. Mondy told us that his daughter, Susanna, was awaiting our visit, and that on the way he and Catherine would lead us in their car to the village where Susanna and Nick lived with their two children. After a delightful tea, it was time to move on, and once again Mondy guided us through the labyrinth of lanes to the motorway and on to Henley.

We ended these exhausting but memorable visits by breaking up the journey back to Southampton to see Jane and Alfred Waller in their beautiful house high in the hills above Henley, overlooking the Thames Valley. Shirley, a talented artist, has always been fascinated by this enchanting view, and I hope that one day she will achieve her ambition of transferring it onto canvas. To my great pleasure, Stewart Crawford, Jane's father and Dick's brother-in-law, joined us for dinner, which made the occasion even more enjoyable.

After dinner, when we were having coffee, I announced to all assembled that I would be moving to Paris to live near Jeannie and Rogue. This indeed surprised them, for like nearly everyone else they were amazed at my willingness to leave England. After some consideration, however, they agreed that it was a wonderful idea, and Stewart, who had spent a number of years in Paris during his time in the diplomatic services, admitted that he felt quite jealous.

While Pompy and Shirley were with me, we decided to drive to the Brushmakers for lunch, our favourite inn in the Meon Valley. As we drove up the steep hill towards it, past a farm where hundreds of piglets were playing in the fields, I thought of how wonderful the English countryside could be, and how much I would miss it. I knew that, although it was unlikely that I would ever return, the memory of it would never fade.

Pompy and Shirley completed their holiday by crossing the Channel to visit Roguey and Jeannie, leaving me to complete the preparations for my departure. The whirlwind expedition symbolised days gone by, and was a kind of farewell to the country in which I had spent nearly all of my life and which I loved so much. Now, quite unexpectedly, fate was leading me back to the Continent, from whence I came as a young child, and I had no doubts that I was following the right course.

At last, the day of the move was upon us. Jeannie and Rogue travelled to Southampton on the night ferry on 9 July and arrived punctually, to my great relief. The removal men were also on time, and so the work began. The men assured me that there was nothing left for me to do, and they took charge of the packing of my books, kitchen equipment, china, silver and ornaments. Even my clothes could be left on hangers and in drawers, ready to be installed with the minimum of inconvenience in my new home.

Our only moments of real anguish occurred when the precious piano had to be manhandled down about ten stone steps to the garden. At one moment, we thought that disaster had struck when one of the team slipped on the grass bordering the steps, but he recovered his balance and, much to our relief, the difficult and dangerous task was accomplished without damage to either a removal man or to the Steinway. Even so, it was a tense moment! After this incident, cups of tea were handed around while we recovered. When the work was finally completed and the van packed to the brim, a very cheerful gang set off to return to their depot. All of my possessions were to be kept in storage until 31 July, when I would actually take possession of my new home in Paris, but for now it was time to move on, and Roguey asked me to close the front door of the home that I was leaving.

I spent the last night in Southampton in a comfortable hotel, and when I was finally alone in my room I could hardly believe that it was all happening. The prospect of living in France – and above all of being near my family – delighted me, and it was wonderful that they wanted me to do so. I felt like I had been launched into a fast-flowing river, and that I was off on an unstoppable cruise. It was all very exciting, and I was determined to enjoy it as much as possible. I only hoped that Jeannie and Roguey felt the same way.

We sailed on the afternoon ferry. It was a beautiful sunny day, and as we passed Portsmouth Harbour and the Isle of Wight I thought of the wonderful times that we had enjoyed sailing in dear old *Maggie* in those very waters. Back then, I could never have foreseen that one day I would be leaving England to live abroad again.

We arrived at Jeannie and Roguey's home in the Avenue des Pages late on the night of 12 July. We were all very tired, and went straight to bed, with the comfortable feeling of having accomplished a difficult mission. As I dropped off to sleep, I remembered that this was the date of my father's birthday, and that the next day was that of his brother, Leo, and that the 14th was not only French National Day but also Mondy's birthday. All of these anniversaries were potentially happy events, and I fell into a deep and contented slumber.

I had been given many descriptions of my new flat, and had been sent beautifully-drawn plans of the interior, which comprised a spacious sitting room and two bedrooms. I also knew that large French windows opened onto a garden. I had pictured it all in my mind, and I could hardly wait to see it, but I refused the kind invitation of the current inhabitants to inspect it whenever I wished before their departure on 30 July. The actual entrance to the flat was in a courtyard, which pleased me enormously, as the Route de Montesson, on which the building is situated, is very busy and noisy. My flat was in an annexe on the opposite side of the courtyard, and I was assured that it was absolutely free from the sound of traffic. Jean and Rogue were so worried that I might be disappointed in their choice, but I assured them that, from what I had heard, the flat sounded perfect, and that I could hardly wait for the day when it would be empty and I could finally be introduced to my new home.

Coda

The great day finally arrived. The keys were handed over and, accompanied by Jean and Rogue, I walked into the courtyard, up three stairs, opened the heavy glass door and walked into the entrance of the building, where I opened my new front door for the first time. There were no surprises. I loved my new home on sight. It was just as I had imagined it, with large windows, parquet flooring, built-in cupboards, and shelves from floor to ceiling in which to keep my office equipment. It was all there, just as they had described it, and I told my children that if they had searched for years they couldn't have found anything more perfect.

Jeannie did nearly all of the redecorating herself, a mammoth undertaking which she accomplished magnificently. Meanwhile, Roguey performed the rewiring, changing the plugs on my British appliances to the French versions, and Christopher, who at the time was working in St Germain, accumulating funds for his future sailing activities, redecorated my delightful bedroom, which has large windows looking out onto the garden. We had received the keys only three days before the van's arrival from England, on 31 July, so it was a race against time to get the decoration completed!

The removers arrived early on the appointed morning with my furniture, having crossed from England on the night ferry. I must say that, considering this, the men seemed in fine form, and were obviously all set to enjoy their little expedition to the Continent. They were typical English workmen, cheerful, patient and careful, and by about two o'clock they had emptied the van of all of my possessions. After that, it was time to deliver the Steinway to the house in the Avenue des Pages. Roguey was beside himself with excitement, for he had been waiting for this moment for years. We piled into the car and led the way to the Corbett residence around the corner.

Before we did any more work, we were all invited to sit at a table in the garden to enjoy the excellent meal that Jeannie had prepared, goodness knows when, which the hungry and tired removal team set upon with vigour. As soon as the meal was over, the men approached the van, closely followed by Roguey, who watched every second of the operation like a large and curious dog. At last, my beautiful piano stood in its new home, all in one piece, and its owner sat down immediately to try it, followed by the foreman, who performed with much enthusiasm and was obviously delighted to get his fingers on the keyboard at last! We were exhausted but happy as we waved cheerfully to our well-fed and -rewarded team, and agreed that they had done a splendid job. In spite of the fact that we were all feeling very tired, it had been a most successful and memorable day.

We spent the next day reorganising the shelves, which had originally covered a section of the walls at Gorse Hill and supported many of my precious books. These dated back to early purchases I had made as a young girl, and there were other treasured volumes, many beautifully bound, which had belonged to Dick and his family. I placed the statue of St Cecilia that Katie had given me on the small circular table which she had always occupied, and under the influence of her benign and gentle smile I felt completely at home. Apart from the chairs, the only other pieces of furniture in the living room were my two large speakers (essential to my way of life) and the desk, which I still remember standing in my father's study in Milan. There were also two landscapes that Dick's grandfather, Francesco Dracopoli, had painted during the Impressionist period, while on the wall facing the garden were hung two superb silk paintings of monkeys which Uncle Fred had brought back from China in 1899.

Opposite my favourite chair, there is an alcove which is shelved from floor to ceiling, and this is useful for placing gifts from friends and relatives. My favourite of these is a model of a fierce little Chinese soldier on horseback, which found its way into my keeping after Uncle Fred's death. I guard this little fellow carefully, for he has a very special place in my heart and I am fearful that my brave warrior may have a fall and injure one of his horse's legs – he would be in a bad way then, and so would I – and so he is placed on high, as though on a mountain peak in his native land, surveying us from afar.

I began my story with the words, "From my earliest days, my life was filled with music." I now have time to think of this, as I listen to the wonderful music that I can hear at the touch of a button, whenever I wish.

This itself is largely due to the foresight and determination shown by Uncle Fred and his colleagues at the turn of the last century, in their development of Emile Berliner's invention of the "talking machine", and their faith in its potential. This enterprise actually developed into recording as we know it, and served to immortalise for posterity the greatest music performed by the leading artists of their period.

As I write these words I am conscious of the almost incomprehensible developments that have taken place in the world of communication. What would Uncle Fred say now? I know the answer to this question well: he would have studied and assimilated its implications and gone forth to use its potential for his own work.

I ponder on this as I remember the great performances I attended with Uncle Fred, and I think about the artists that I knew, many of them personally, including Furtwängler; Toscanini; Bruno Walter; von Karajan; Elgar, conducting his own great violin concerto, with Yehudi Menuhin as the soloist; Schnabel; Fischer; Lipatti; Horowitz; Rachmaninov; Lotte Lehmann; Elizabeth Schumann; Frida Leider; Lauritz Melchior; and the immortal Feodor Chaliapin. Now I can switch on the television and actually see some of them performing again. If only the gramophone had been invented at the time of the great masters – how marvellous it would have been to have heard Mozart and Beethoven playing their own concerti. Even Uncle Fred didn't quite manage that!

Index